Doodle London

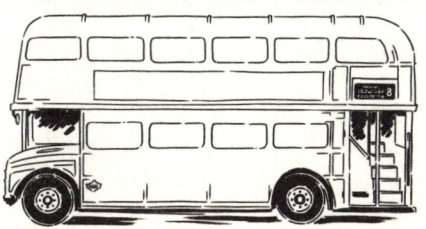

Published in 2013 by Dog 'n' Bone Books
An imprint of Ryland Peters & Small Ltd

20–21 Jockey's Fields
London WC1R 4BW

519 Broadway, 5th Floor
New York, NY 10012

www.rylandpeters.com

10 9 8 7 6 5 4 3 2 1

Text © Rob Merrett 2013
Design and illustration © Dog 'n' Bone Books 2013

The author's moral rights have been asserted. All rights reserved. No part of this publication may be reproduced, stored in a retrieval system, or transmitted in any form or by any means, electronic, mechanical, photocopying, or otherwise, without the prior permission of the publisher.

A CIP catalog record for this book is available from the Library of Congress and the British Library.

ISBN: 978 1 909313 09 5

Printed in China

Editor: Pete Jorgensen
Design: Alison Fenton
Illustration: Rob Merrett

For digital editions, visit
www.cicobooks.com/apps.php

Doodle London

Doodle a day in one of the world's greatest cities

ROB MERRETT

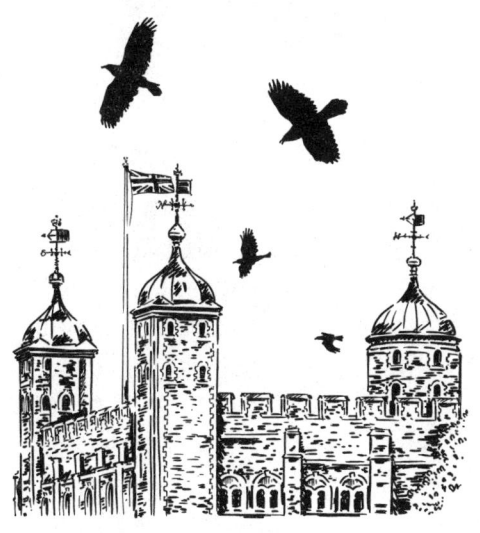

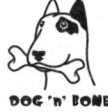

DOG 'n' BONE

Introduction

What is London? London is one of the most culturally vibrant cities in the world. It's also a city of incredible diversity. There are more languages spoken here than almost anywhere else on the planet—it's like a microcosm of the entire world. You can try different kinds of food from all over the globe and enjoy many international festivals and celebrations year in, year out. You certainly won't get bored in this city!

"Why, Sir, you find no man, at all intellectual, who is willing to leave London. No, Sir, when a man is tired of London, he is tired of life; for there is in London all that life can afford."
Samuel Johnson, English writer, poet, and essayist

Whether you prefer history or modernity, you'll find it in London. And it holds just as much appeal for nostalgic adults as it does for curious children. There are Royal palaces, museums, and galleries to visit, handsome and refined shopping arcades in Piccadilly and Mayfair to browse, and crooked streets, quirky grand houses, quaint mews cottages, and quiet leafy squares to discover. And don't forget, afternoon tea at one of London's many fancy hotels will always offer welcome respite from the hectic pace of the capital. For the young and young-at-heart there are ample opportunities to explore the bustling open-air food and vintage markets, binge on late-night bagels in Brick Lane, or sip cocktails with fashionistas at London's most stylish bars.

Experience the city's lovely green spaces, of which Londoners are justifiably proud—from the naturally rambling heaths and the hundreds of tiny neighborhood garden squares to the majestic, manicured Royal parks. The most famous outside space is undoubtedly Hyde Park and although smack-bang in the center of the city, you'll be pleasantly surprised at how lush, lovely, and leisurely it is. Pack a picnic and eat alfresco, or hire a boat or a pedalo and spend a pleasant afternoon afloat on the Serpentine Lake.

Whether you prefer to go by foot, take the tube, grab a cab, or travel on the Thames, take advantage of the many marvels this city has to offer. Even if you are a frequent visitor, I guarantee there will always be something you've not yet seen or done.

This doodle book offers you a fun, informative, and eclectic tour of London at breakneck speed, with well over 100 pages of delightful sketches to complete or create from scratch. There is everything from simple "join the dots" puzzles and adding stick figures to an everyday London scene to designing fashion accessories and concocting mouth-watering culinary delights. If you know London well, draw what you remember from your visits. If you've never been before, this doodle book is guaranteed to whet your appetite for the city and will encourage your imagination to run freely through the quirky cobbled streets, world-class museums, Royal residences, colorful outdoor markets, glamorous fashion boutiques, traditional pubs, and charming green spaces of this hectic, frenetic place.

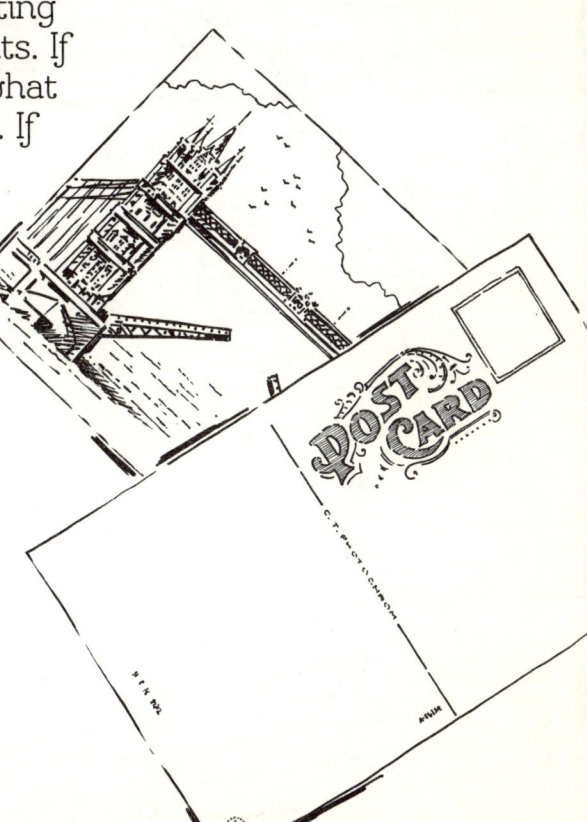

Enjoy your visit!

Create an exotic paradise within Trafalgar Square.

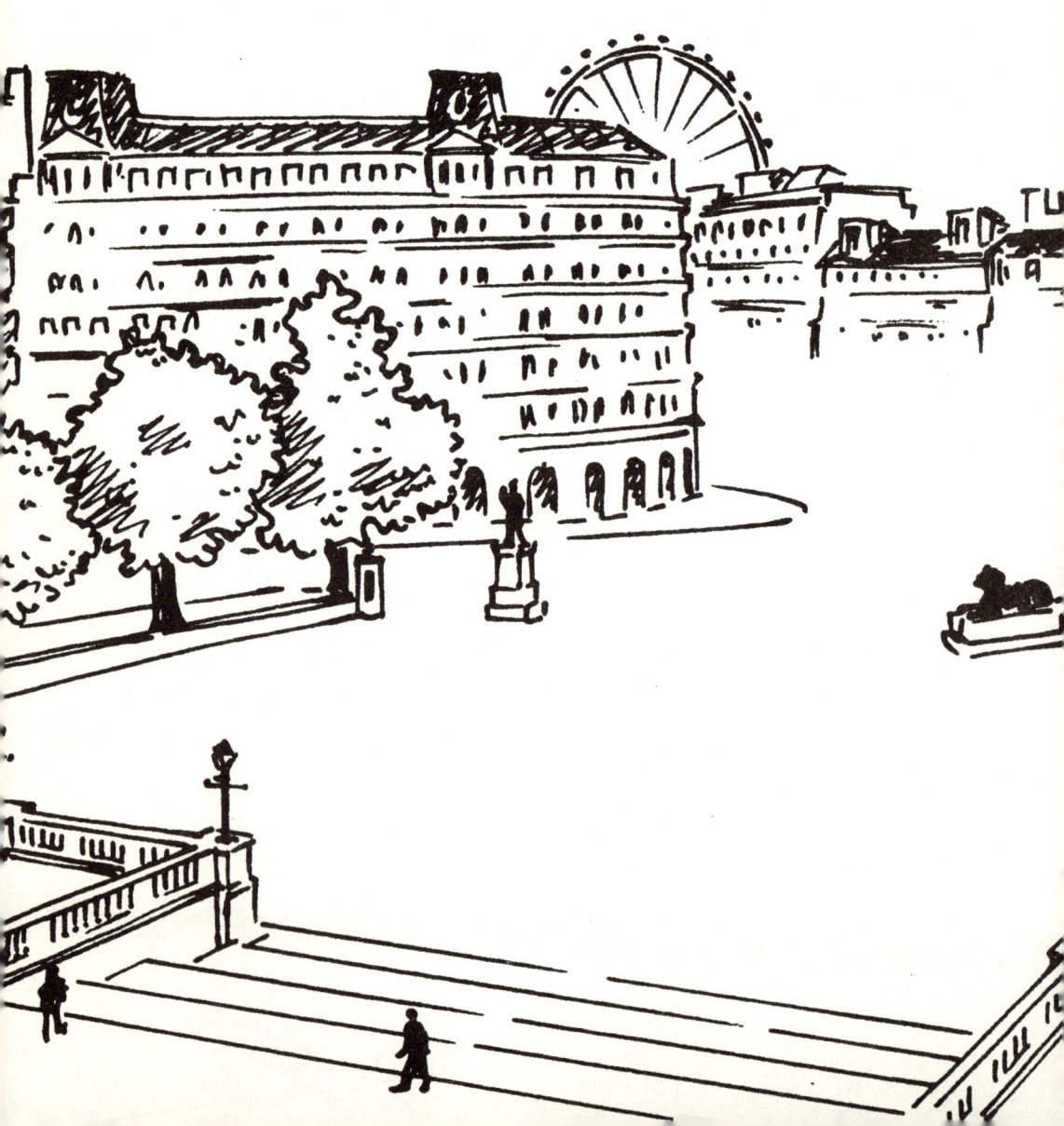

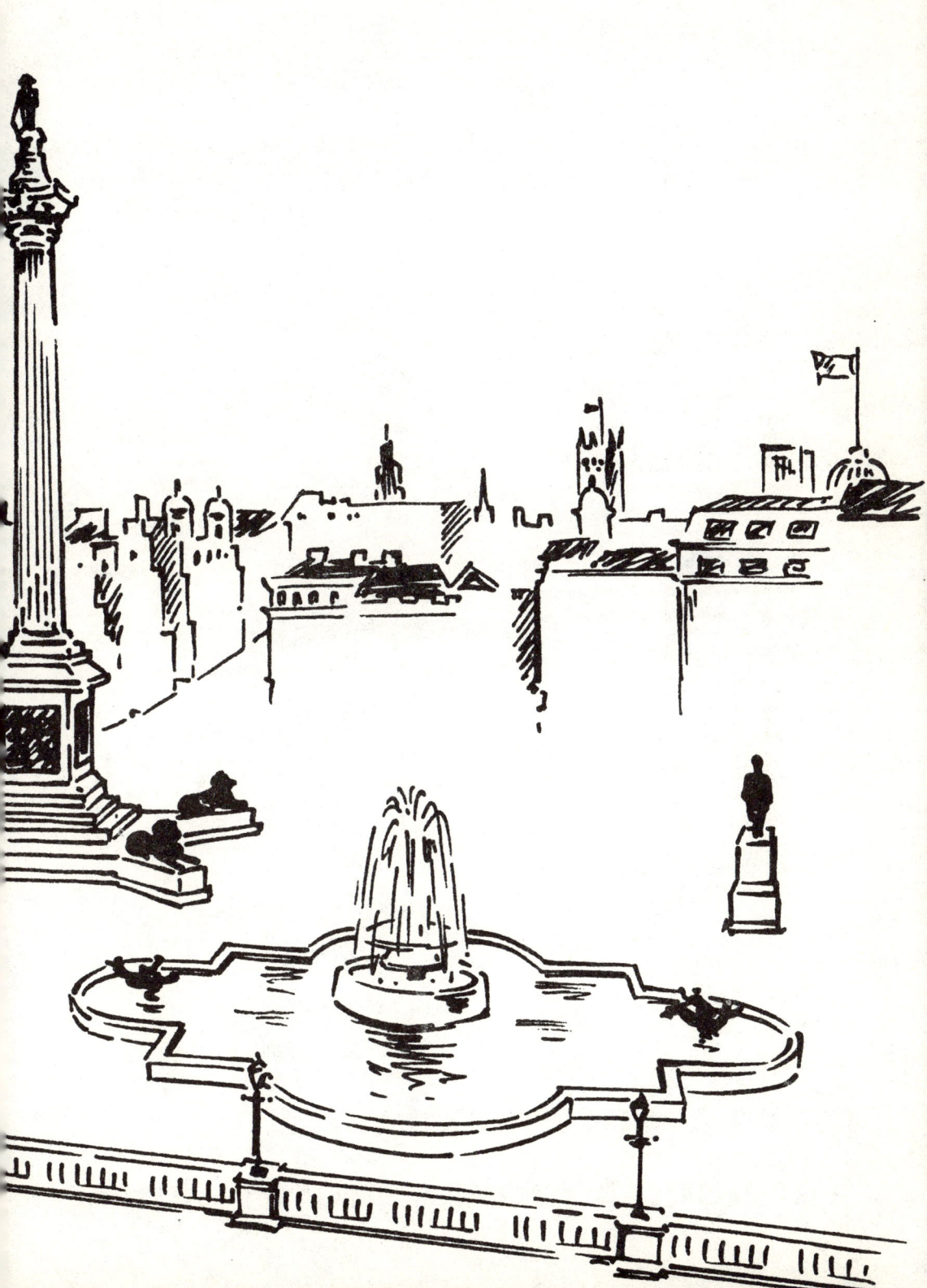

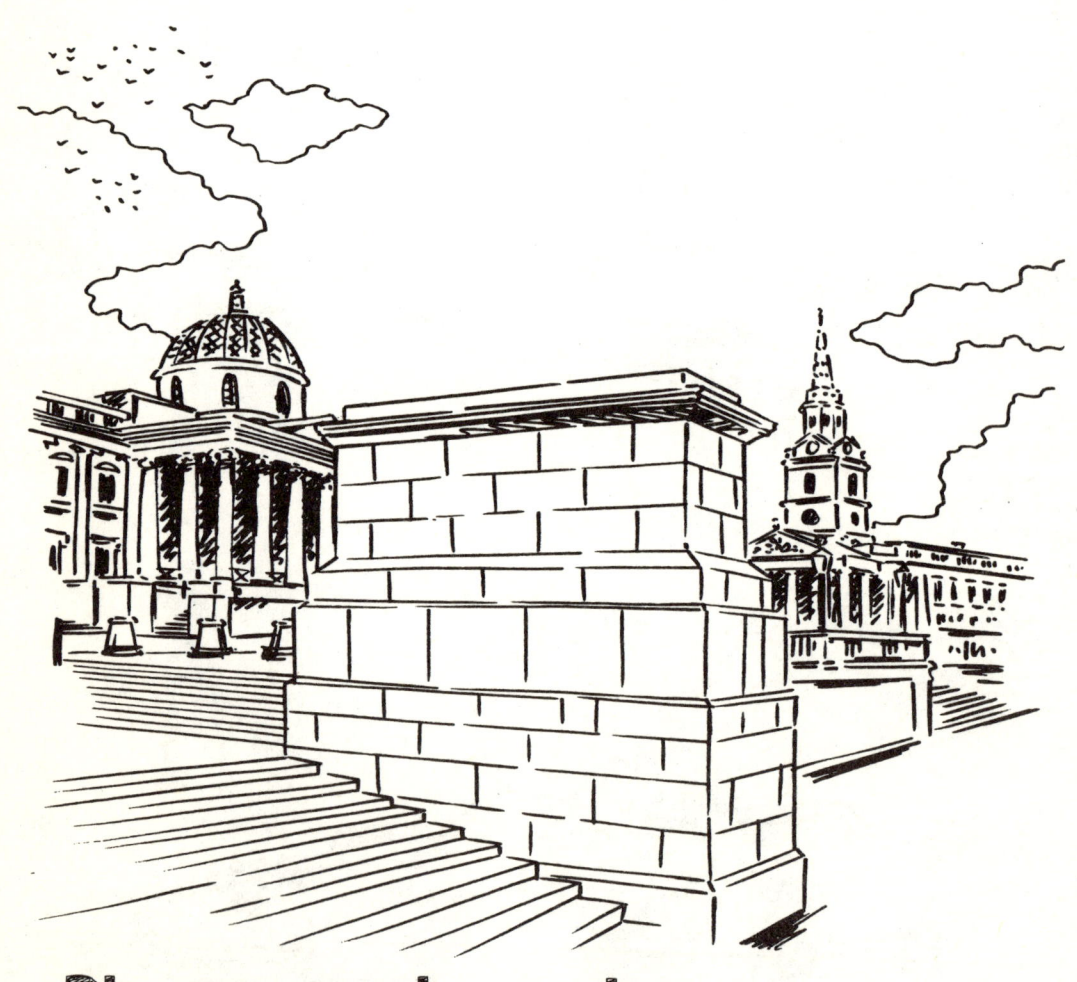

Place a wacky sculpture on Trafalgar Square's fourth plinth.

Decorate the Trafalgar Square Christmas tree.

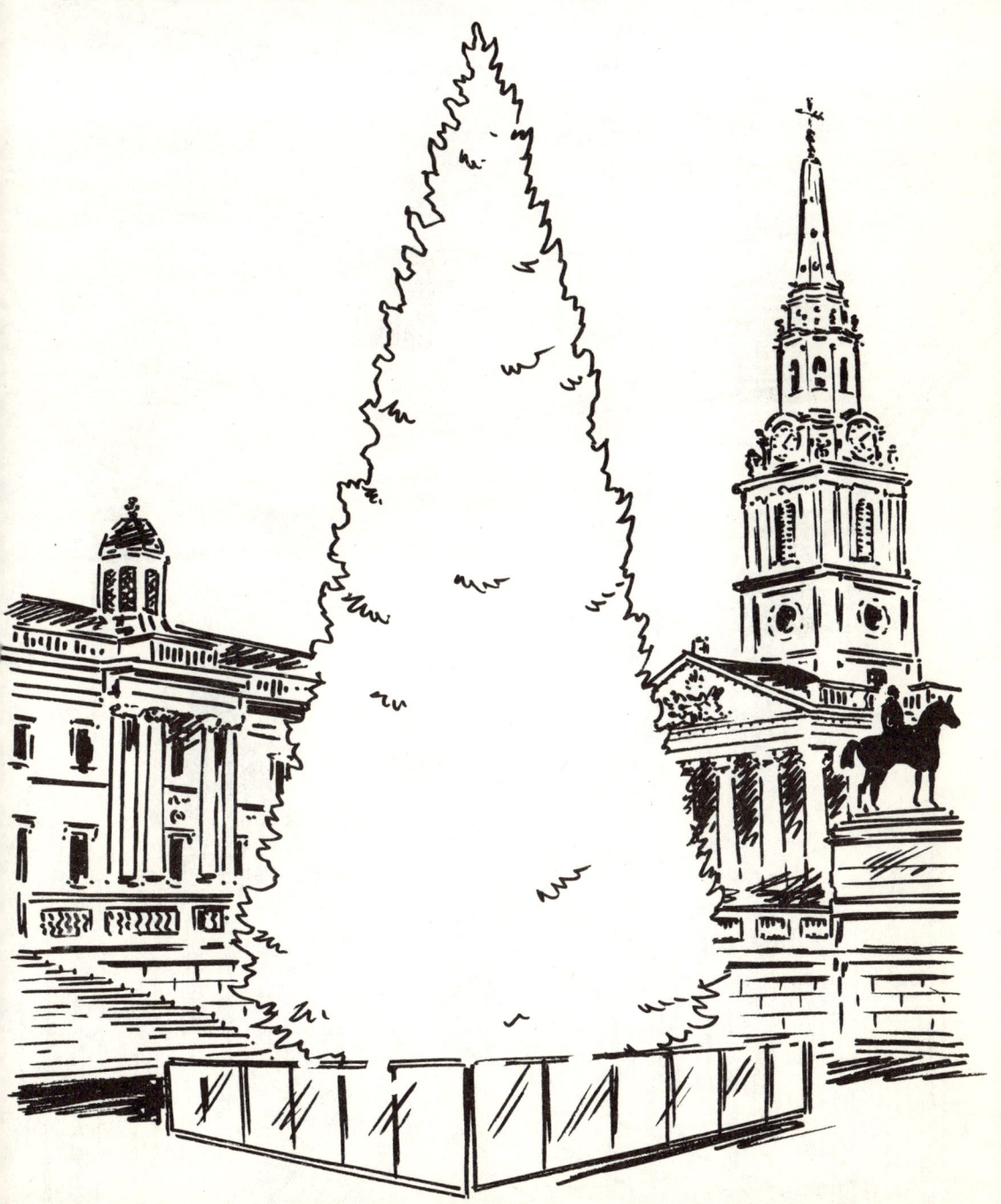

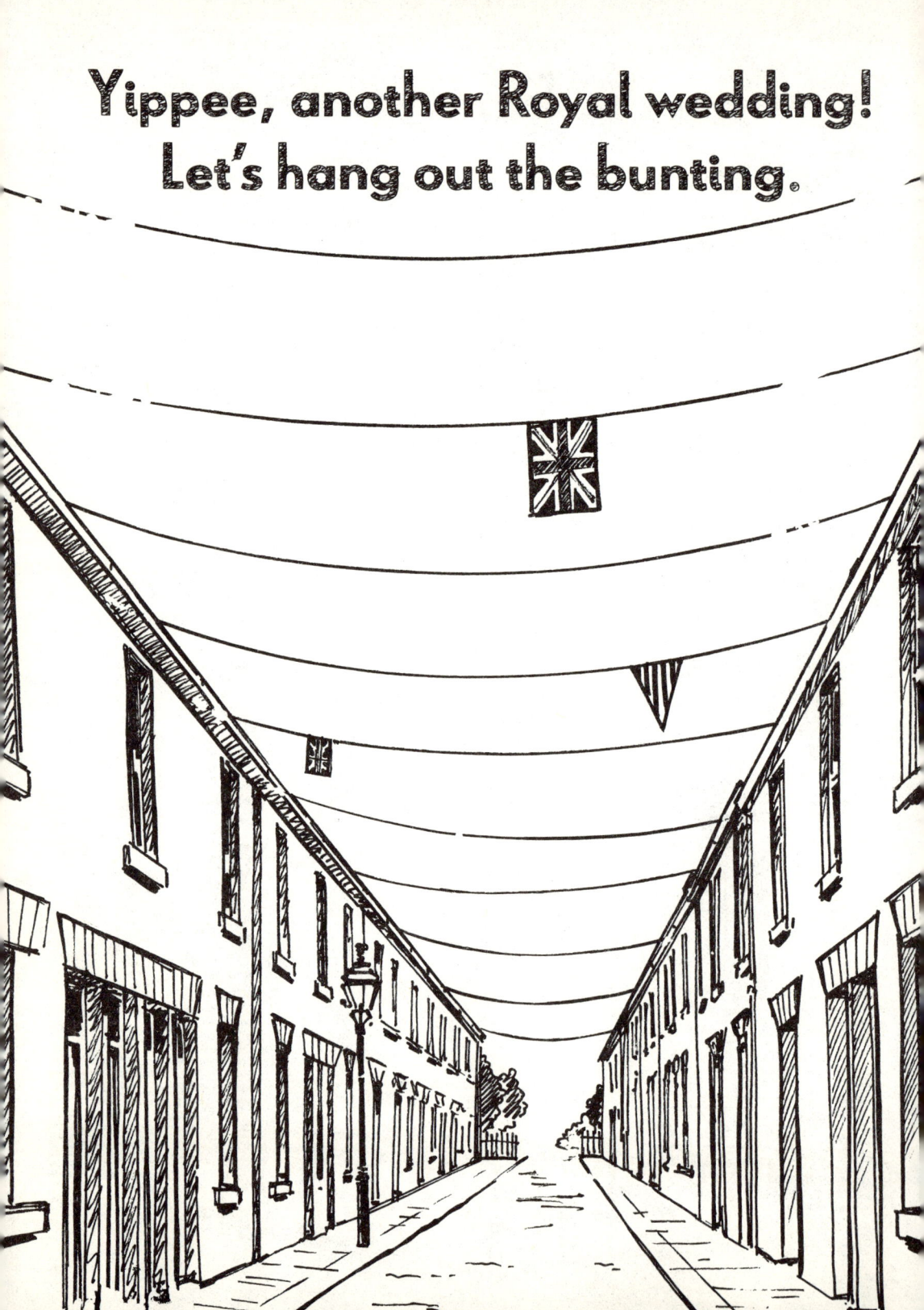

Design elegant hats for the Queen's Garden Party.

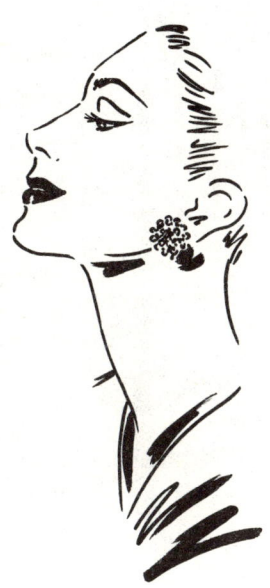
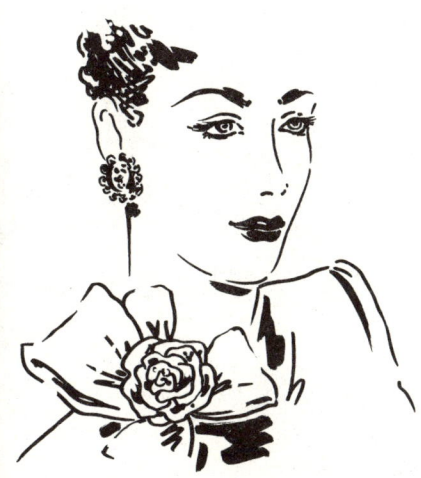
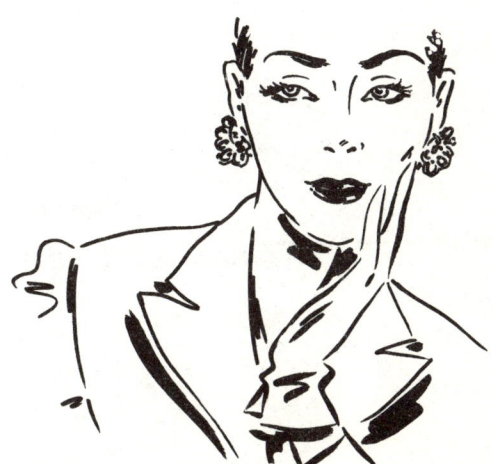

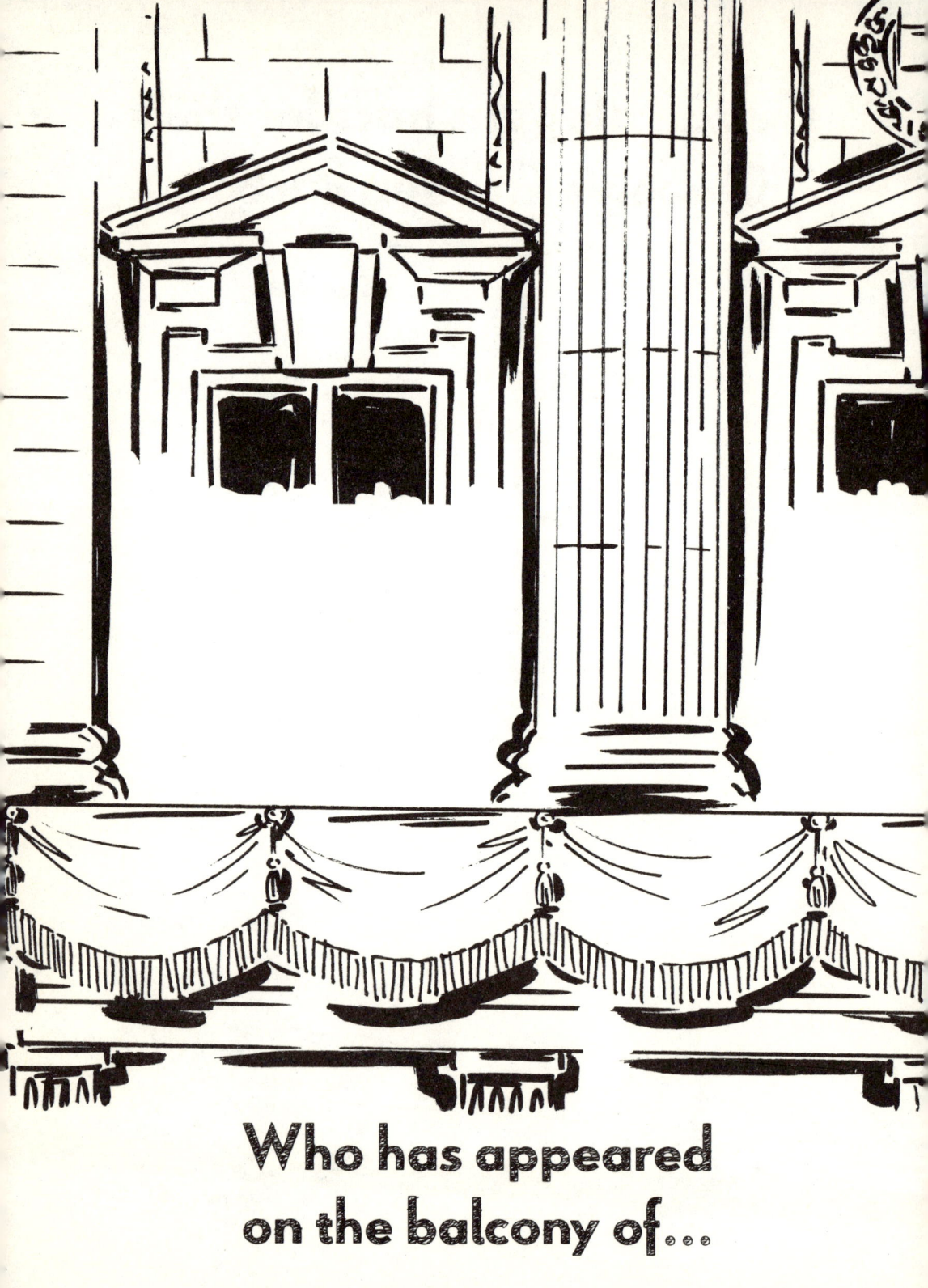

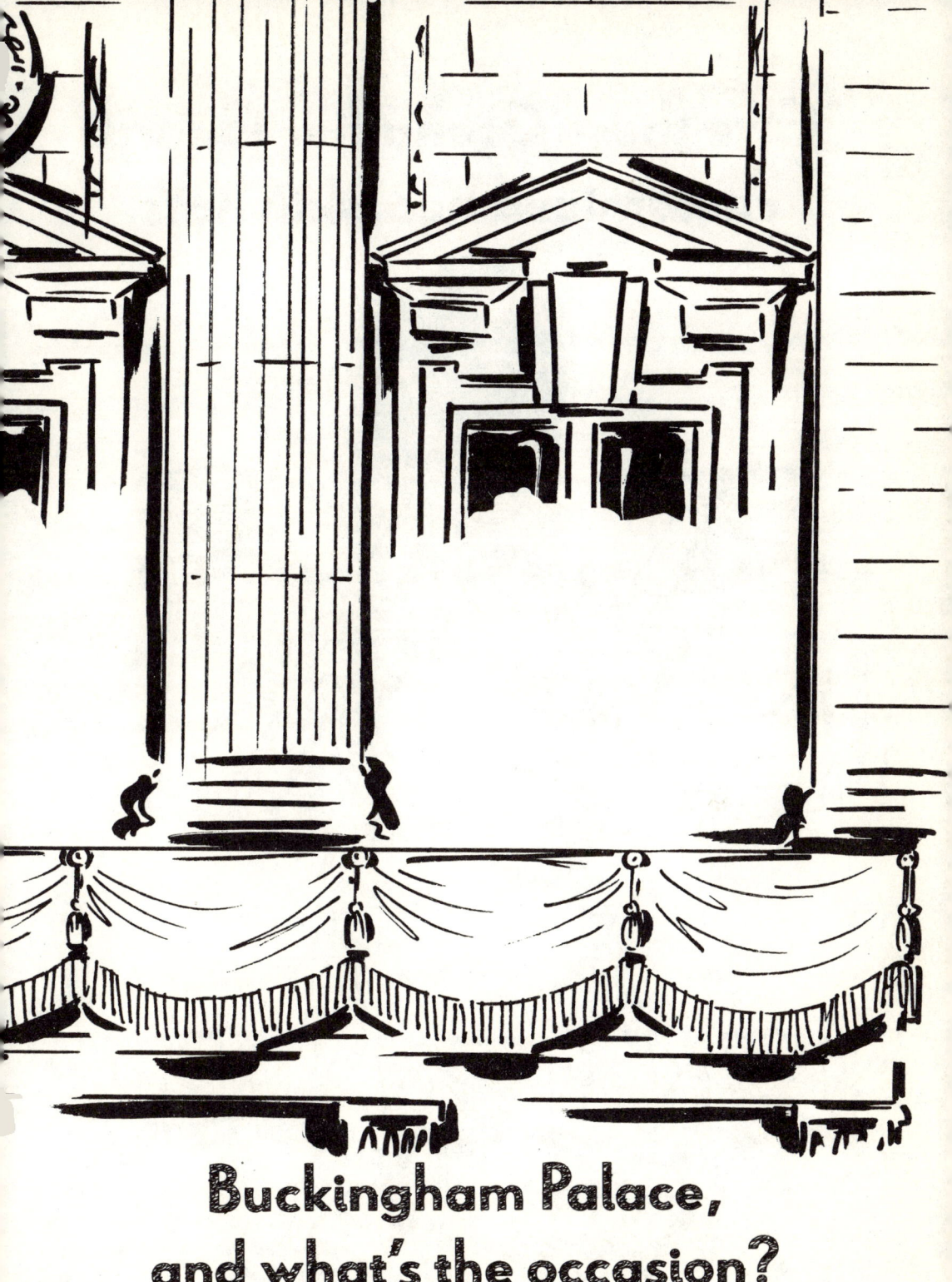

Give these Grenadier Guards customized bearskin hats.

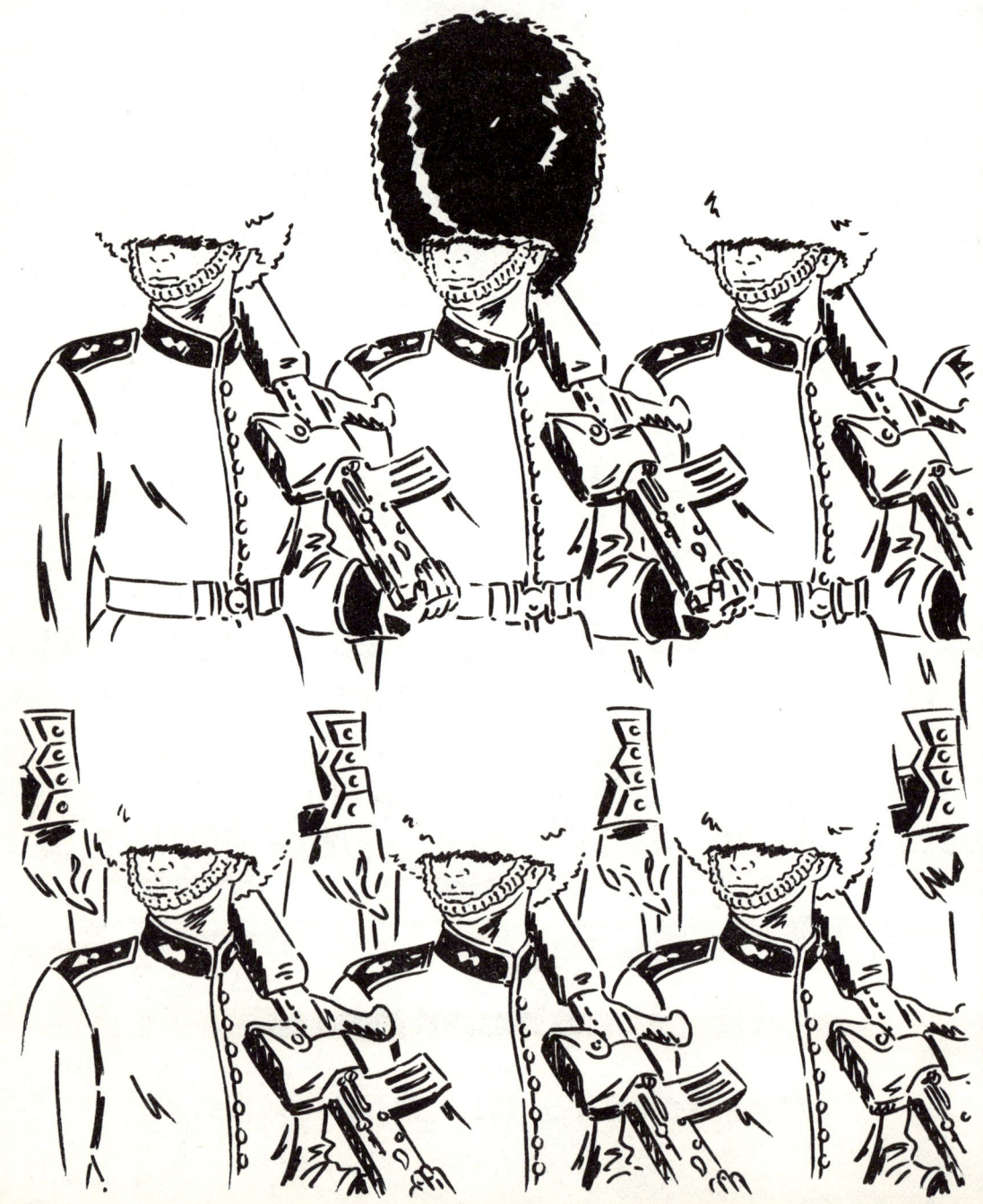

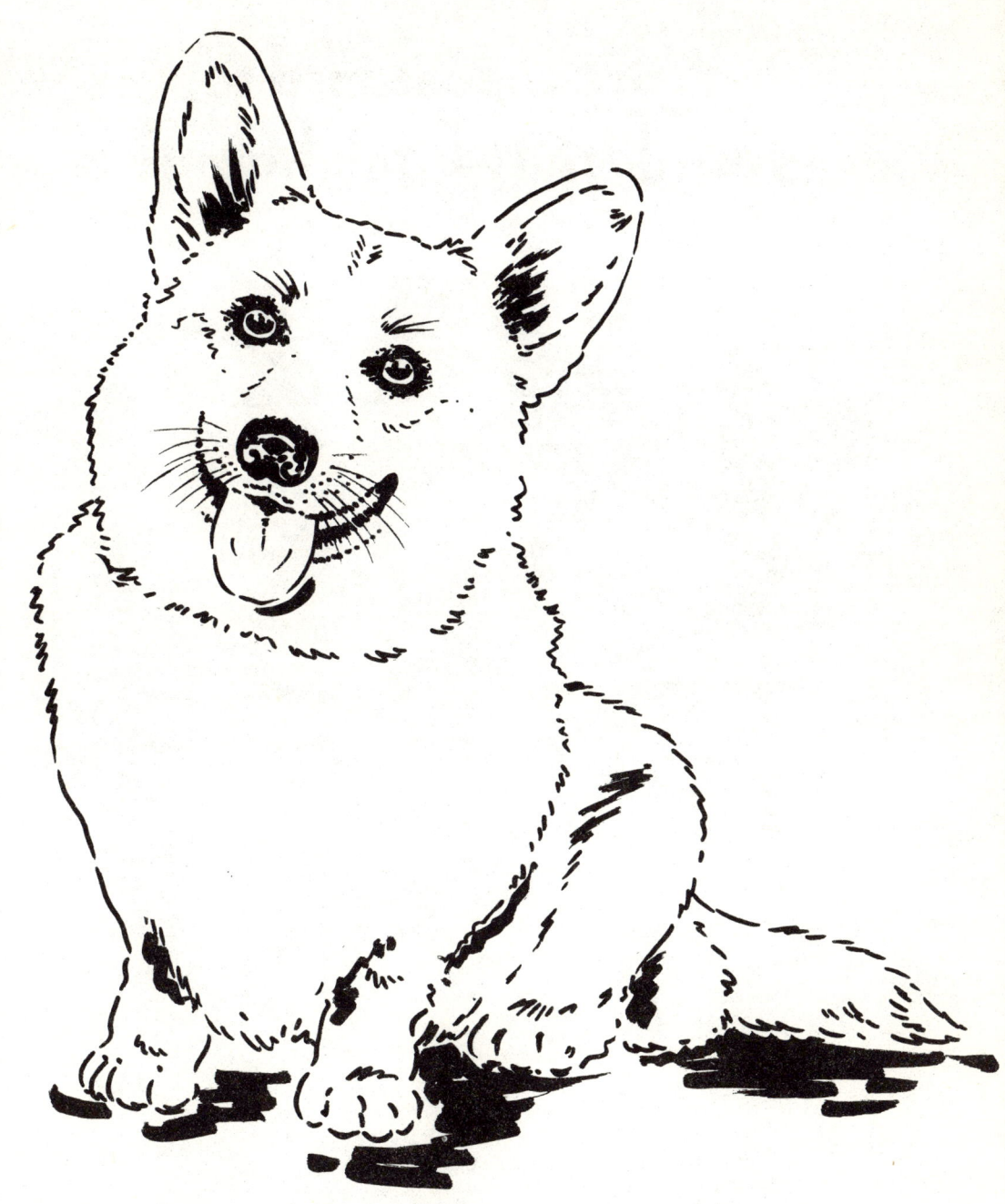

Write a postcard to your family back home!

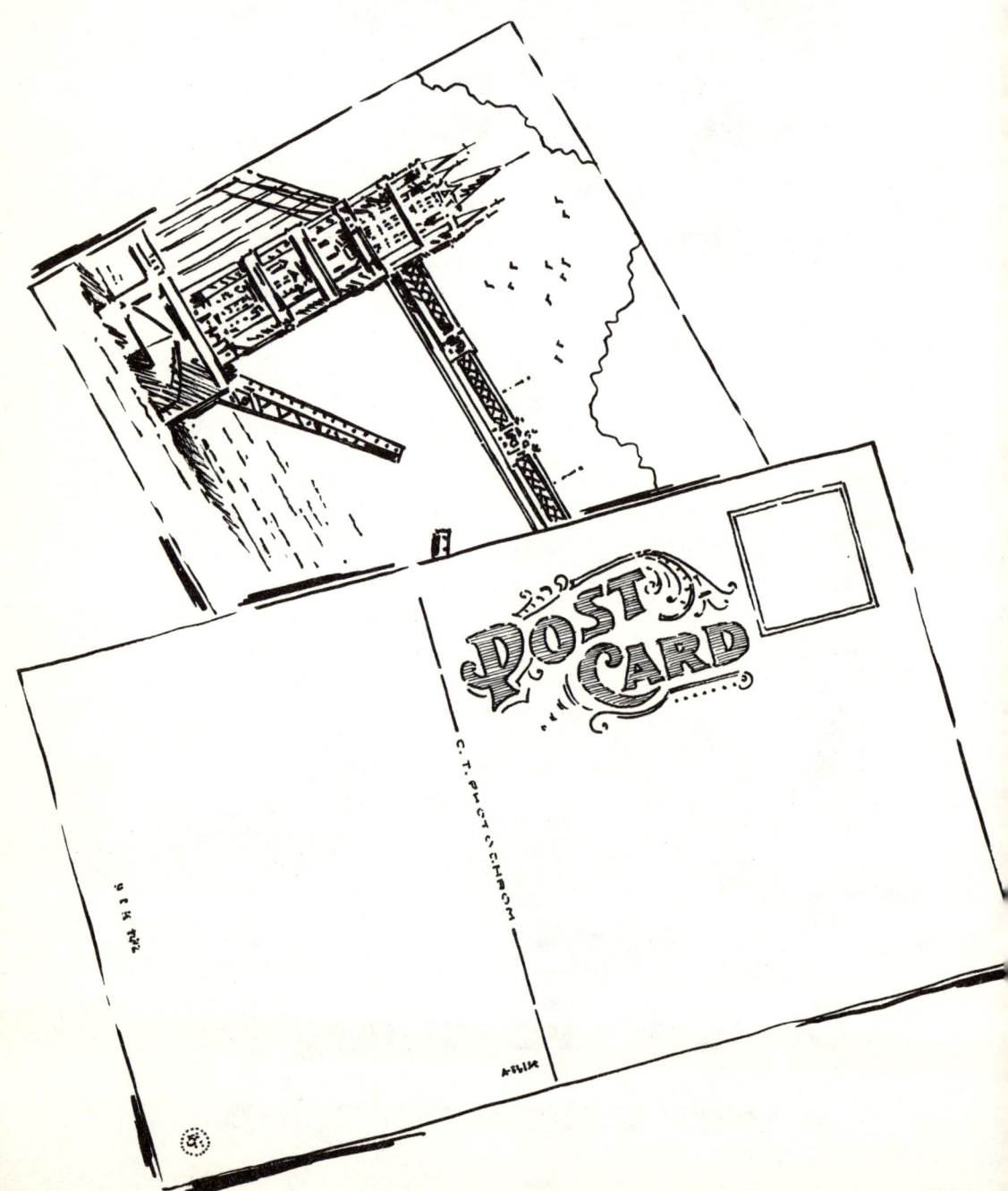

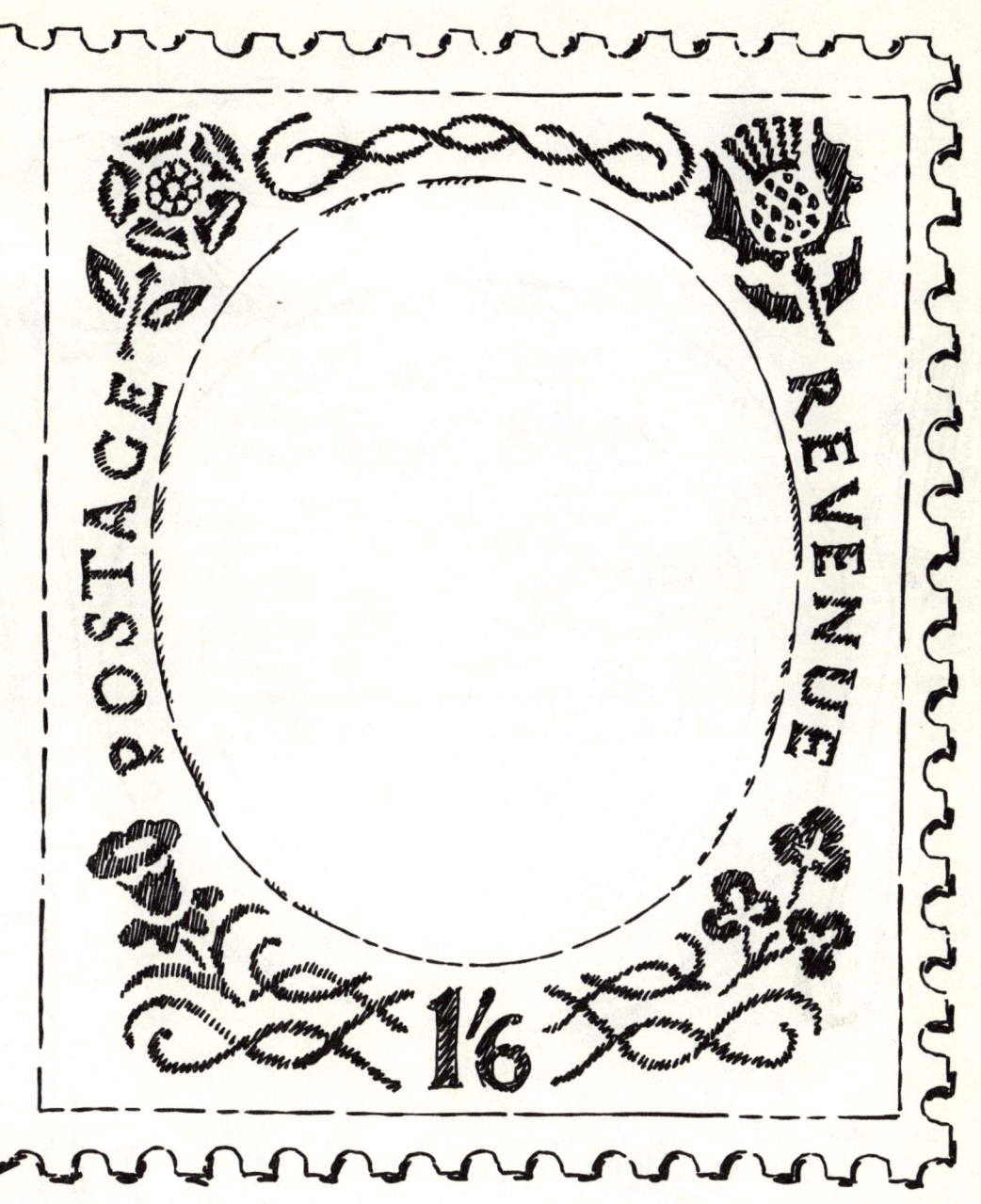

Draw a portrait to decorate this postage stamp.

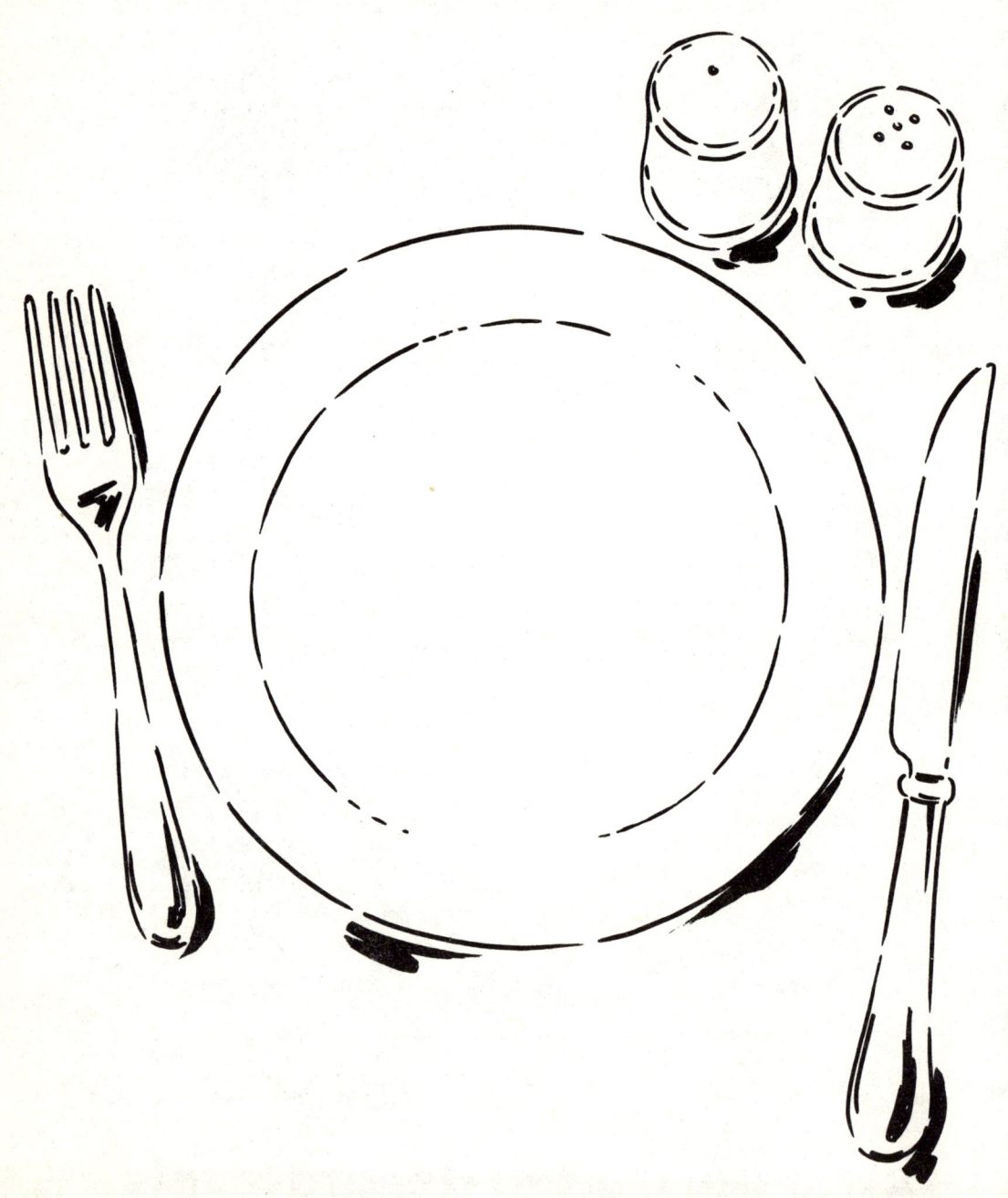

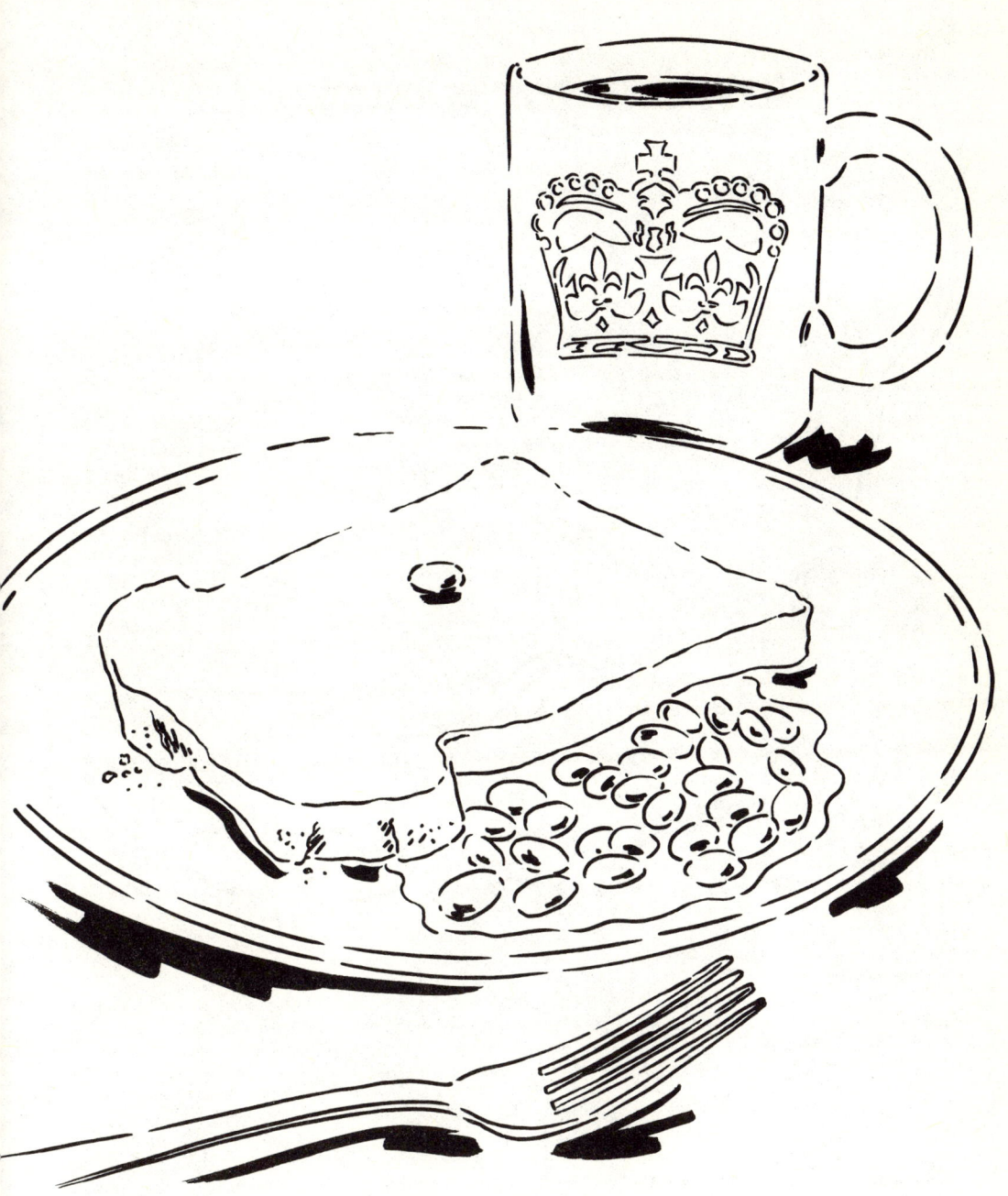

How many baked beans can you get on this slice of toast?

Anyone for a cuppa?

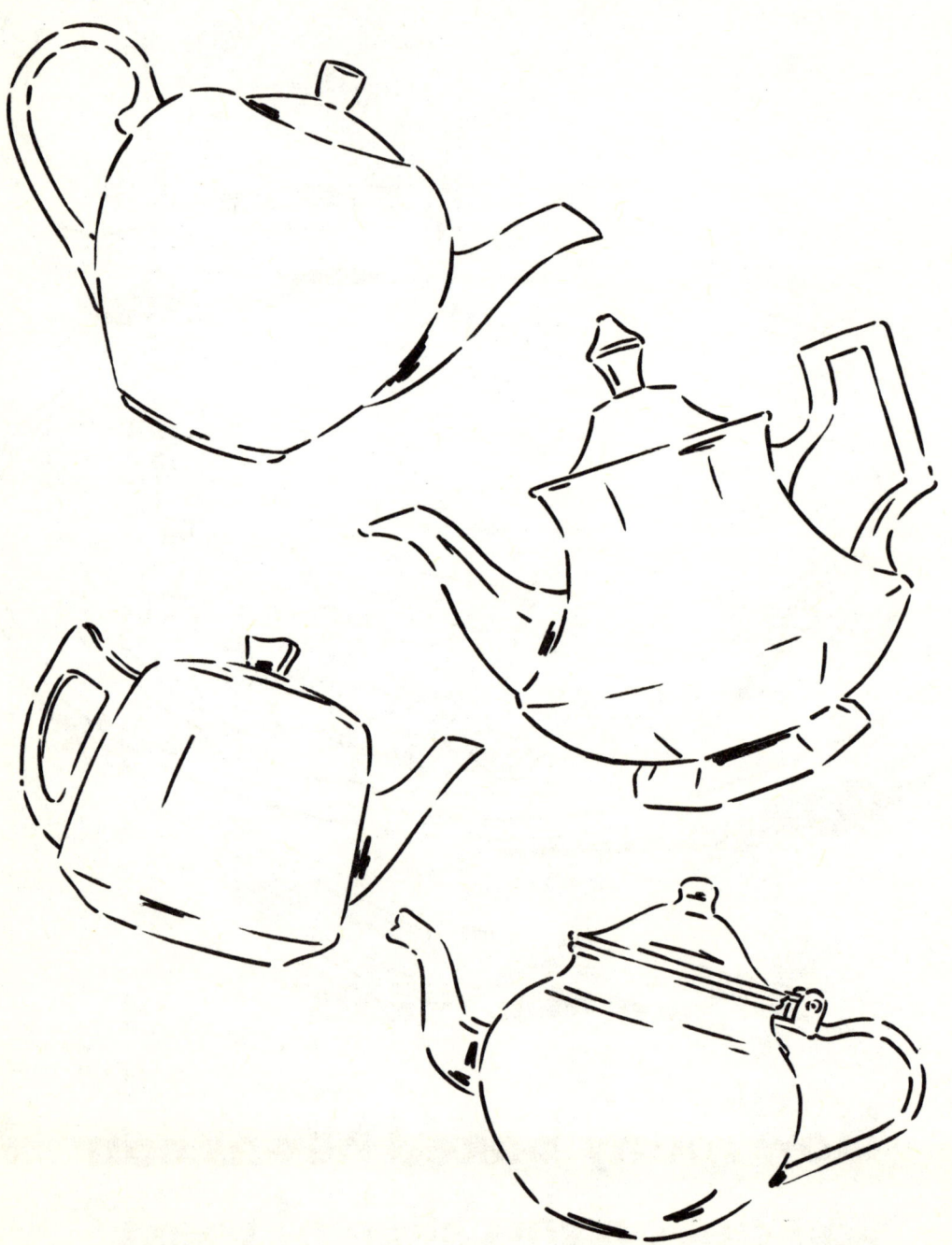

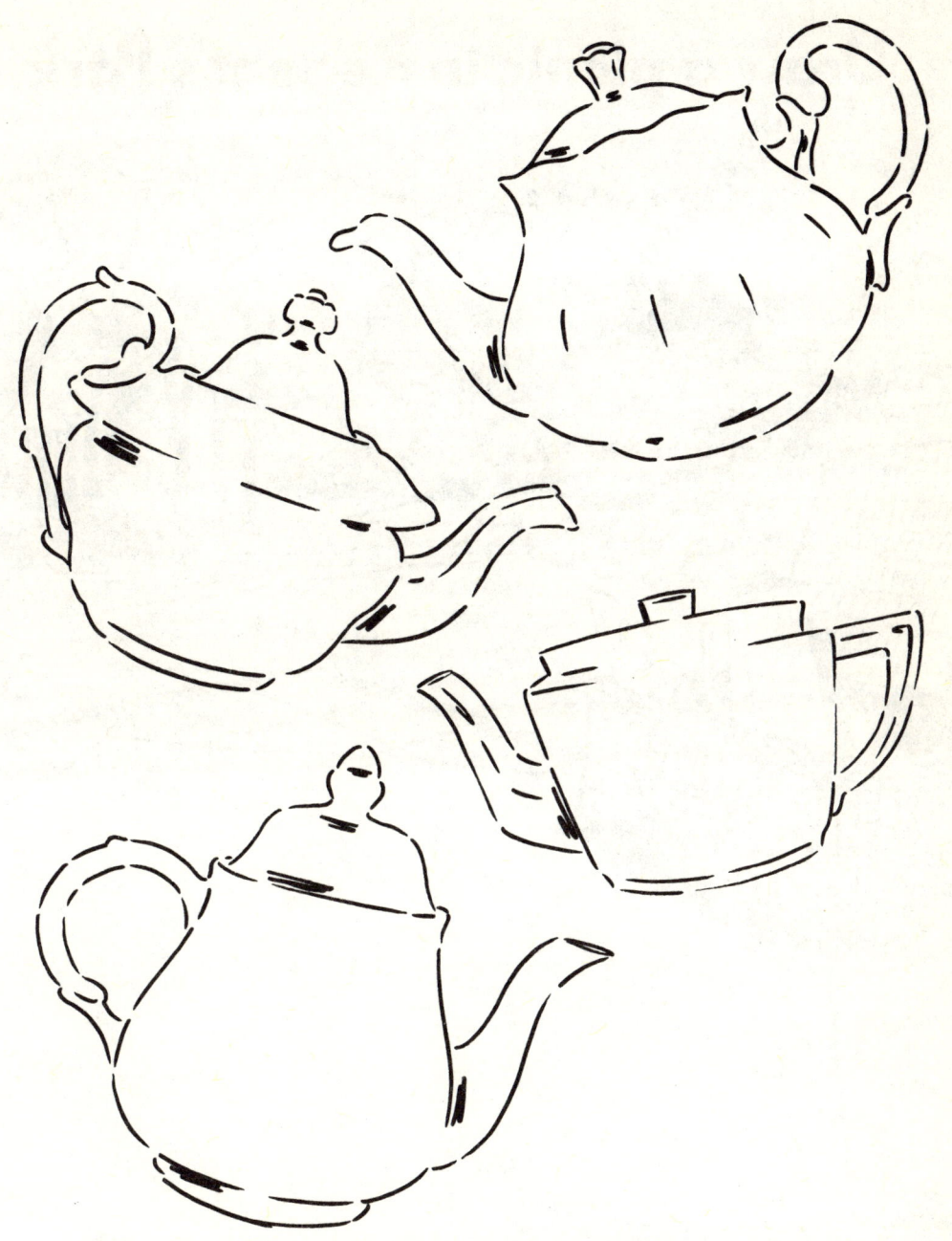

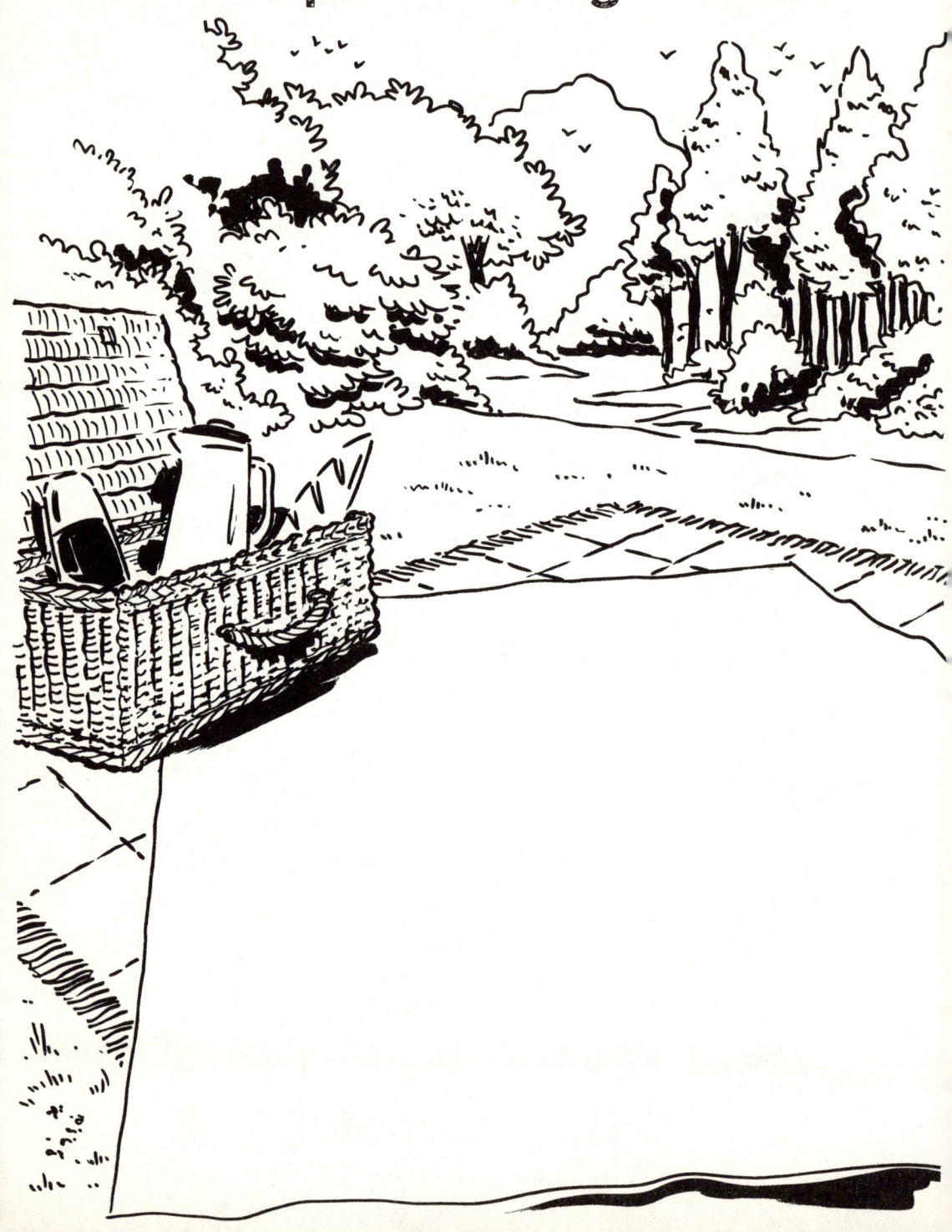

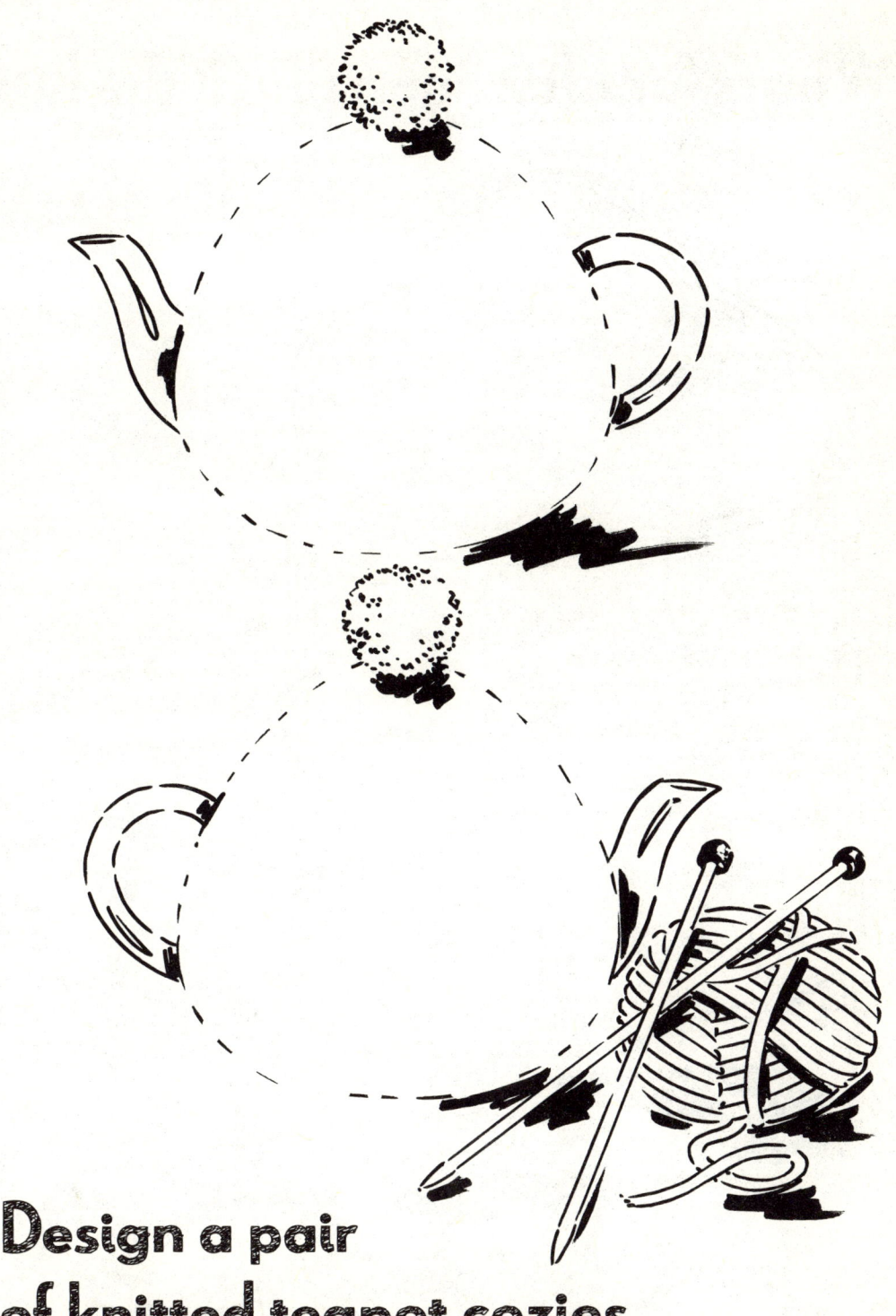

Design a pair of knitted teapot cozies.

What's for afternoon tea at the Ritz?

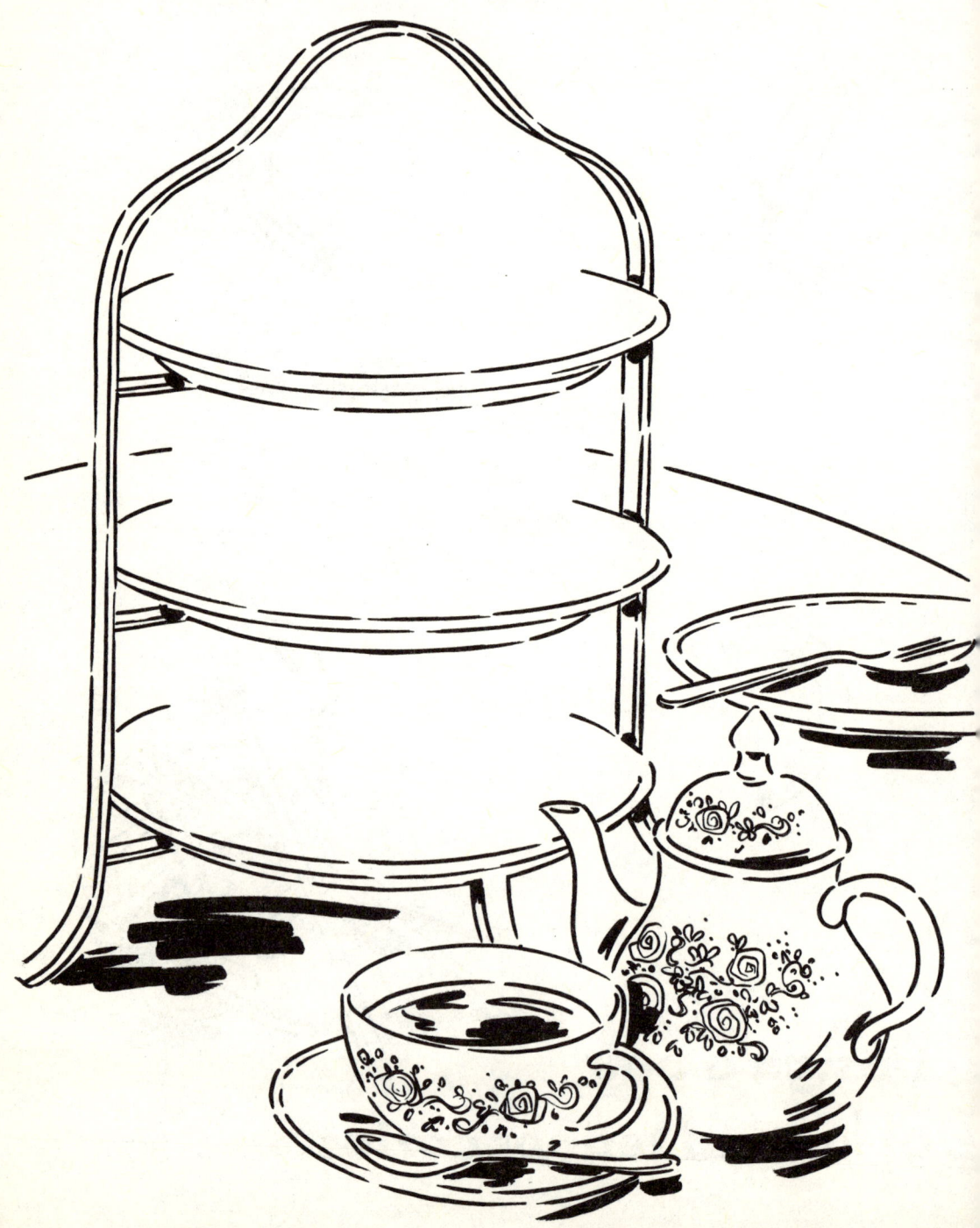

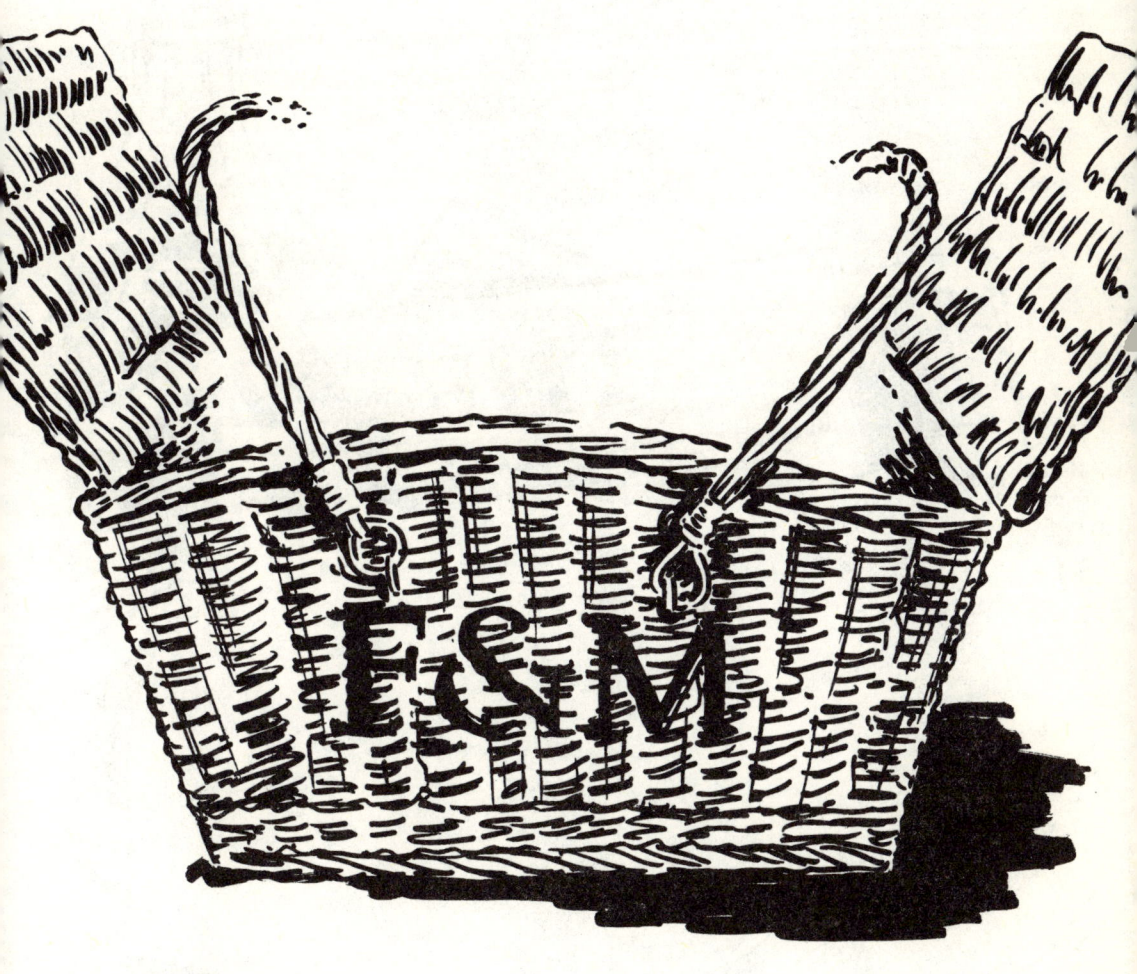

Fill this food hamper with some tasty treats.

It's lunchtime! Draw a portion of the British favorite — fish and chips.

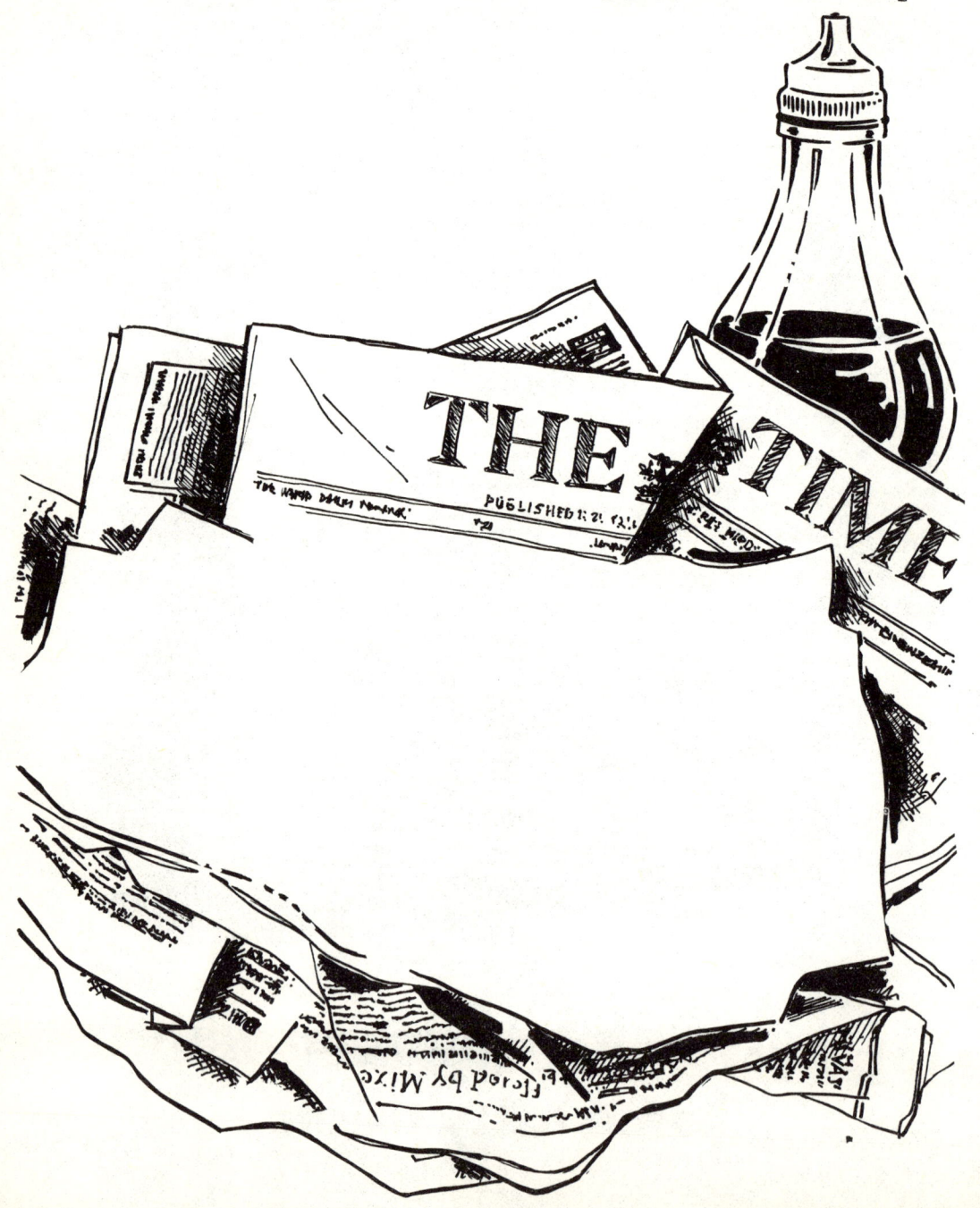

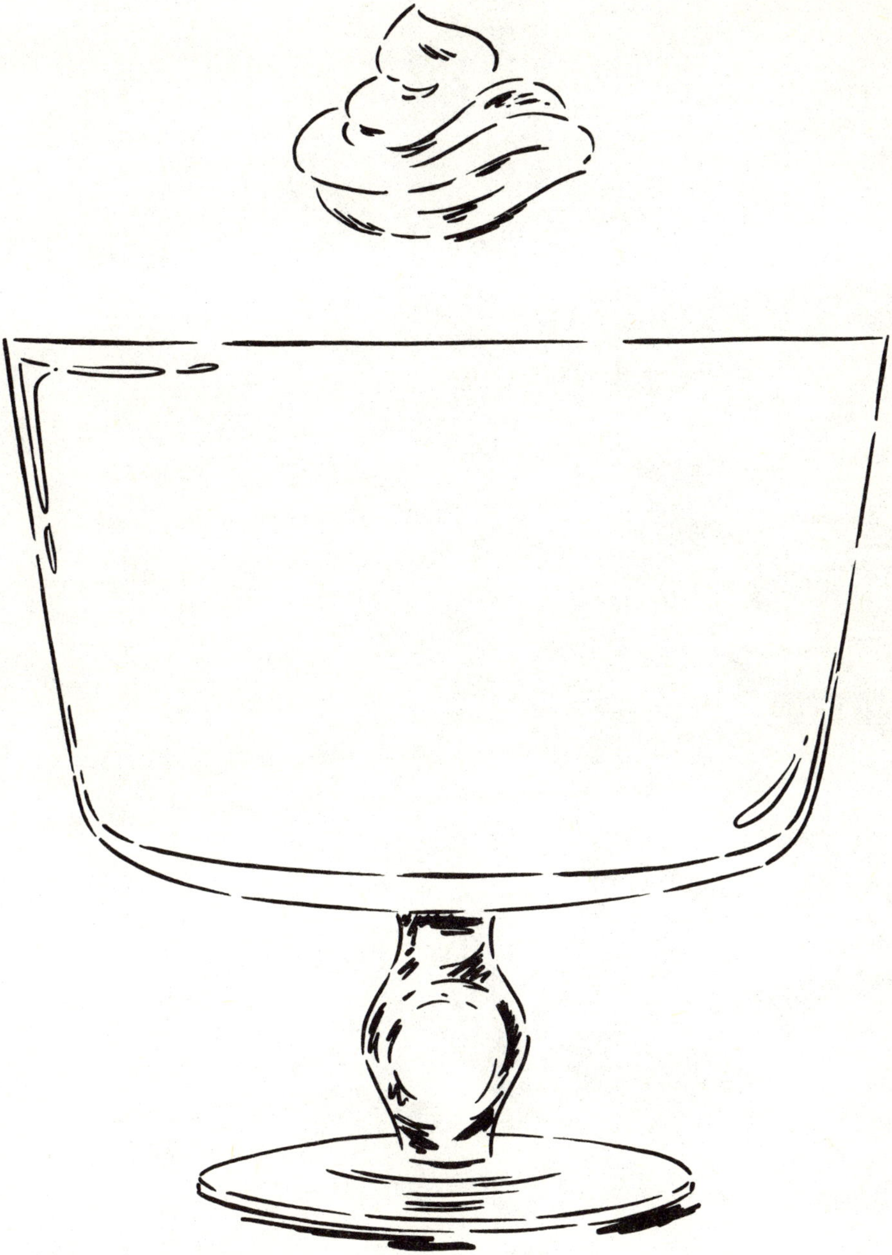

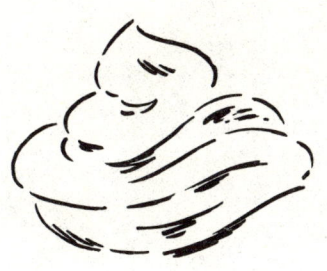

Create the biggest and best sherry trifle EVER!

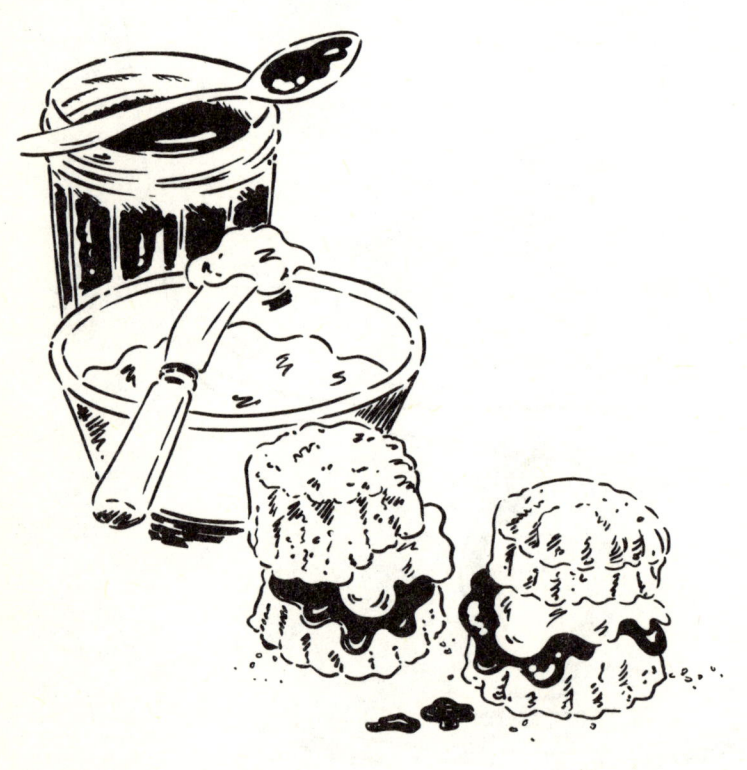

Draw some scones with jam and cream to have for afternoon tea.

How many British biscuits do you know? Add your favorites.

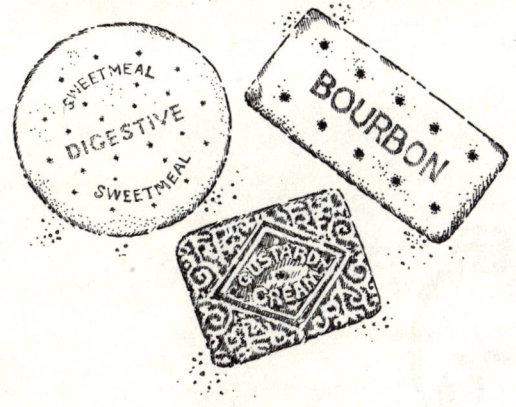

How many pint glasses can...

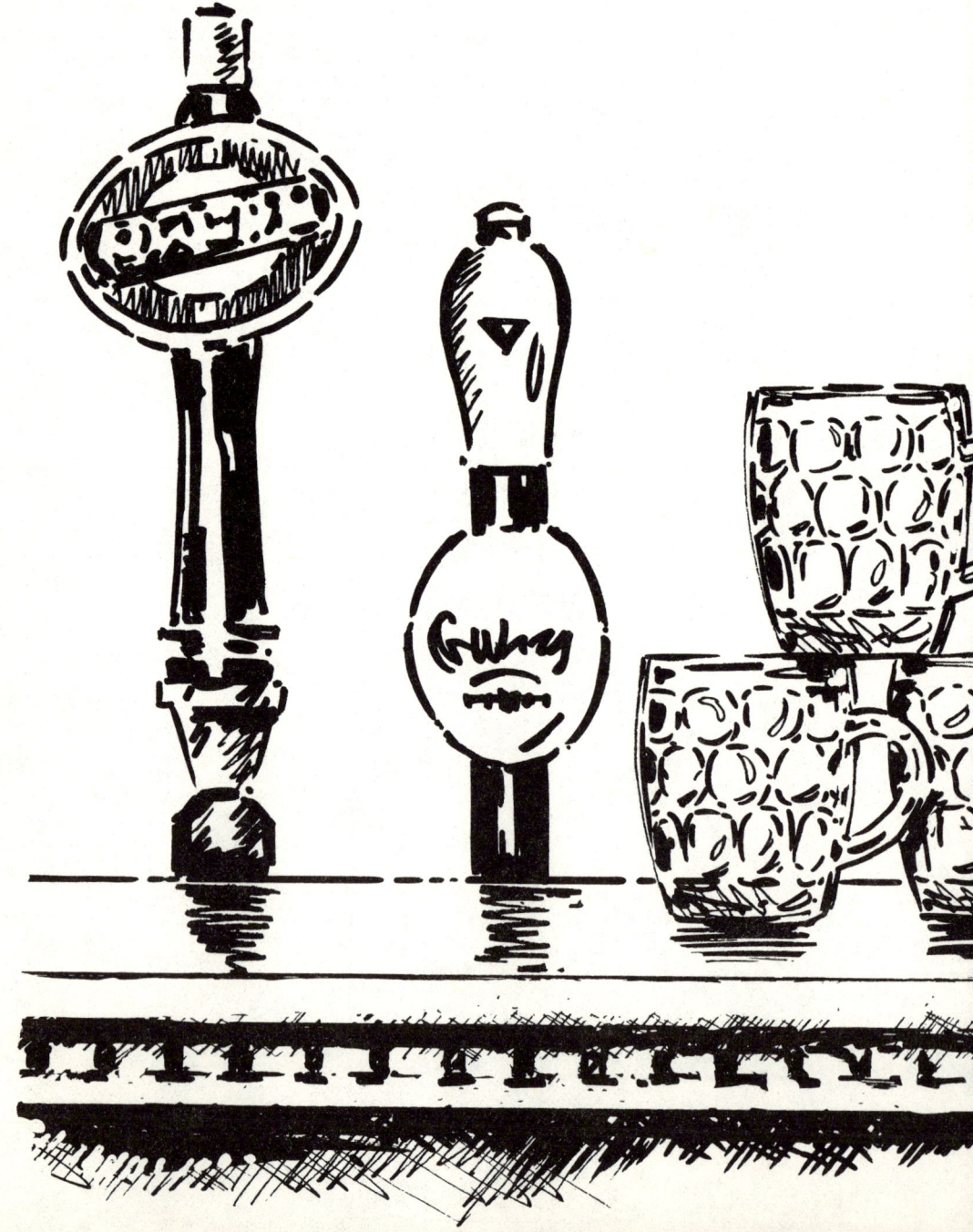

you stack on the bar of this pub?

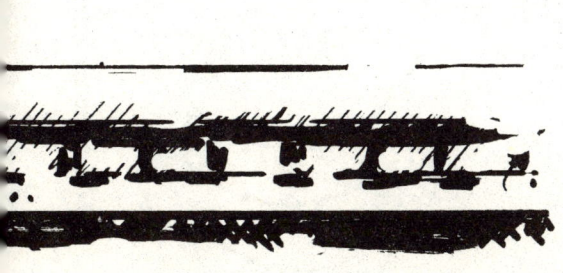

Samuel Pepys described the pub as "the heart of England."

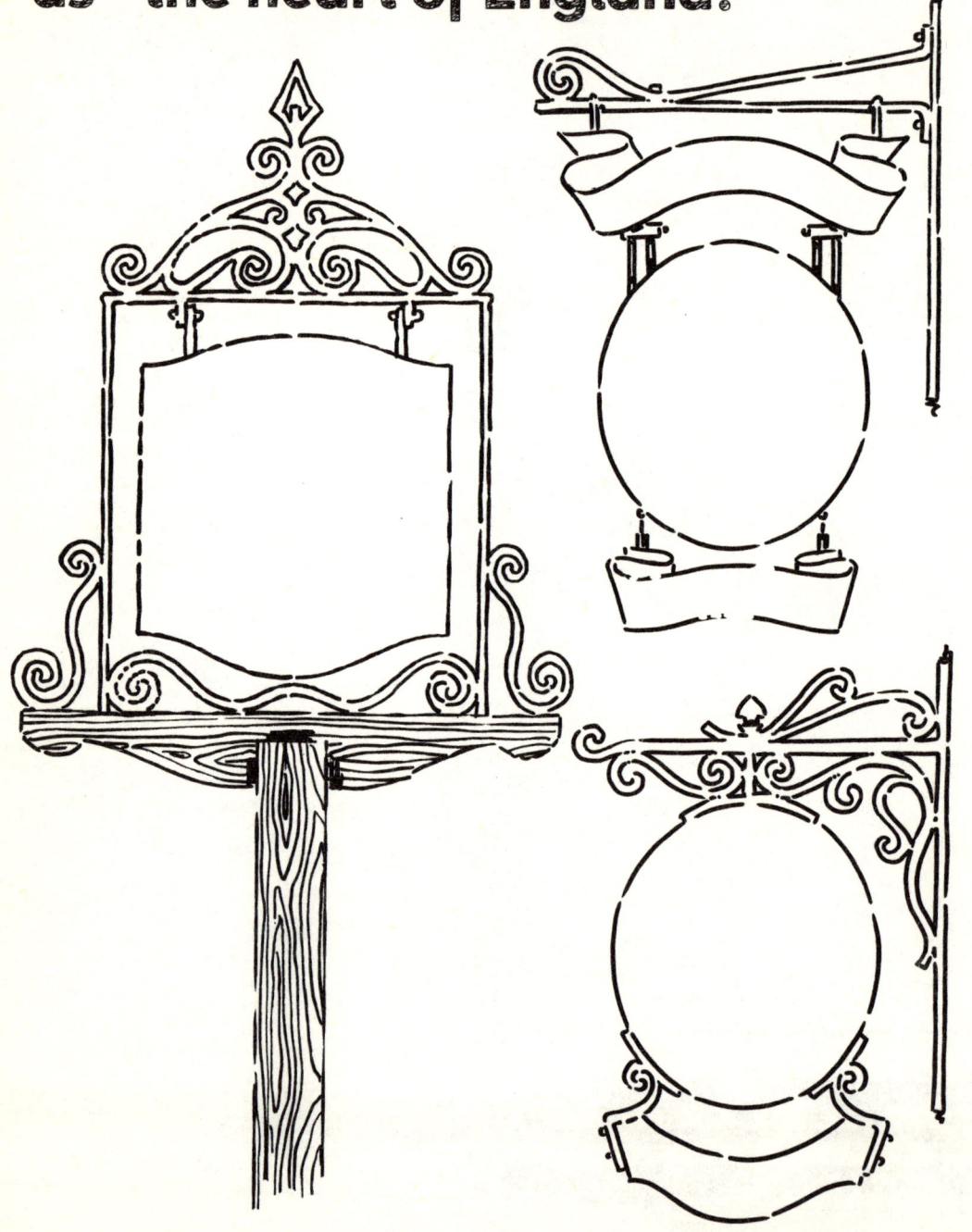

Design a sign for your own boozer.

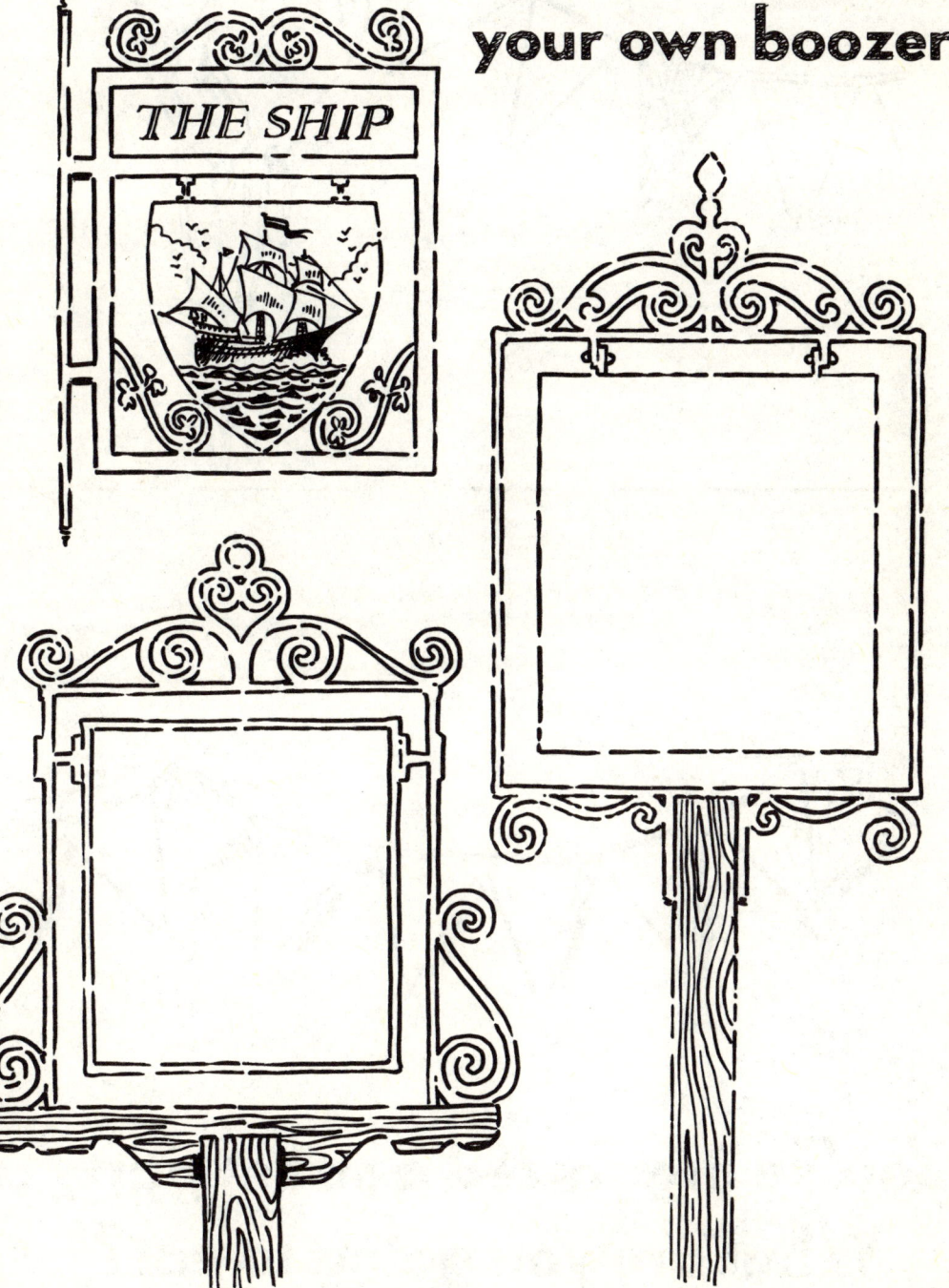

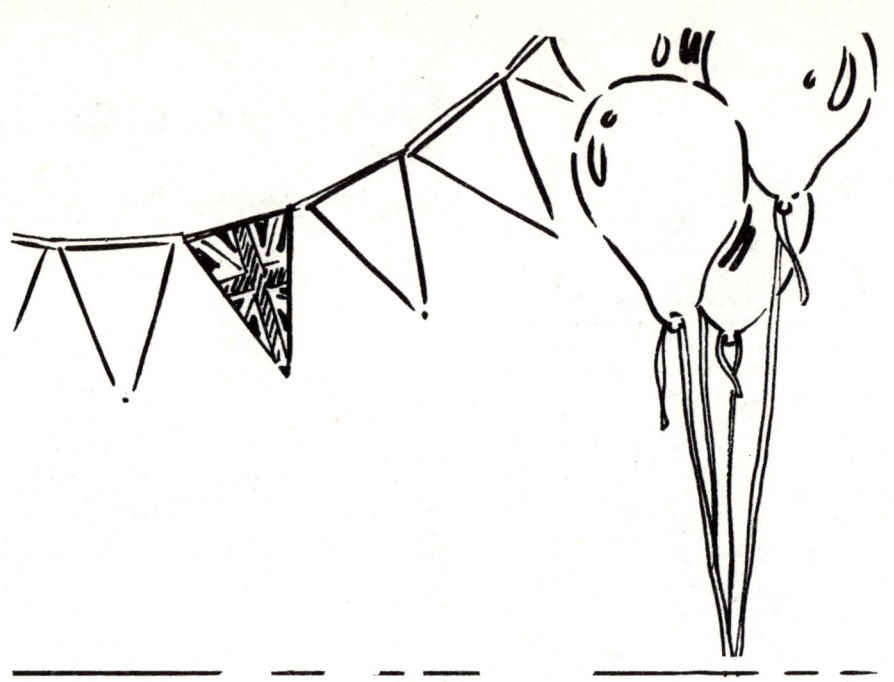
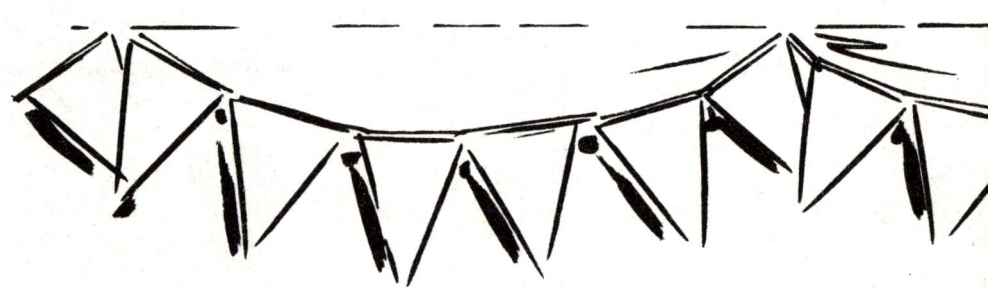

You've organized a street party. What are you going to eat?

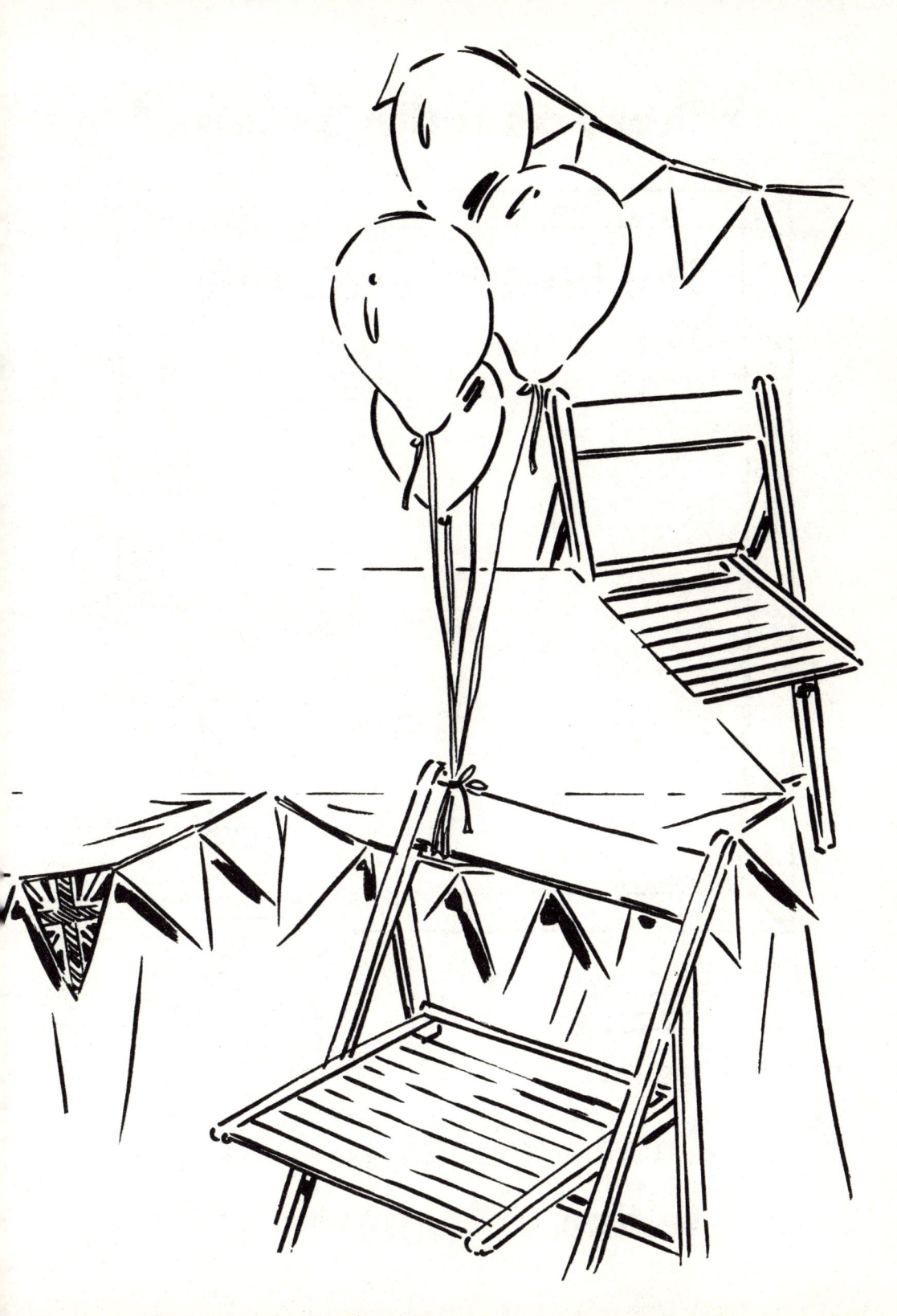

What's on today's menu?

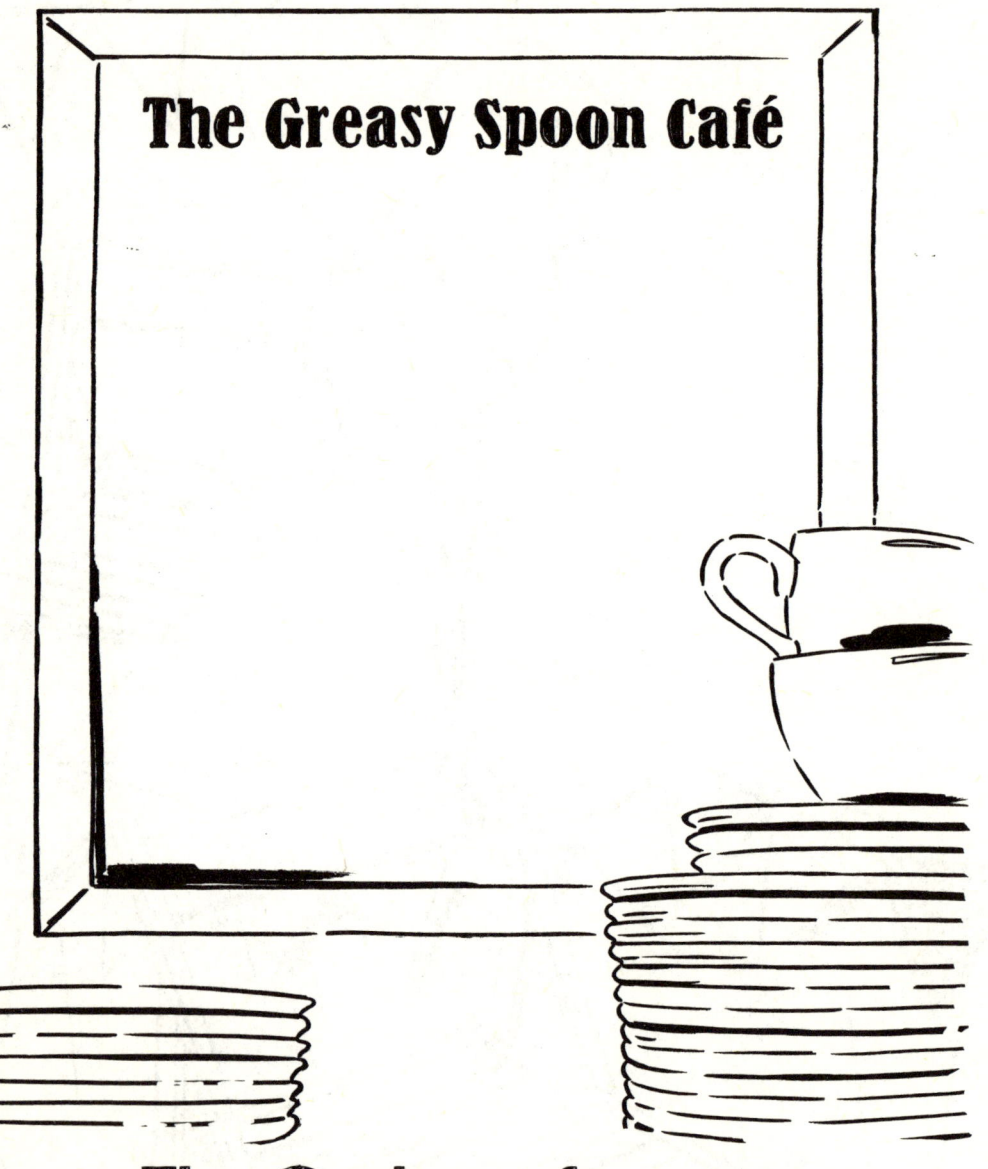

The Greasy Spoon Café

The Cockney favorite, jellied eels, perhaps?

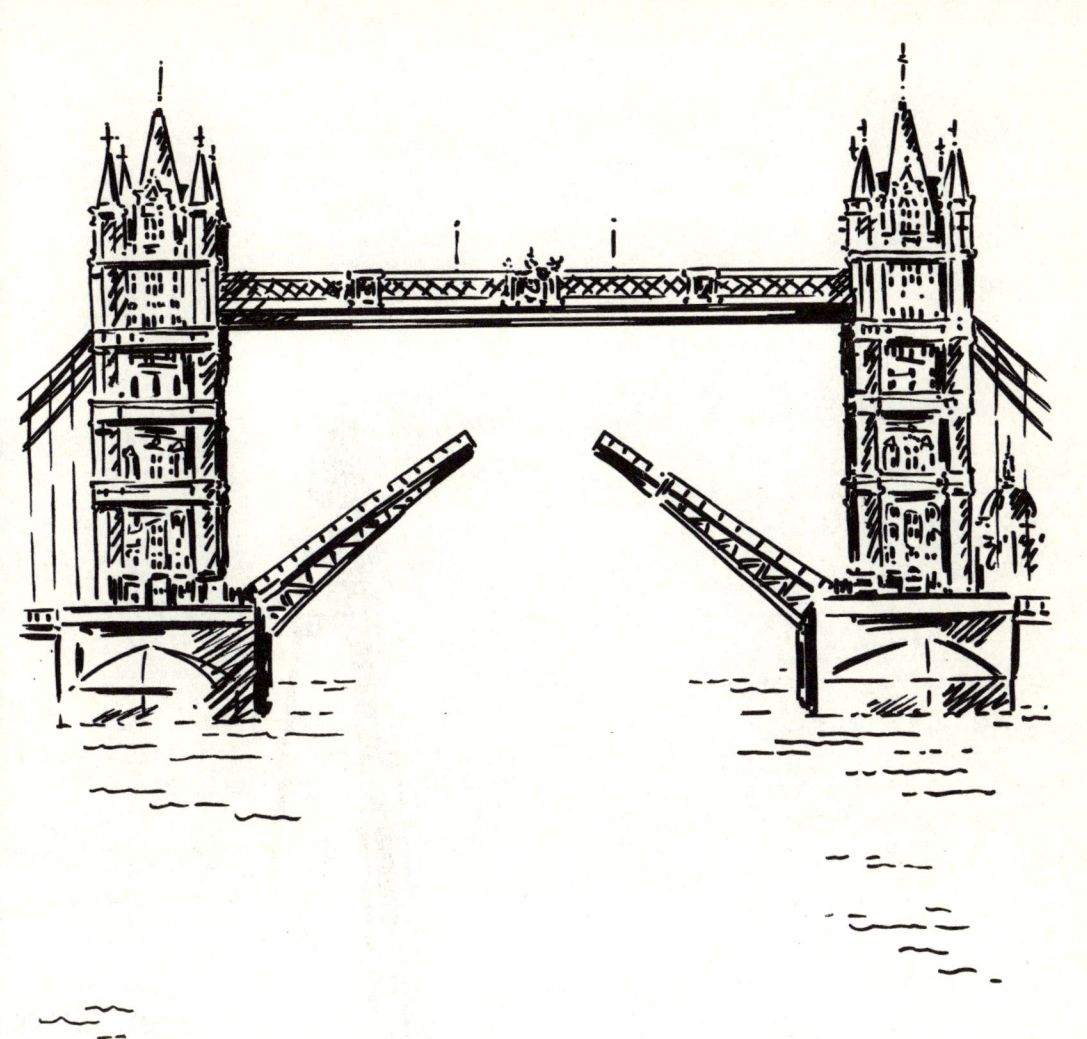

What's passing under Tower Bridge?

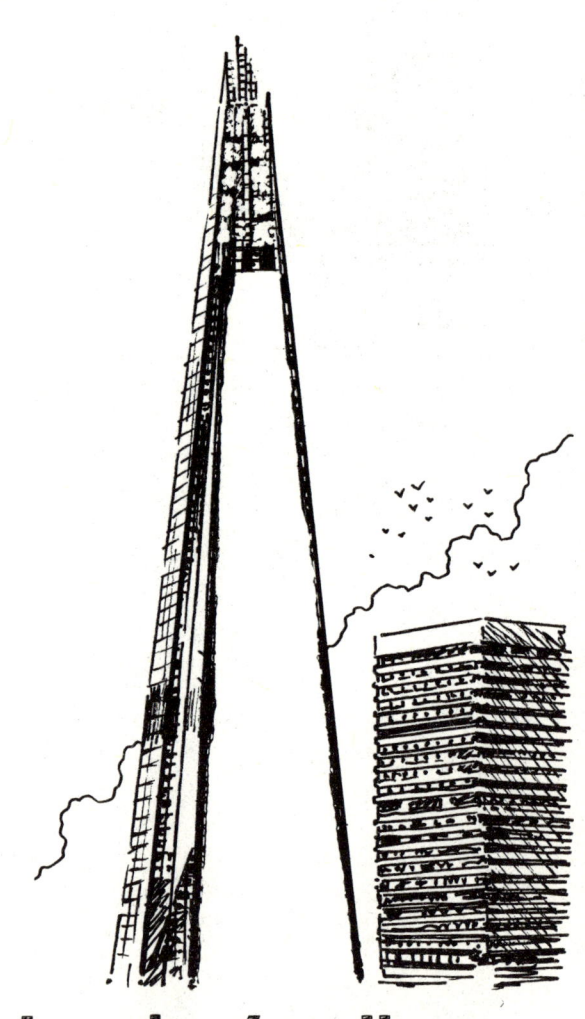

The Shard is London's tallest building. Design an even taller one.

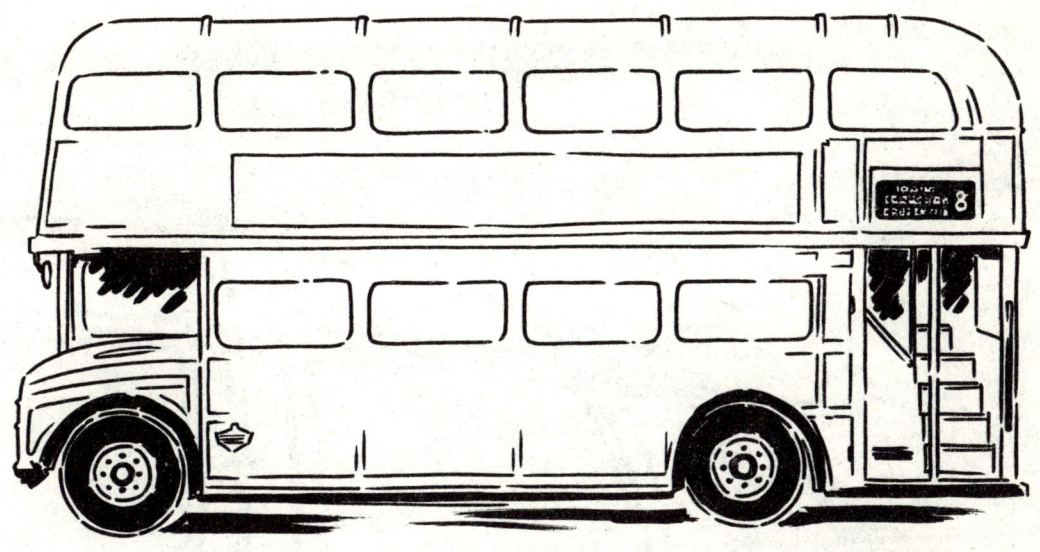

Decorate these iconic London double-decker buses taking you on a tour of the city.

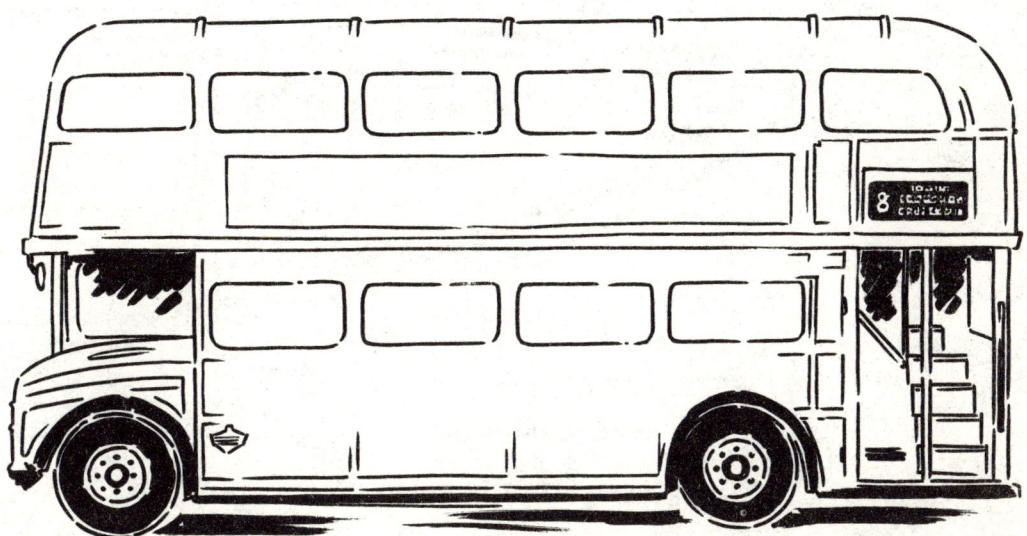

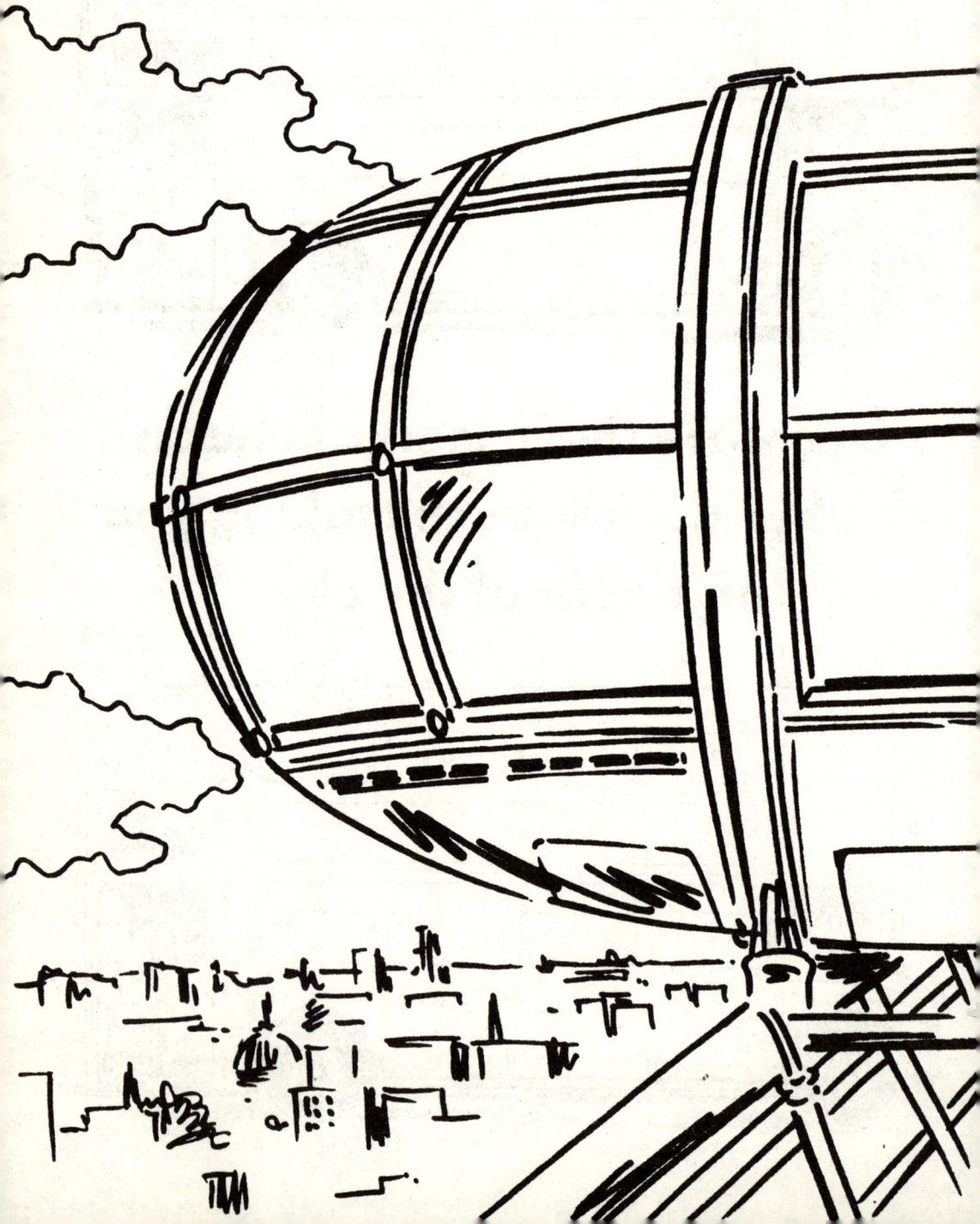

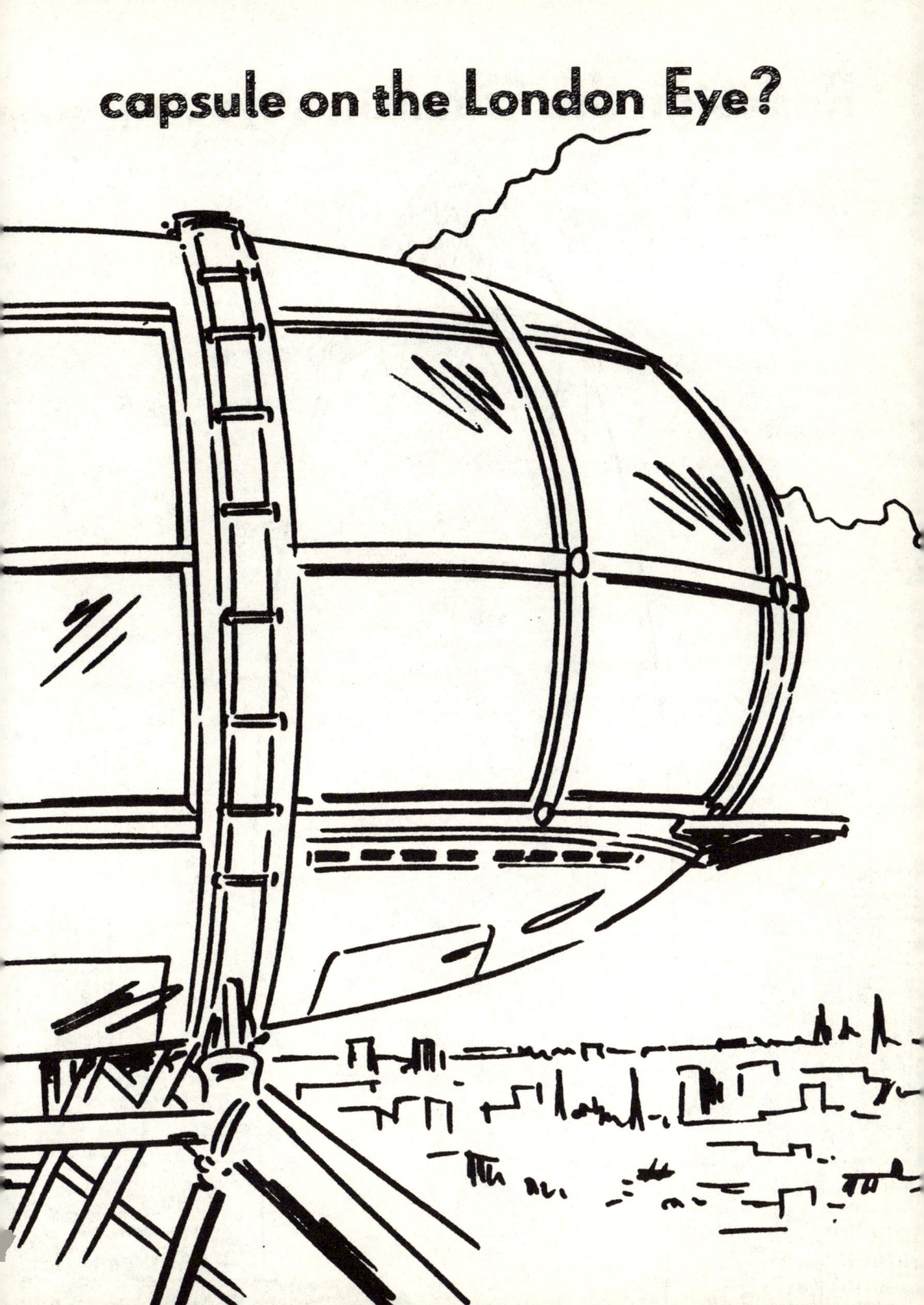

Redesign the Gherkin skyscraper.

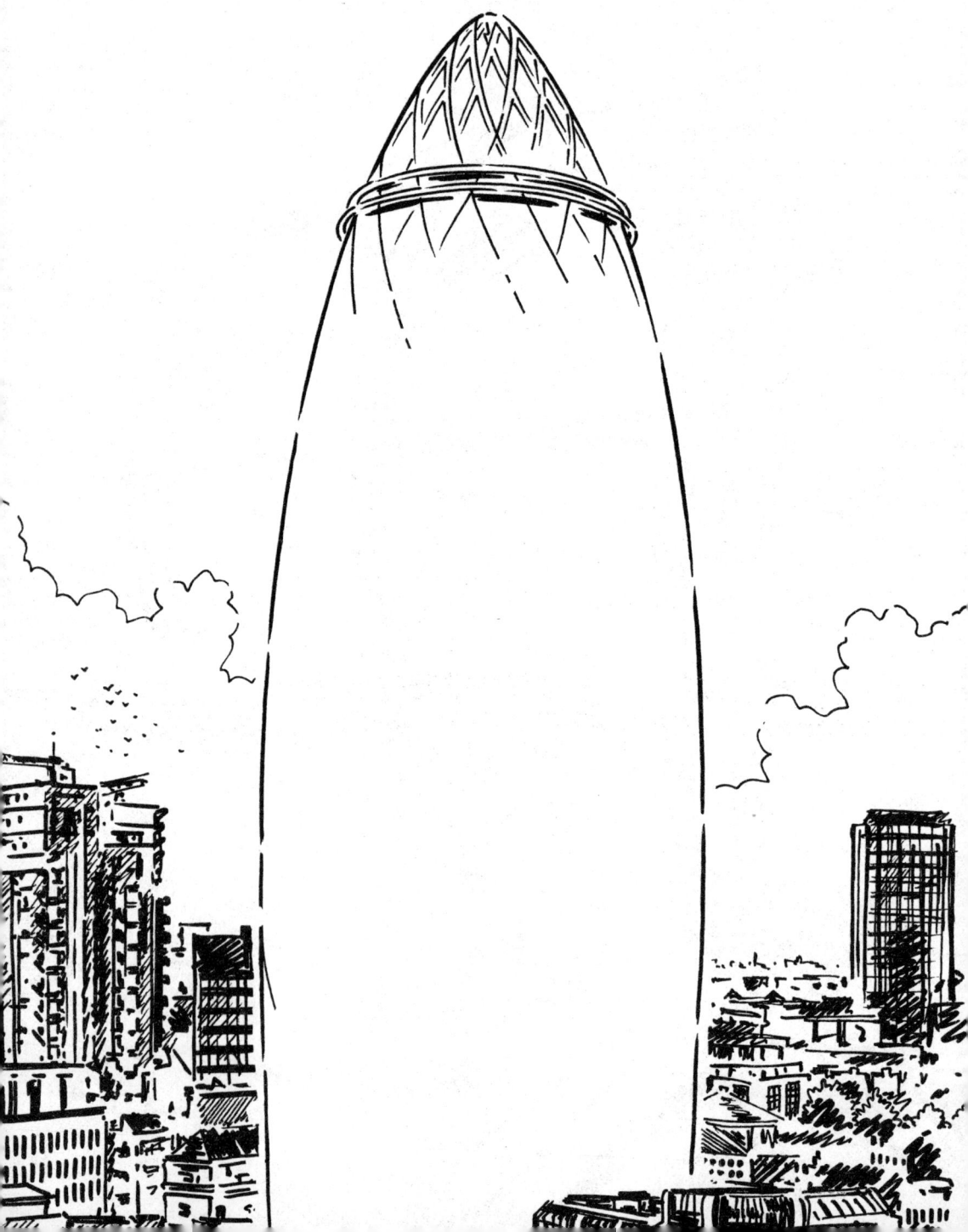

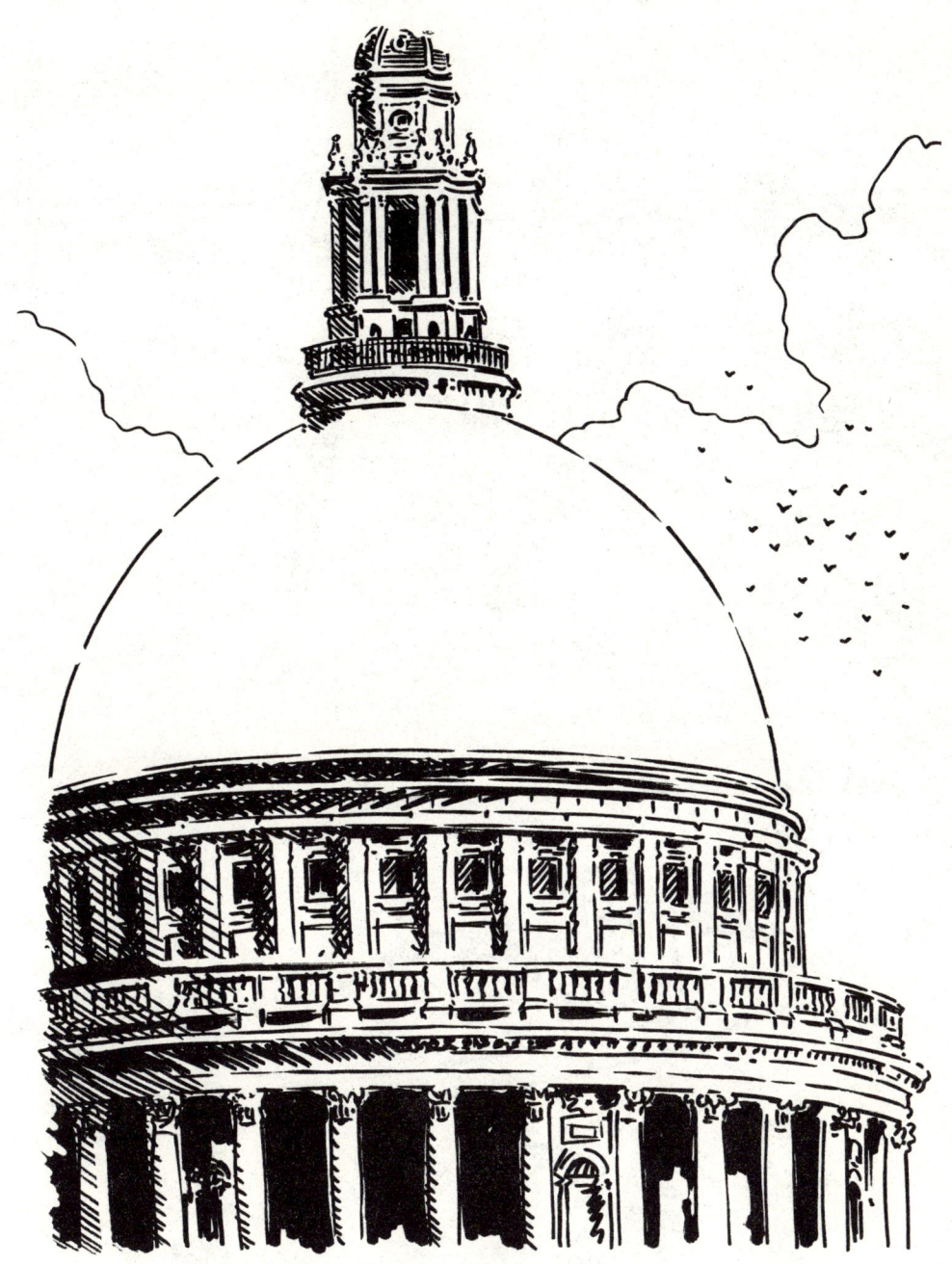

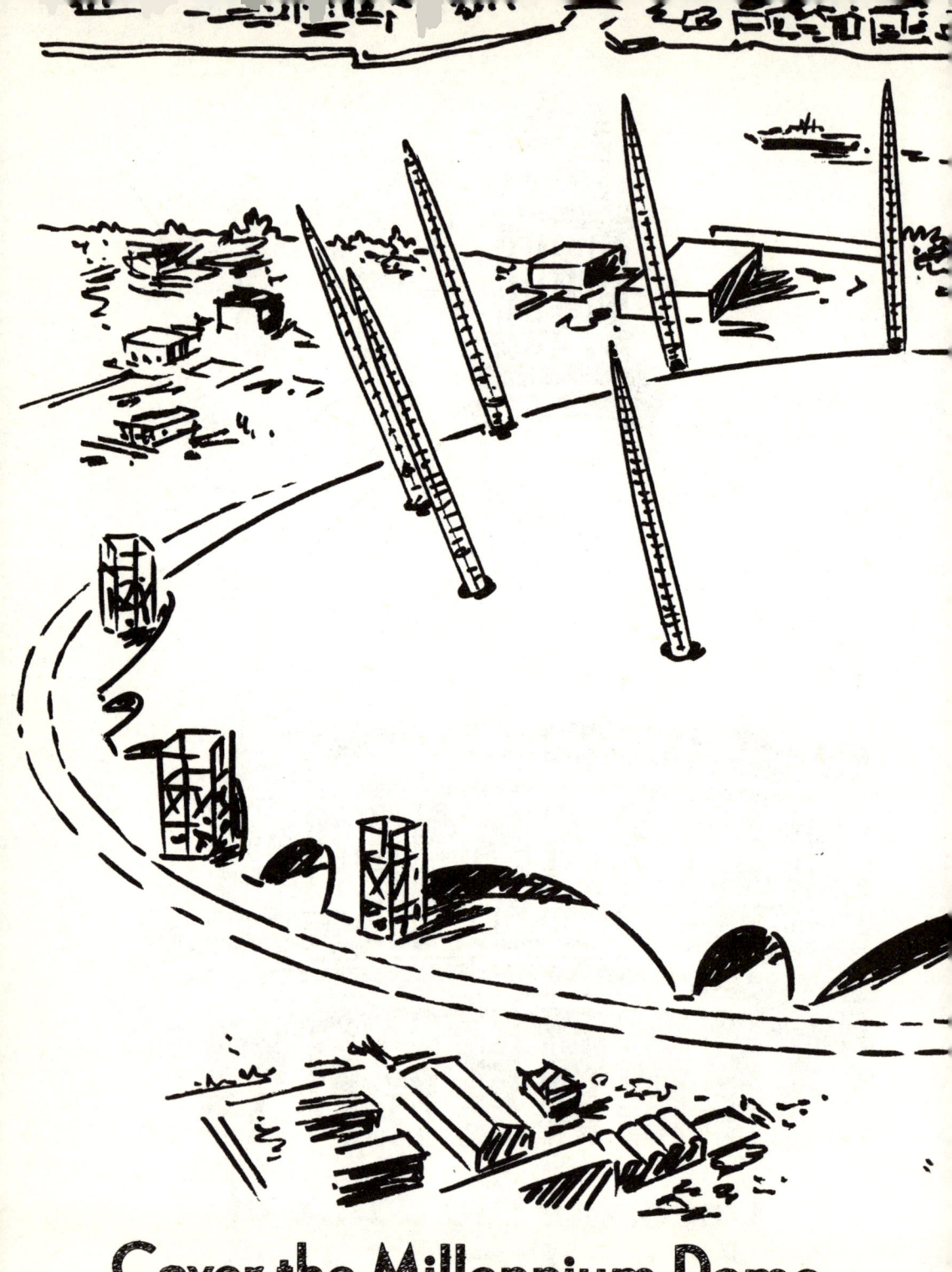

Cover the Millennium Dome...

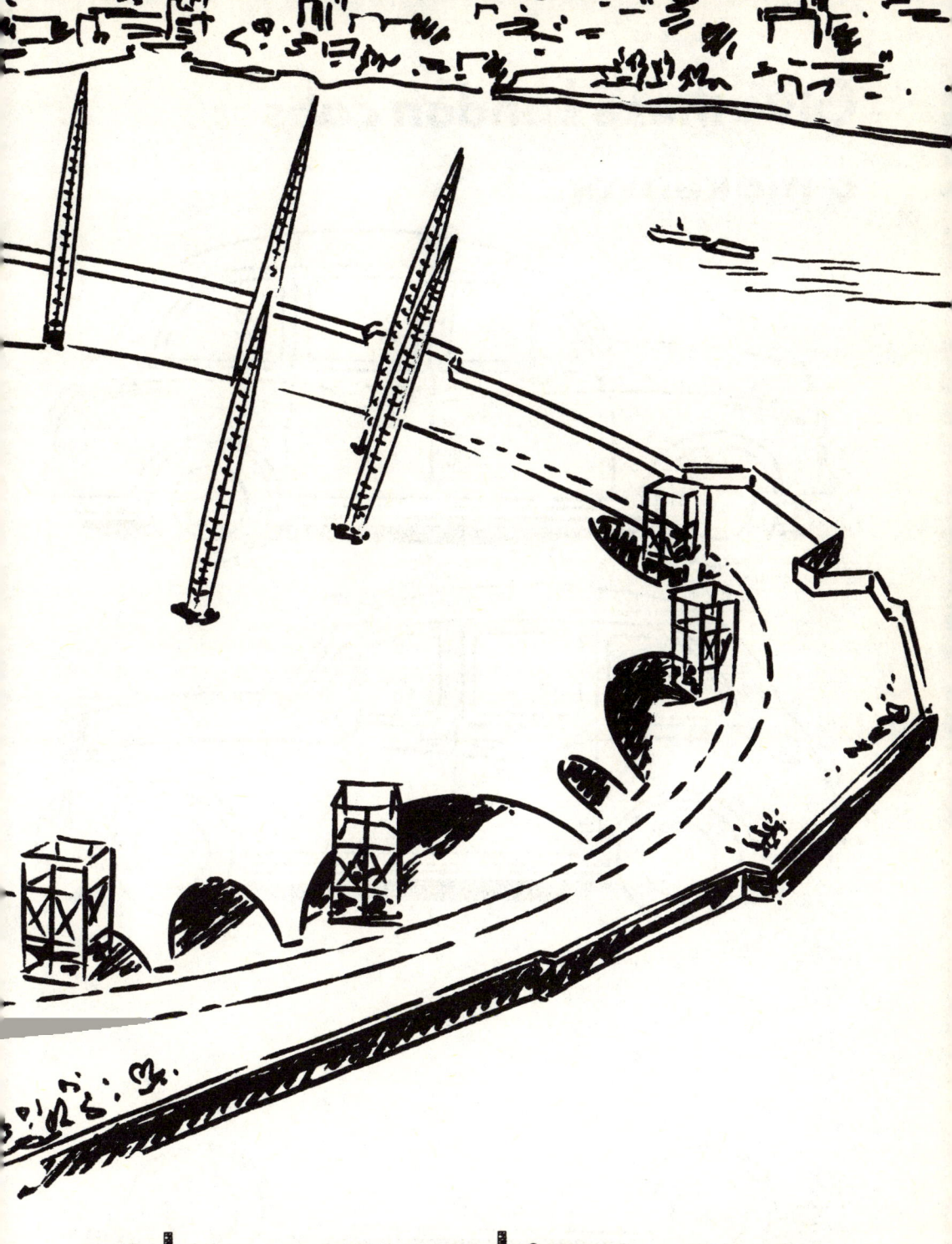

with an eye-catching pattern.

Give these London cabs a makeover.

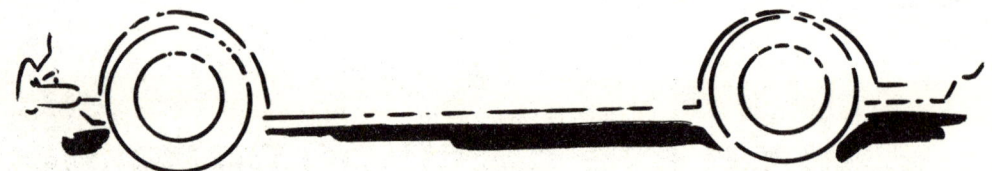

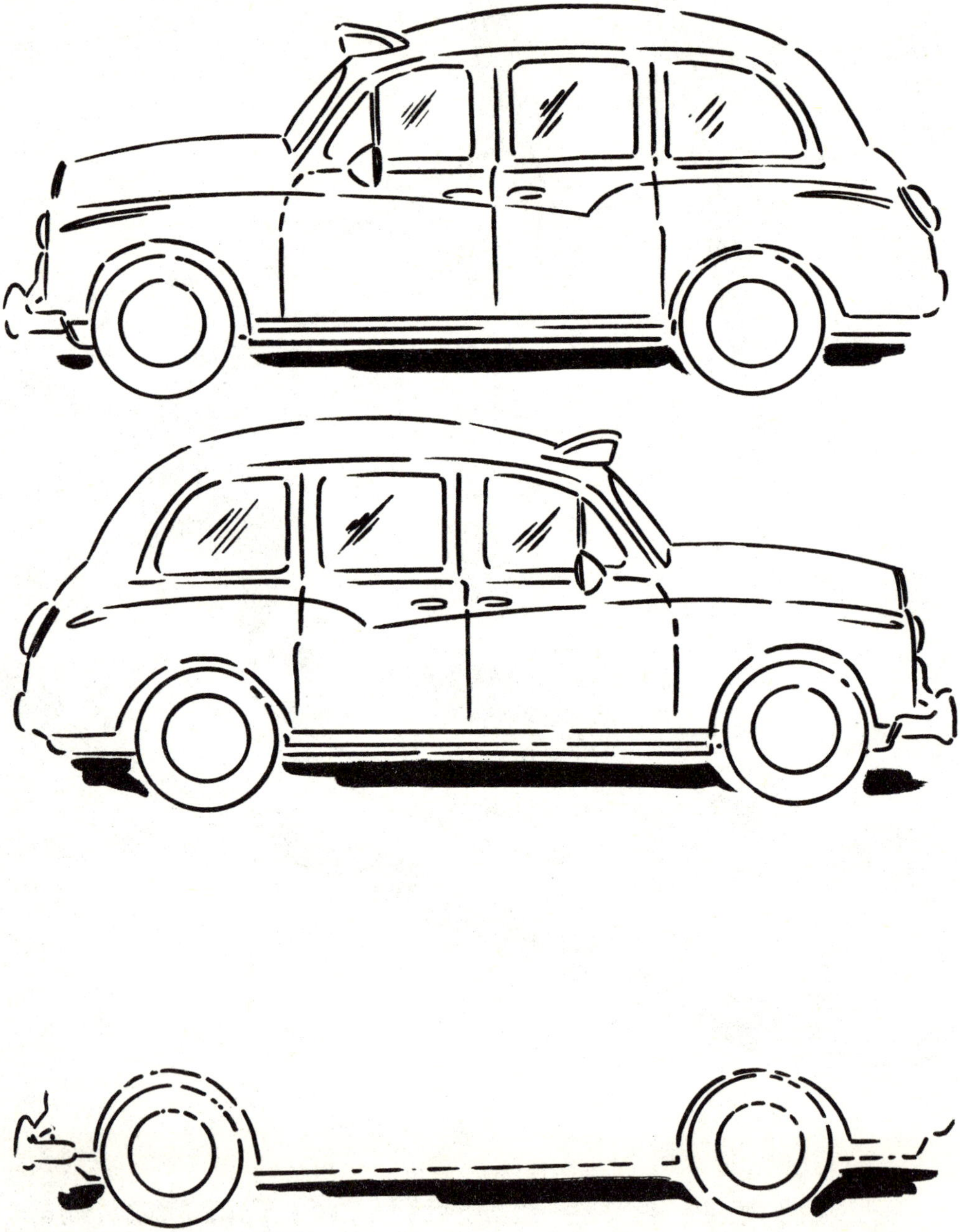

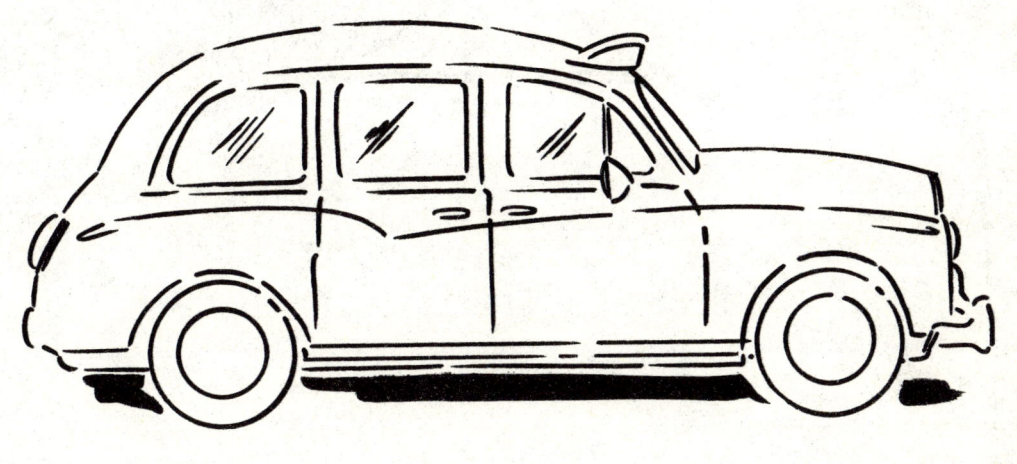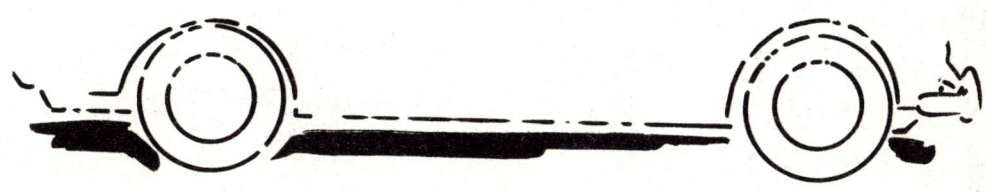

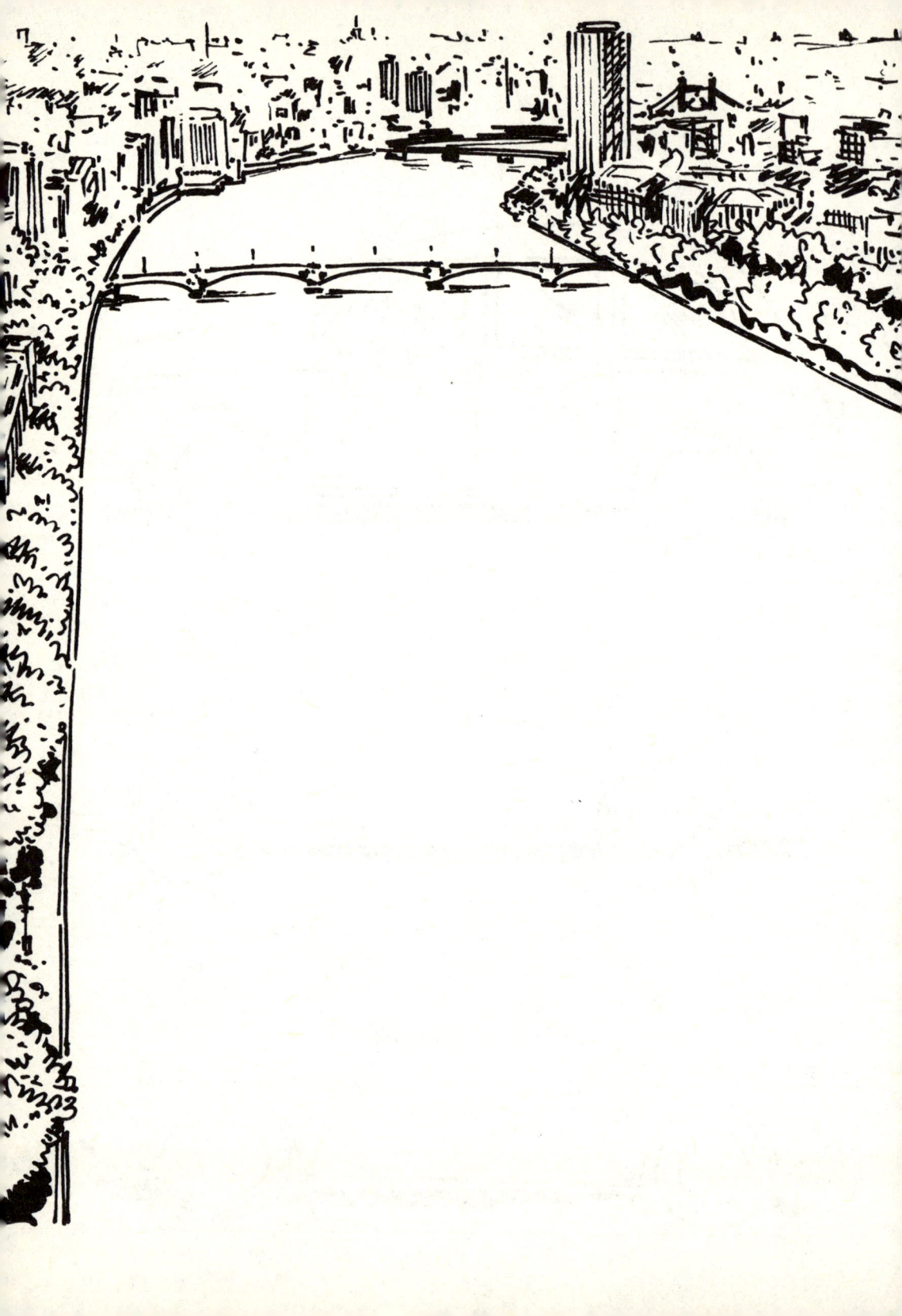

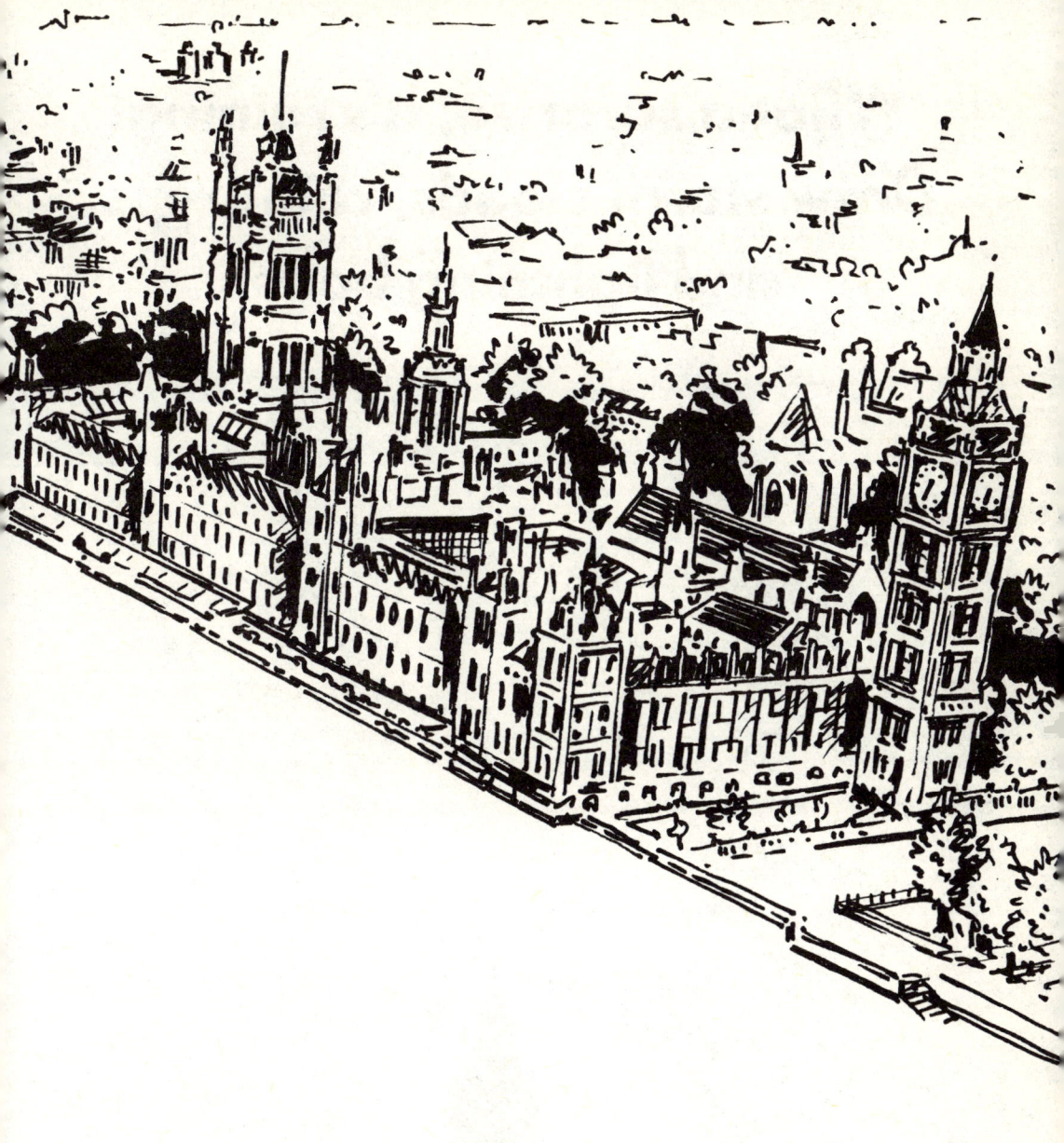

Draw a fantasy island in the River Thames.

What a surprise, it's raining! Draw storm clouds, raindrops, and lightning bolts.

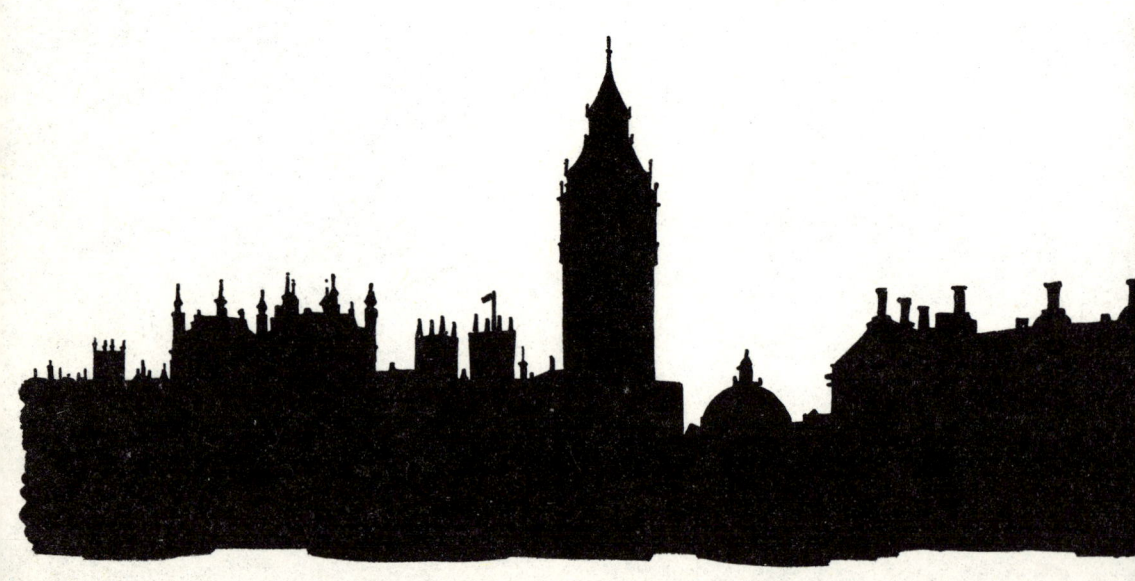

What's in this picture hanging in the National Gallery?

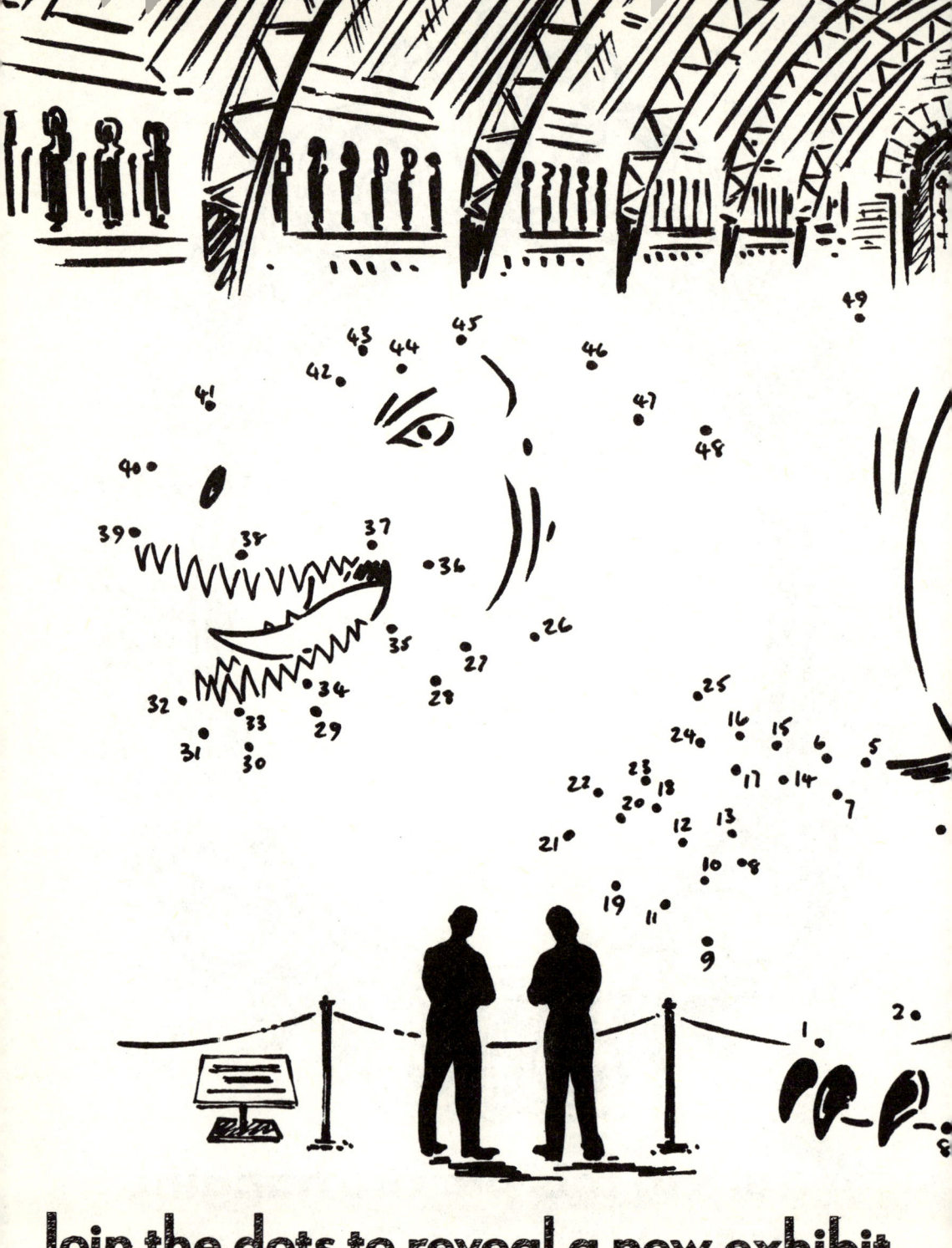

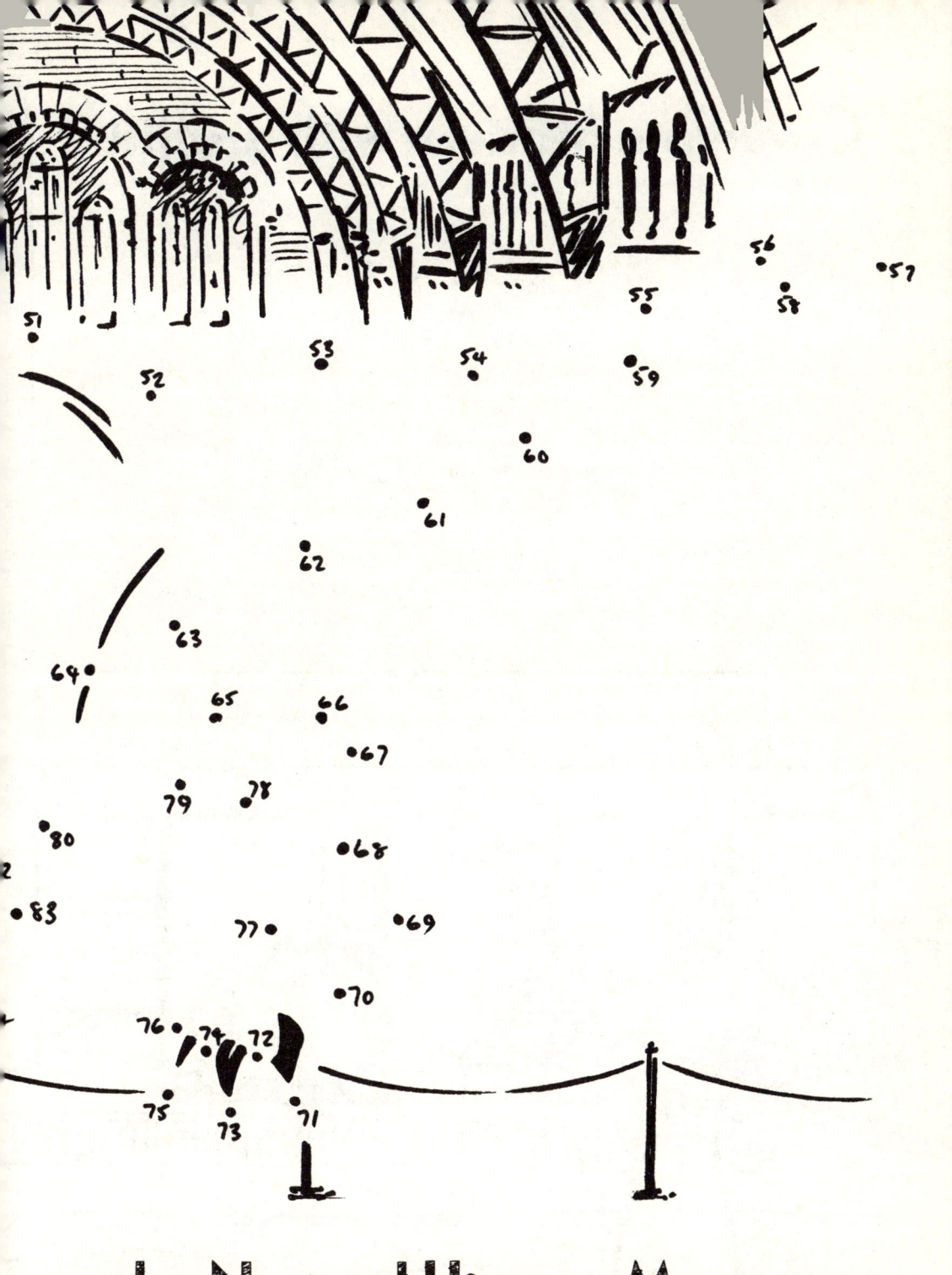

at the Natural History Museum.

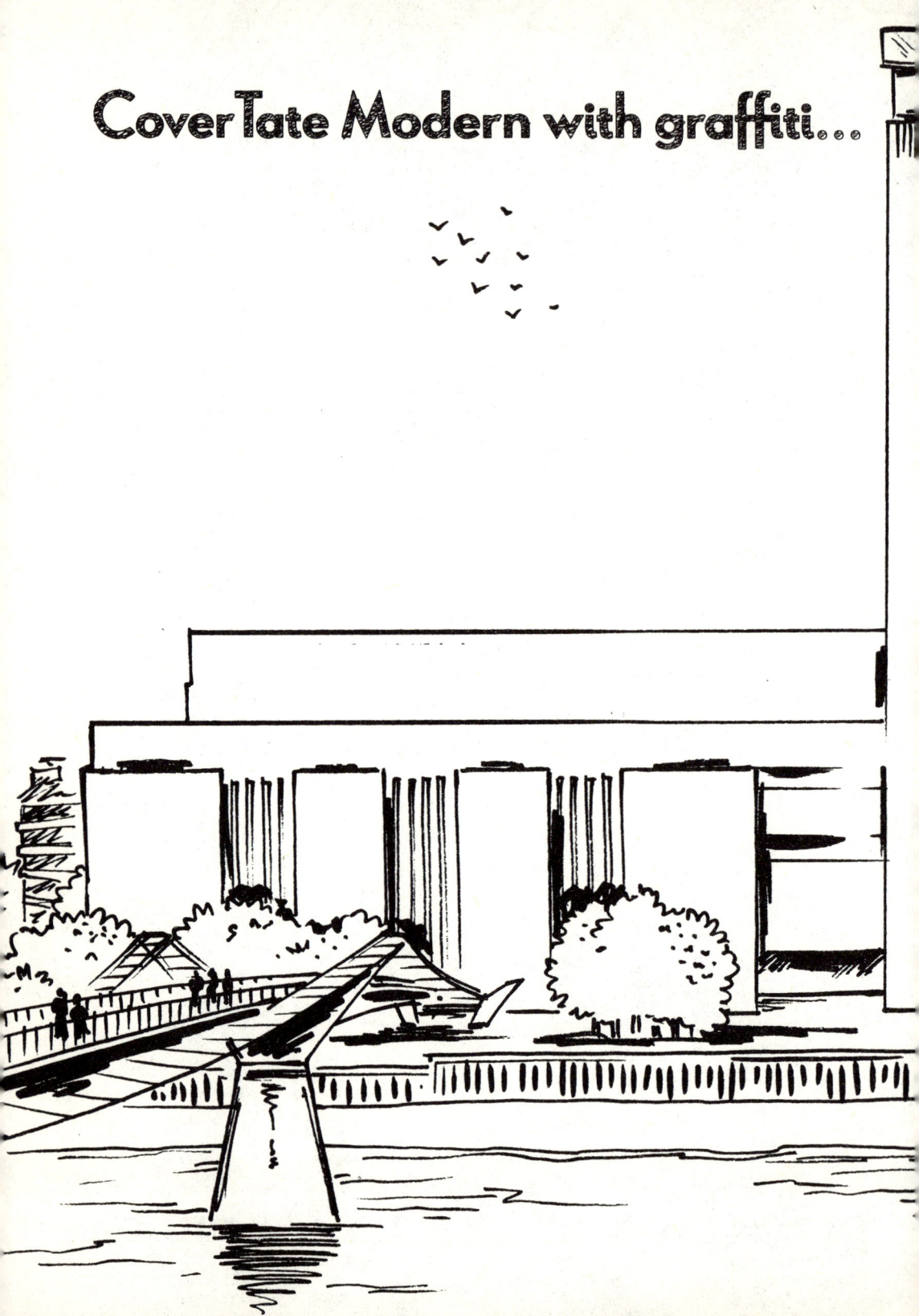

and draw sculptures on the roof.

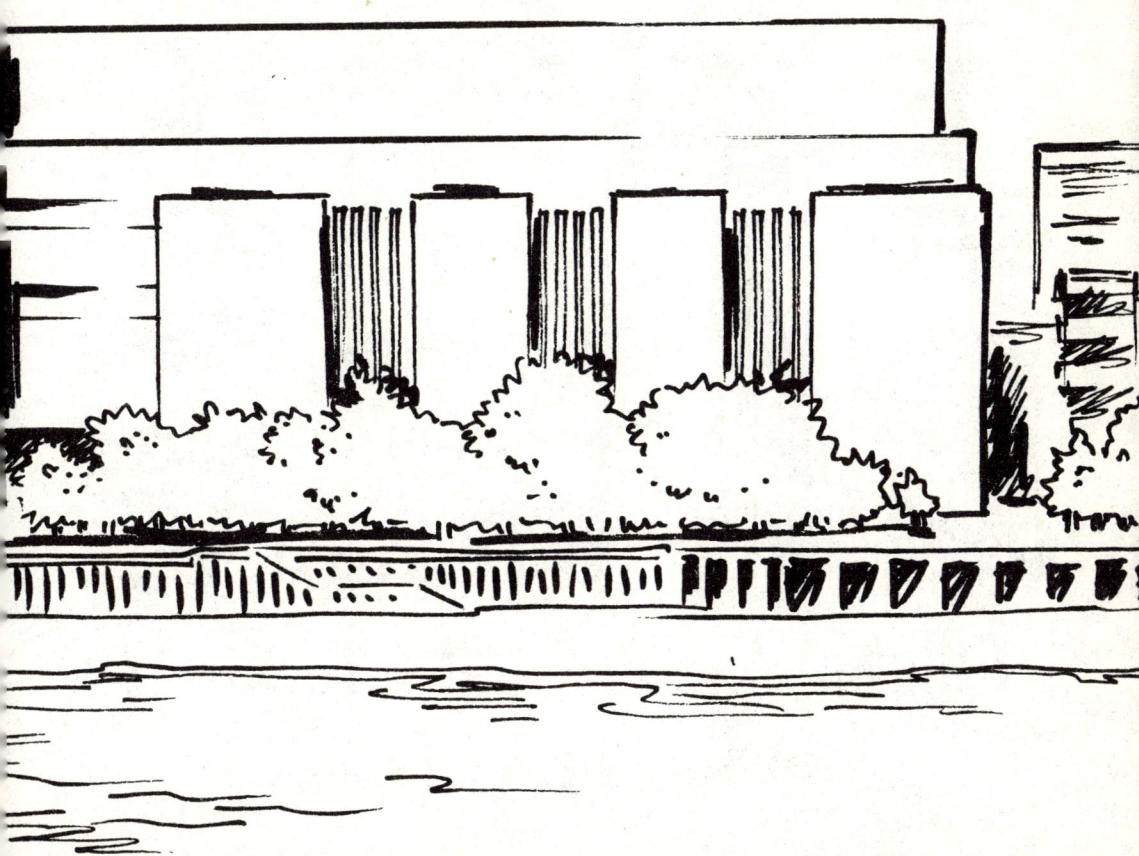

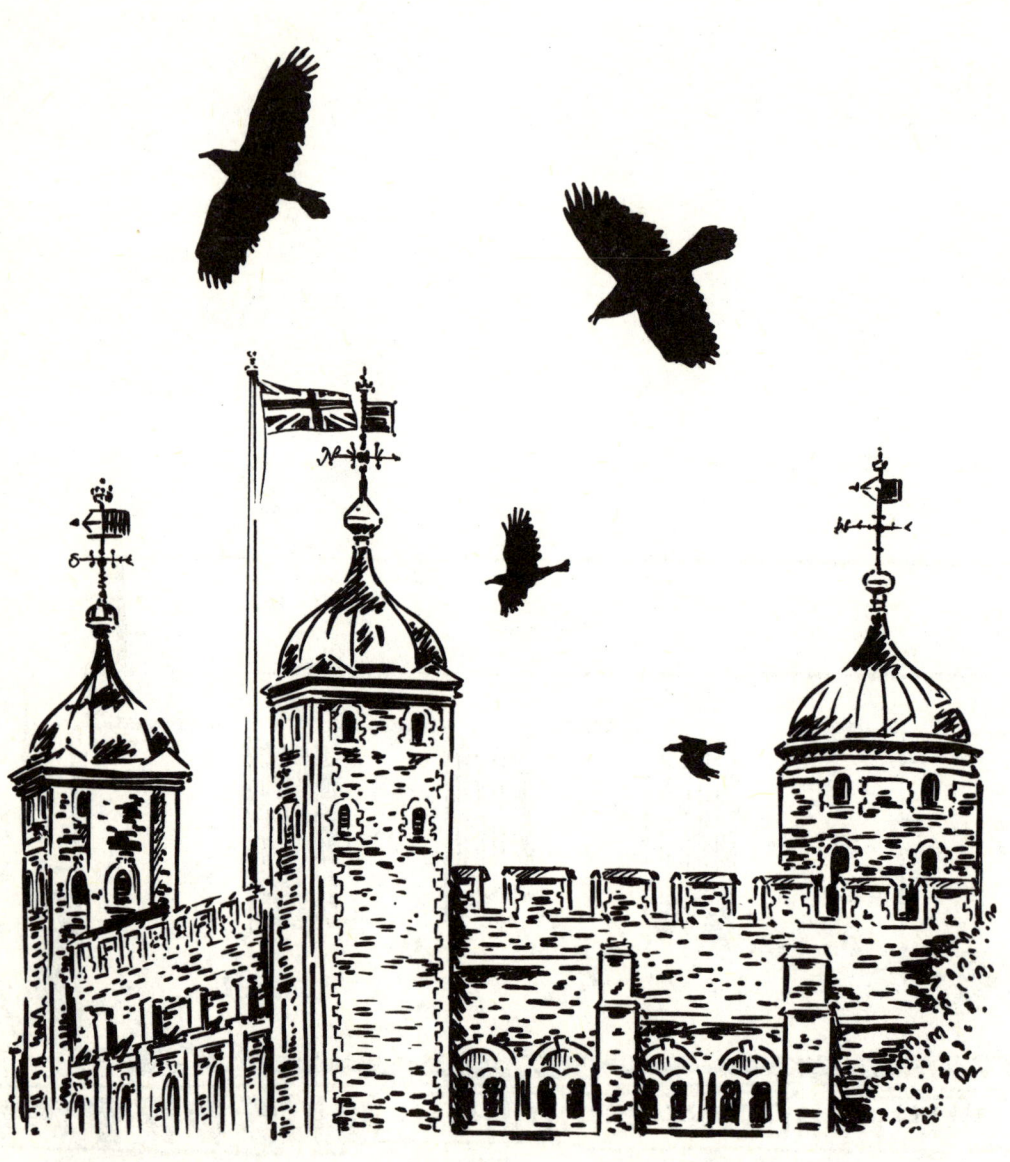

Join the dots to discover this famous London attraction.

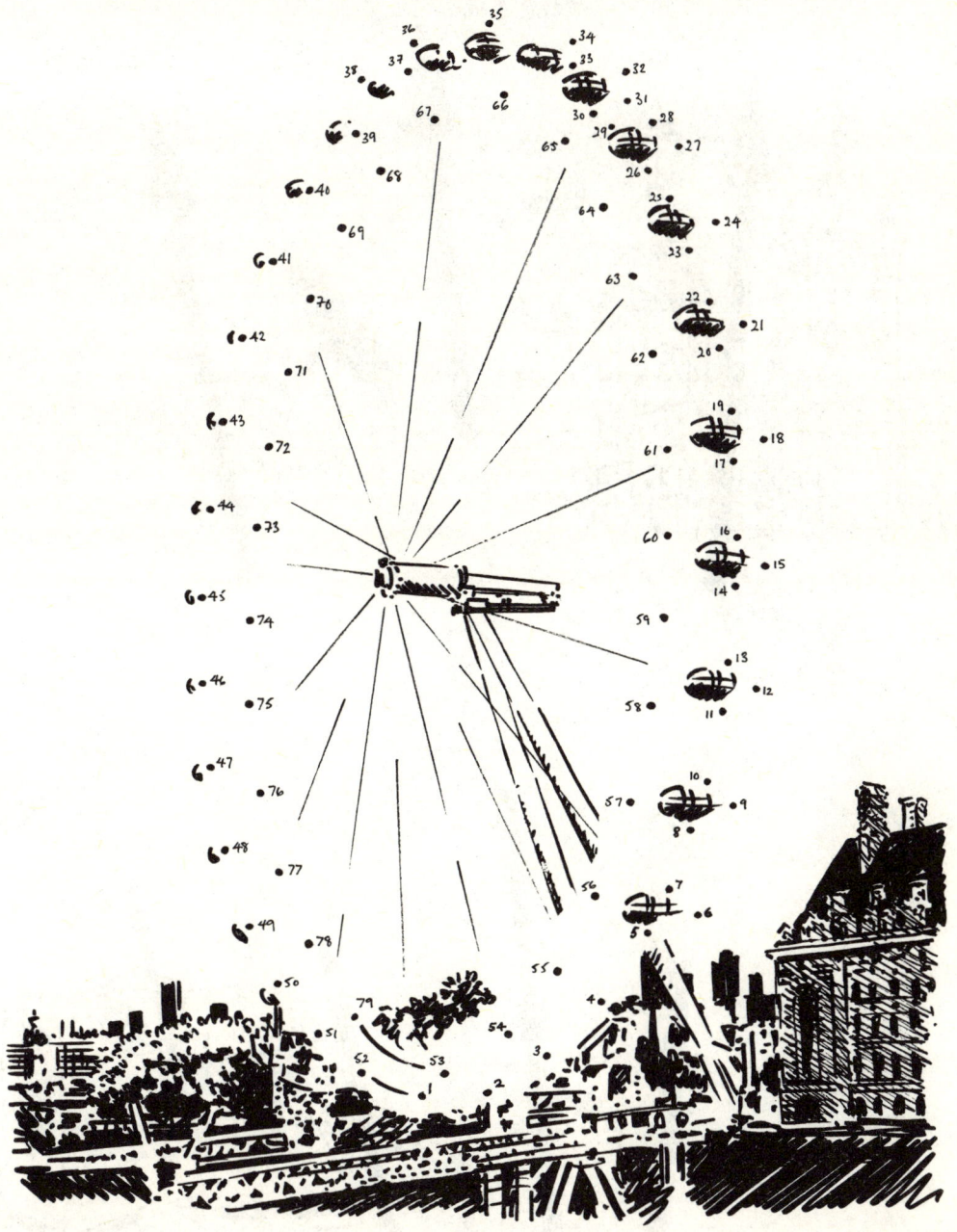

Who has been sent to the Tower and lost their head?

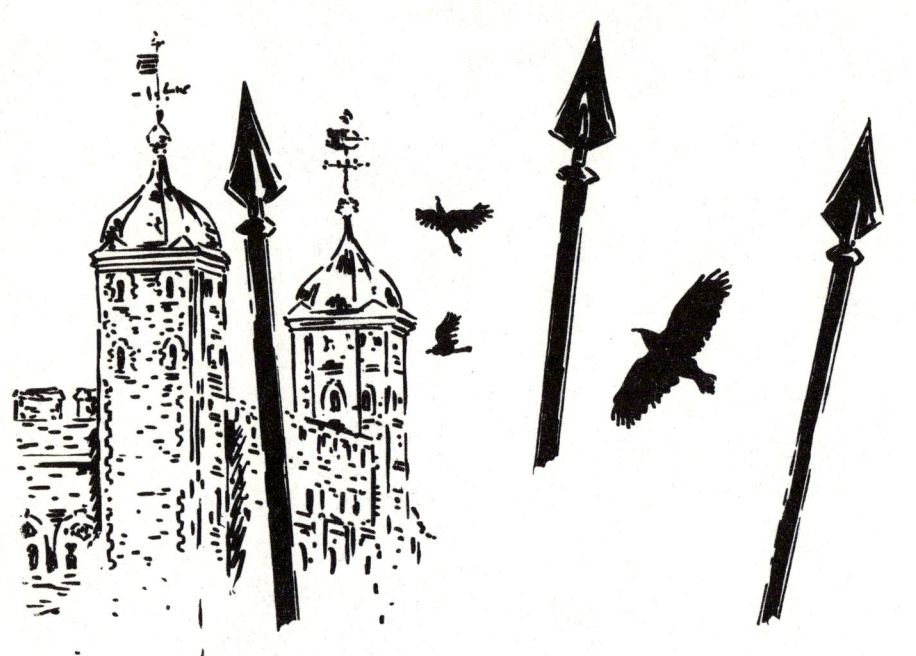
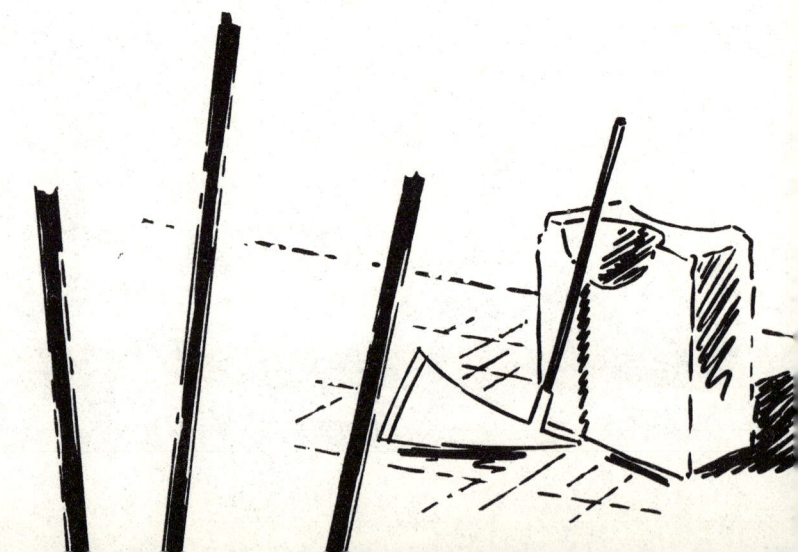

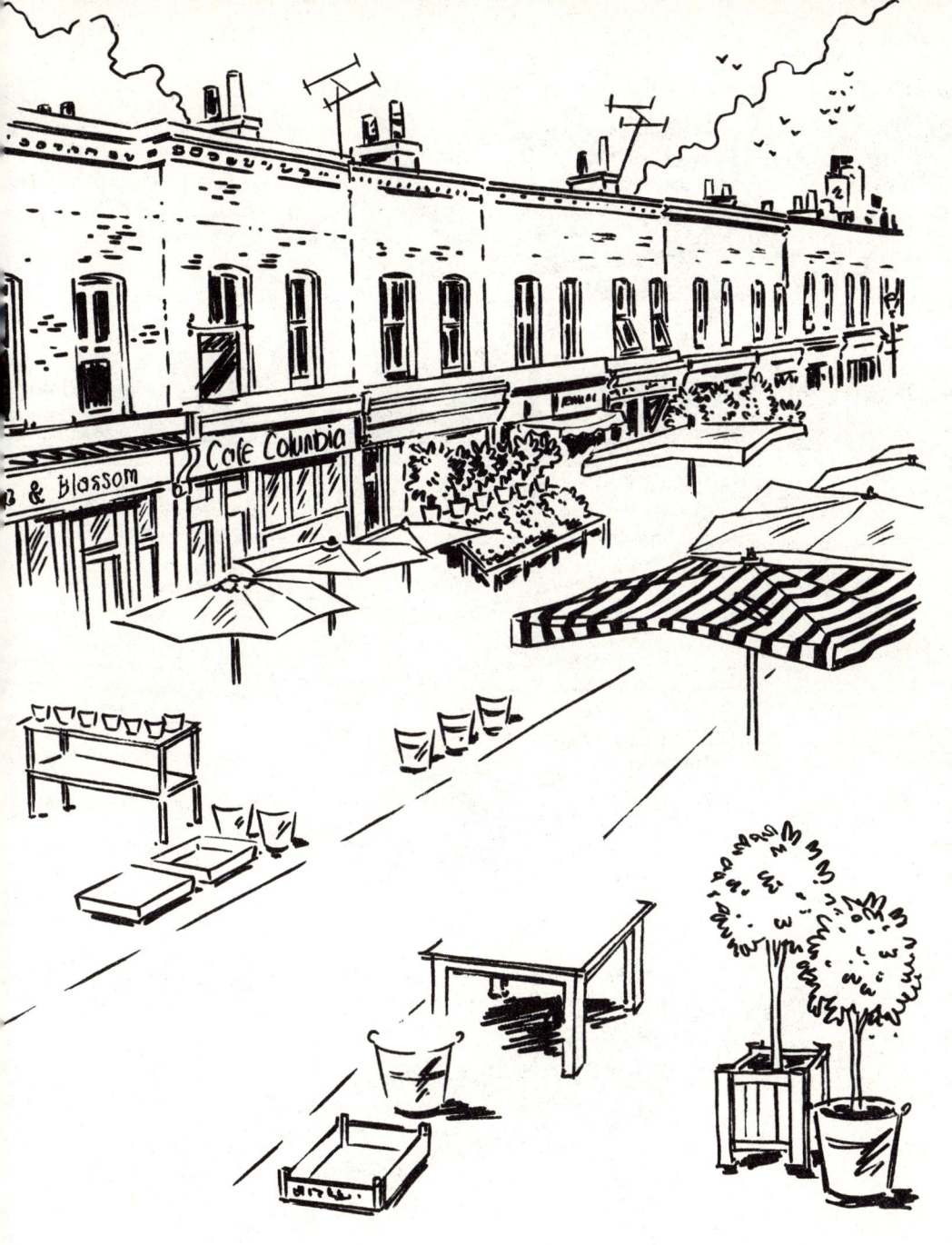

What's for sale at Columbia Road Flower Market?

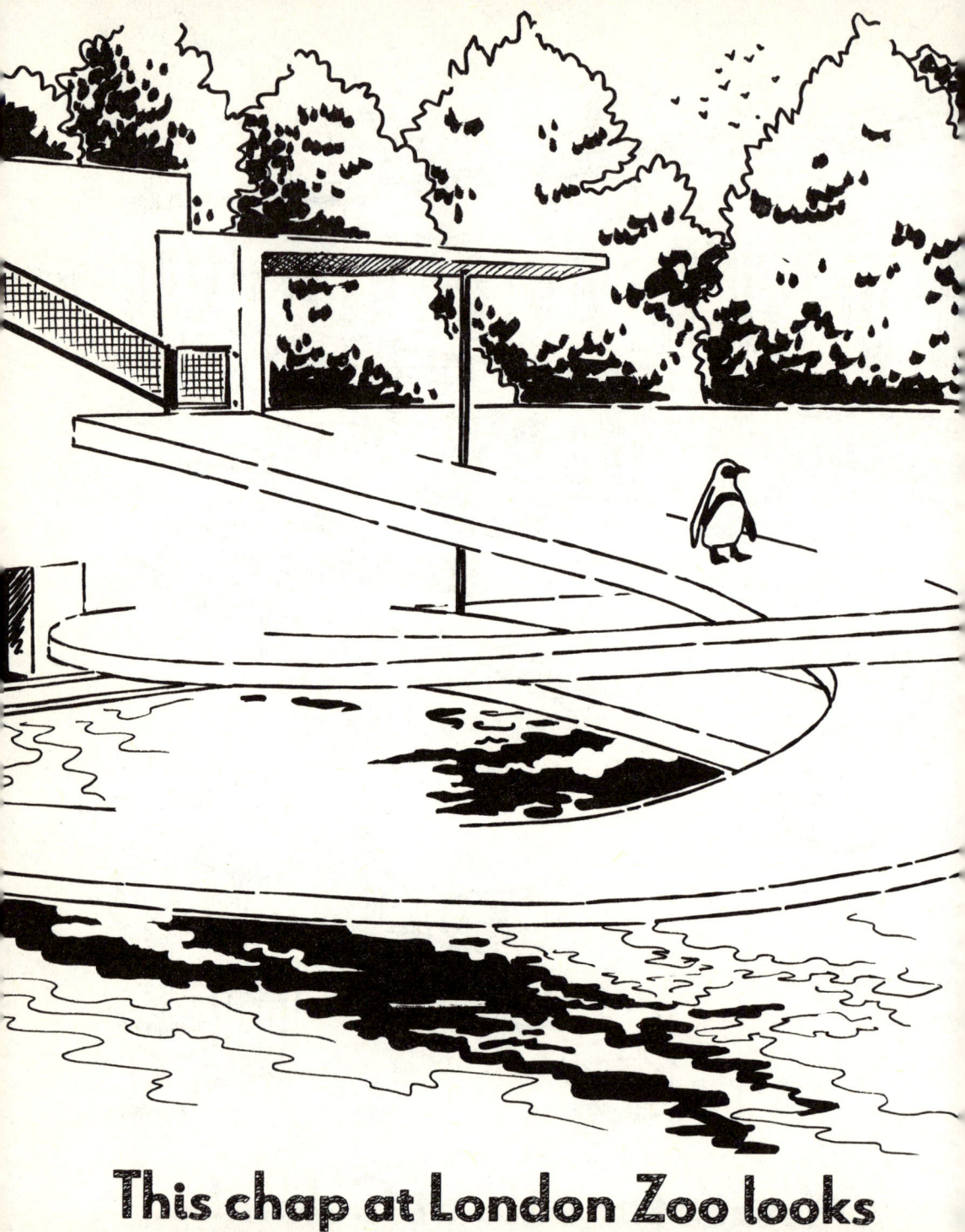

Draw a series of fantastic bridges to span the River Thames.

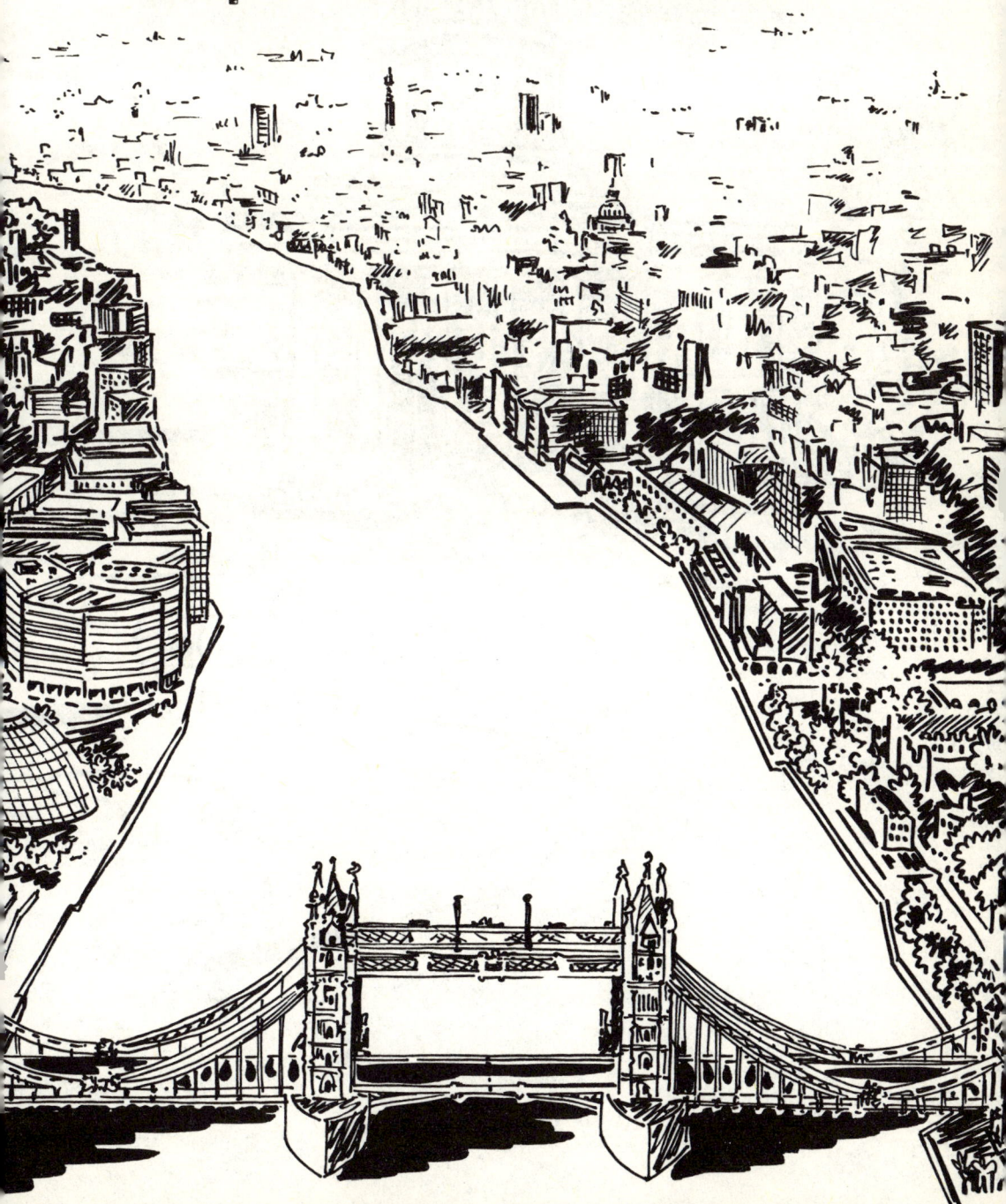

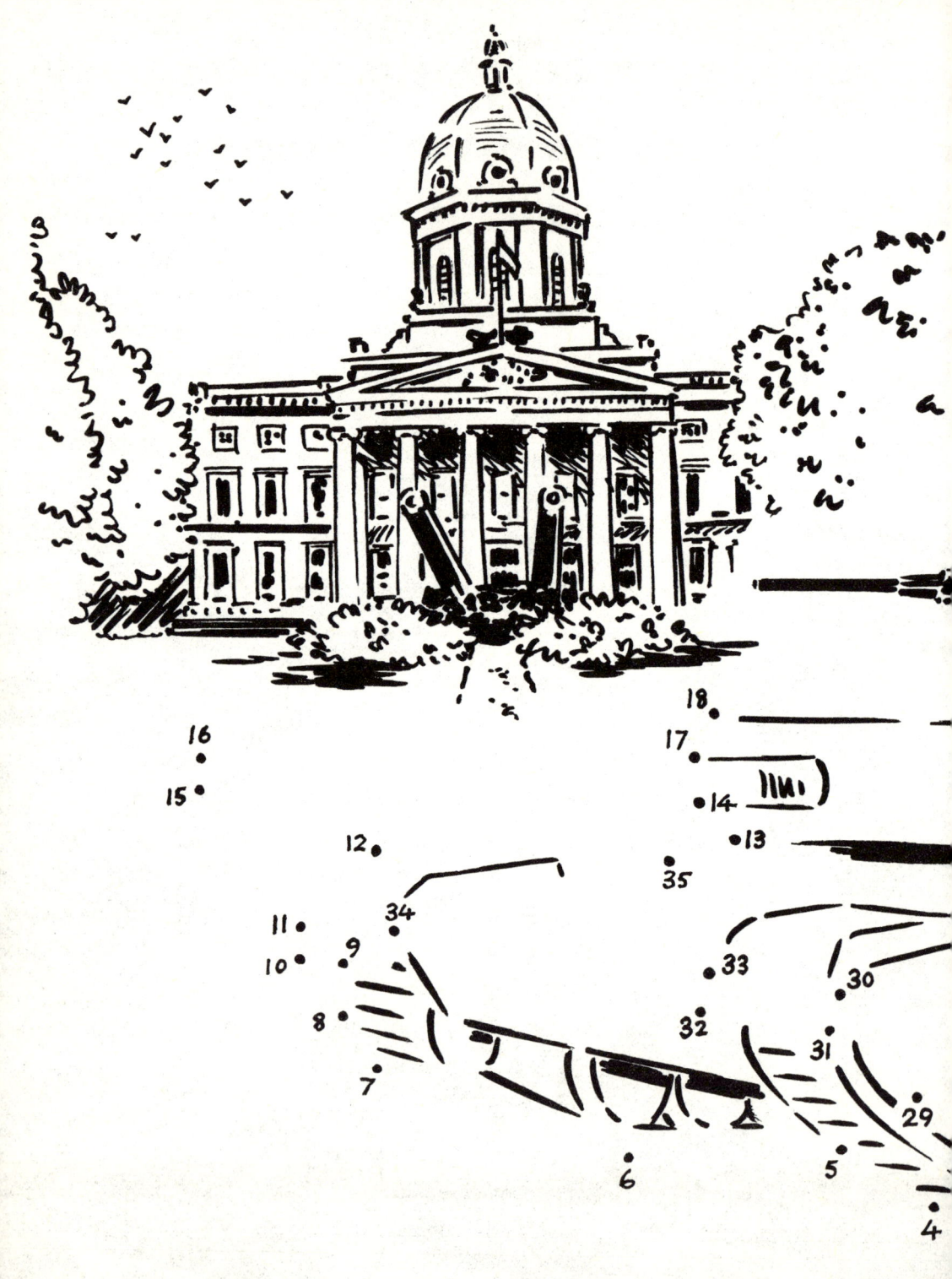

Join the dots to discover what's in front of the Imperial War Museum.

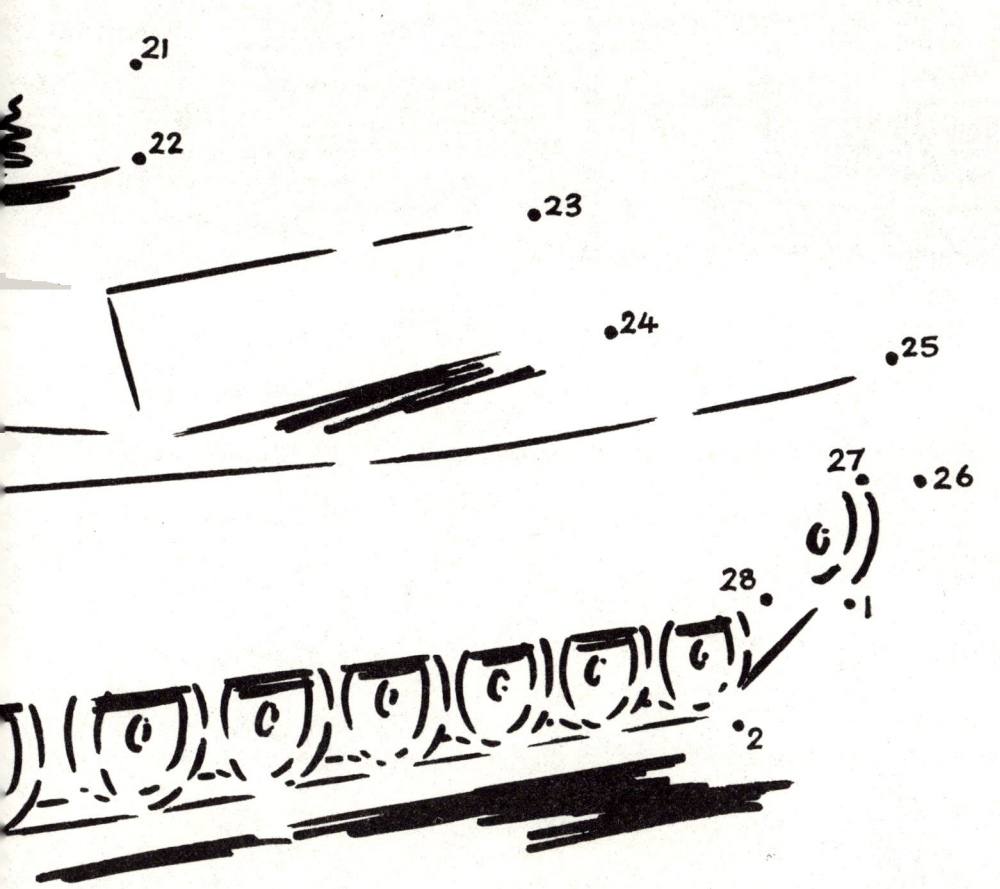

How many skaters can you get...

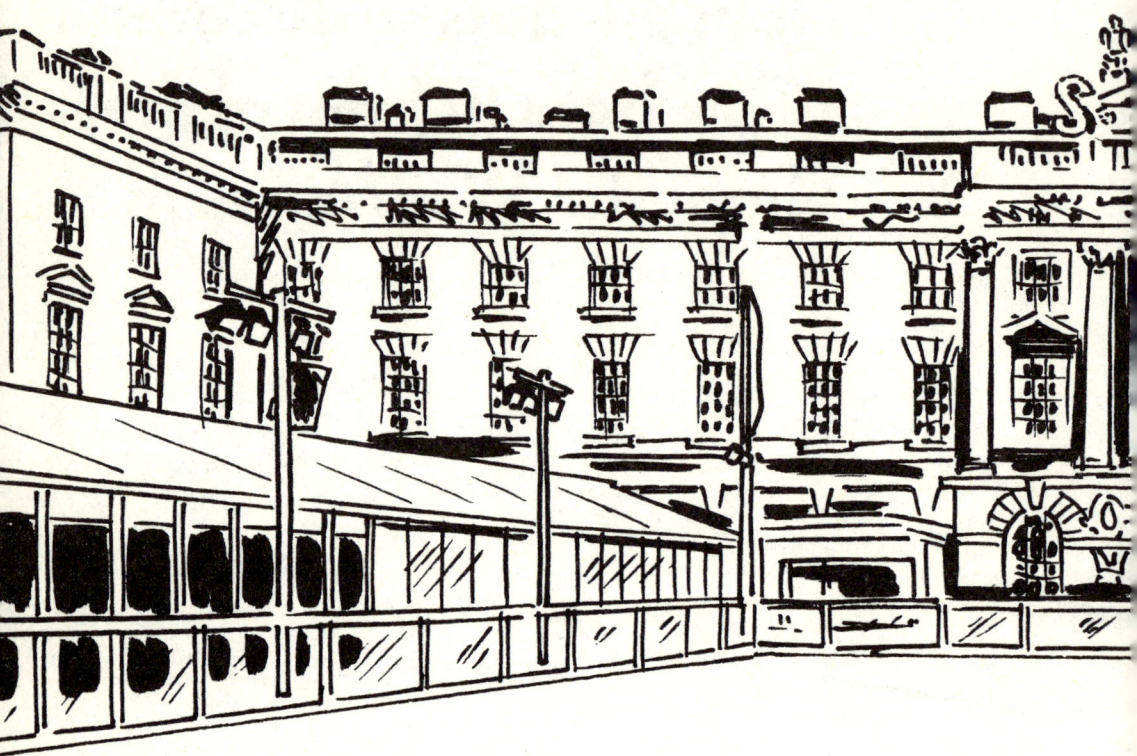

on the ice rink at Somerset House?

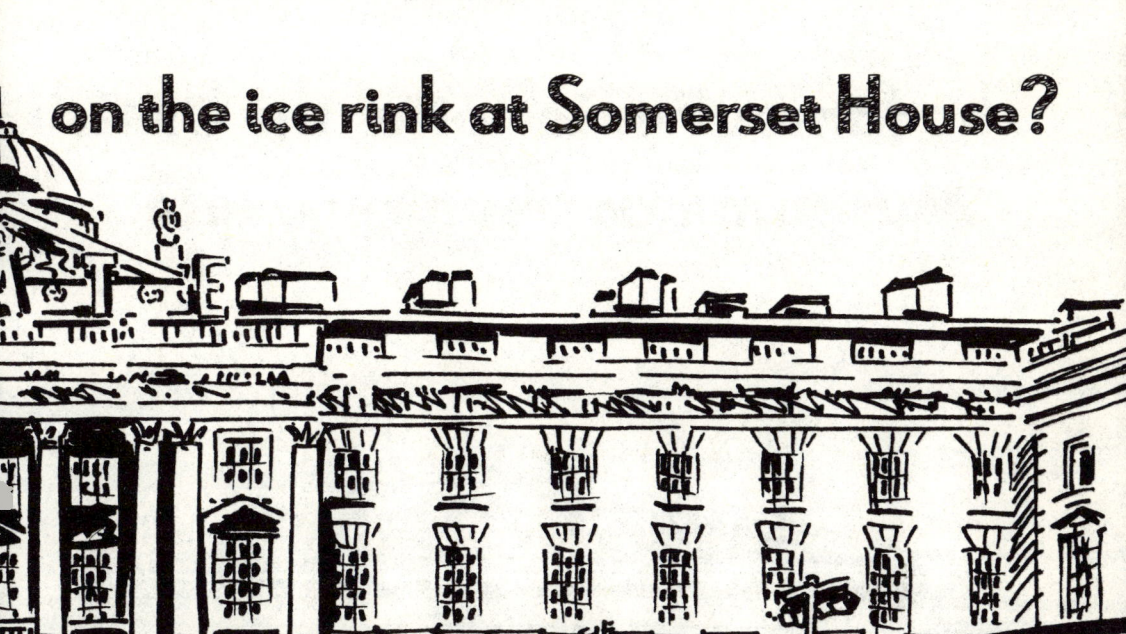

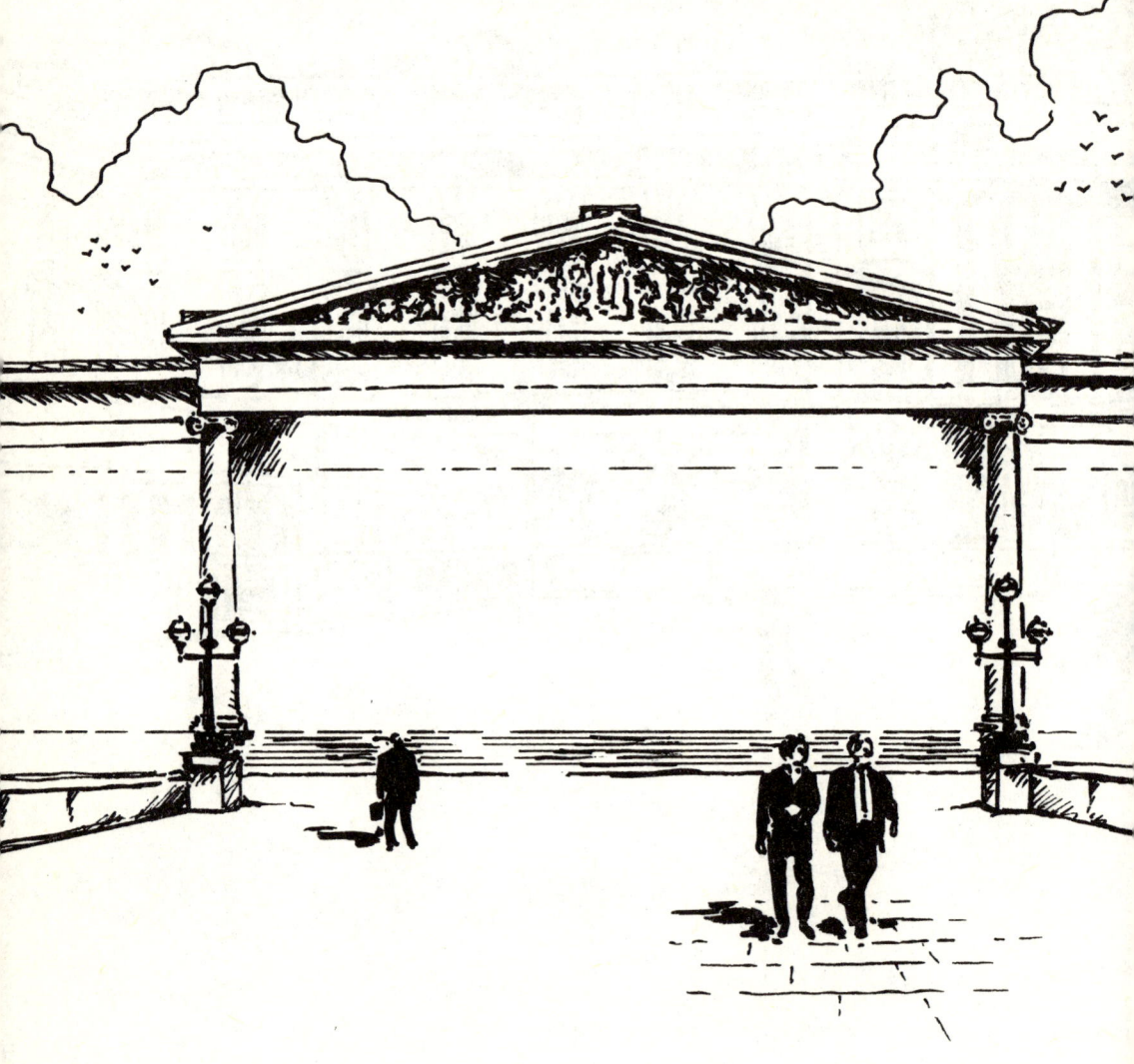

Create a prize-winning garden...

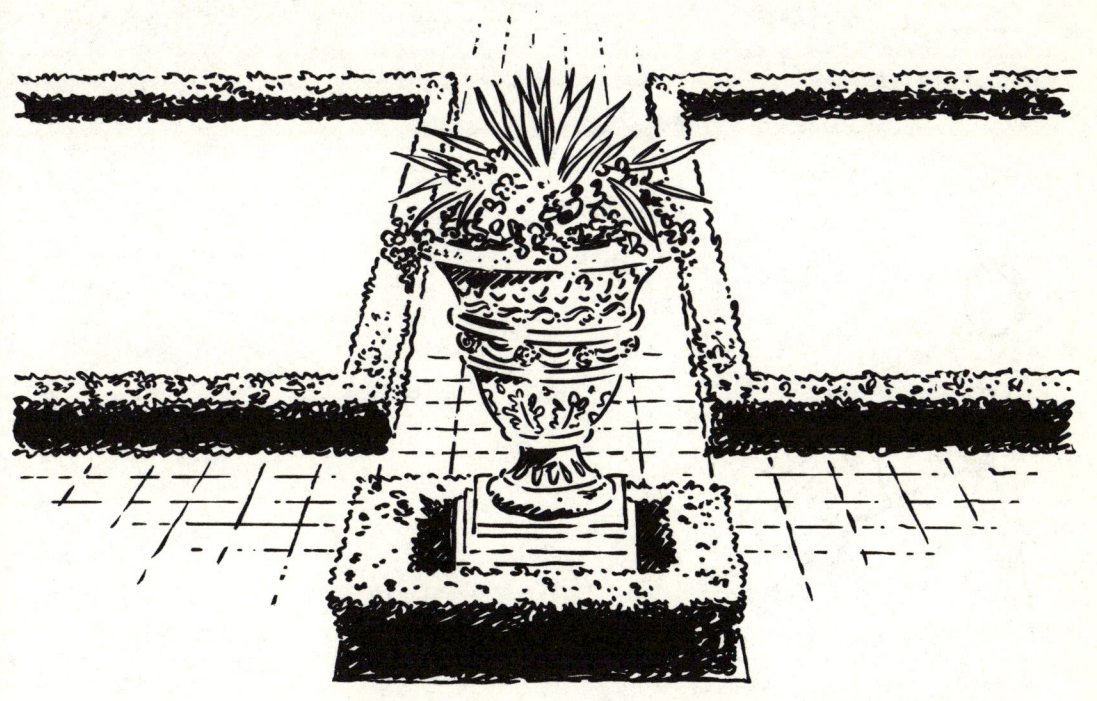

for the Chelsea Flower Show.

Create a stage set for this ballet at the Royal Opera House.

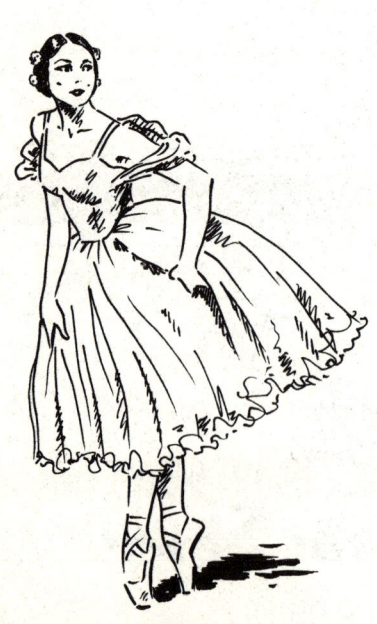

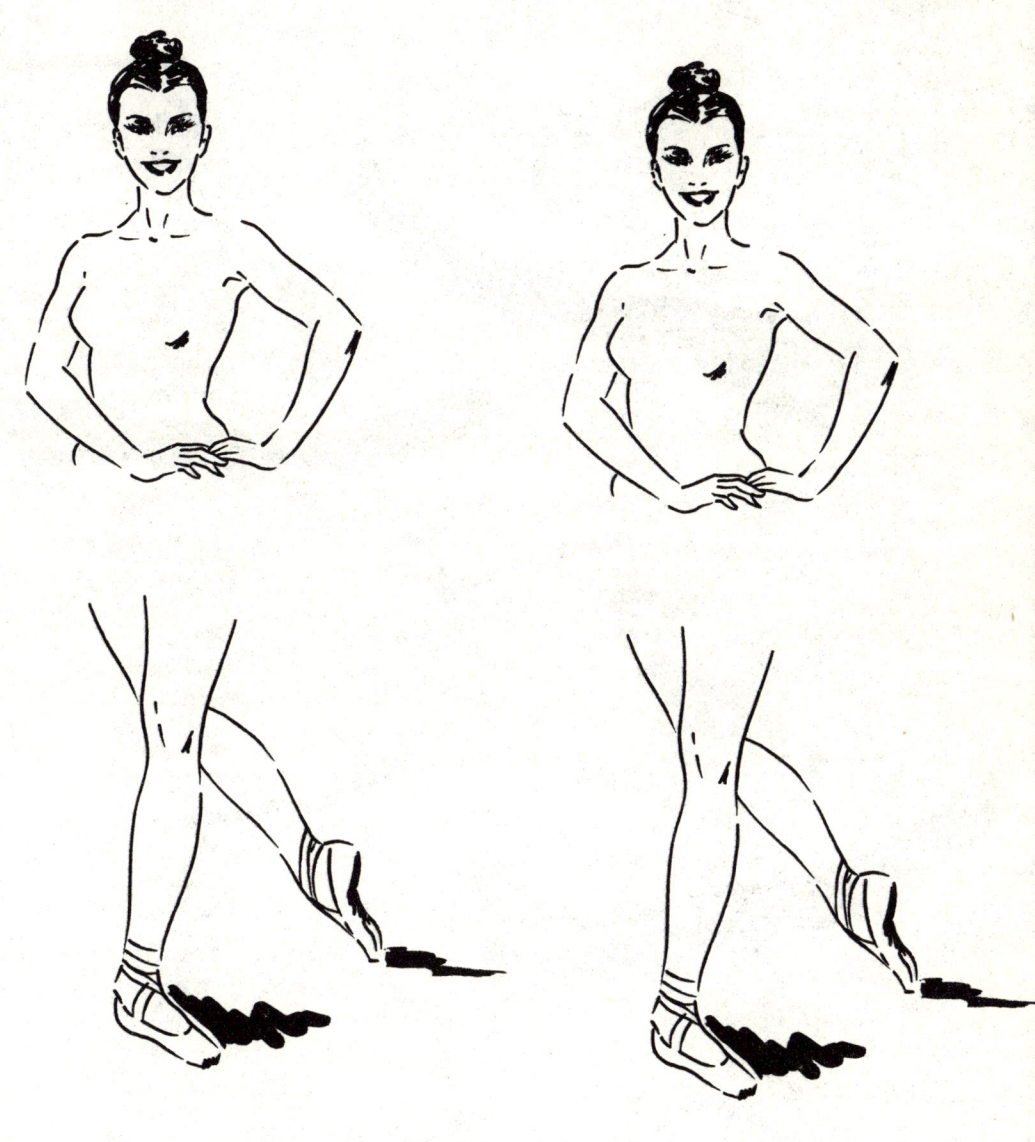

Design two pretty tutus for these dancers in the Royal Ballet.

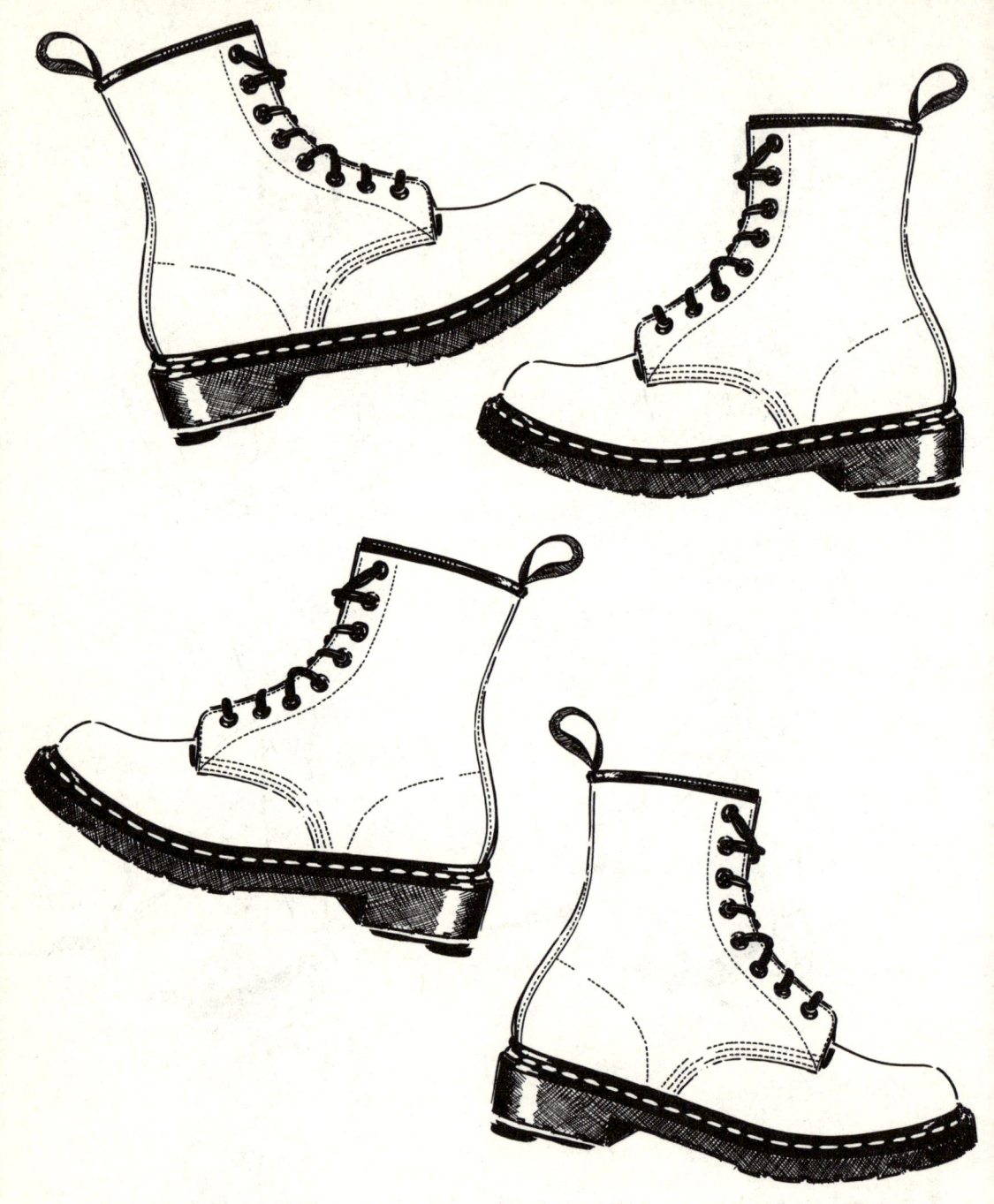

These boots are cool in Camden.

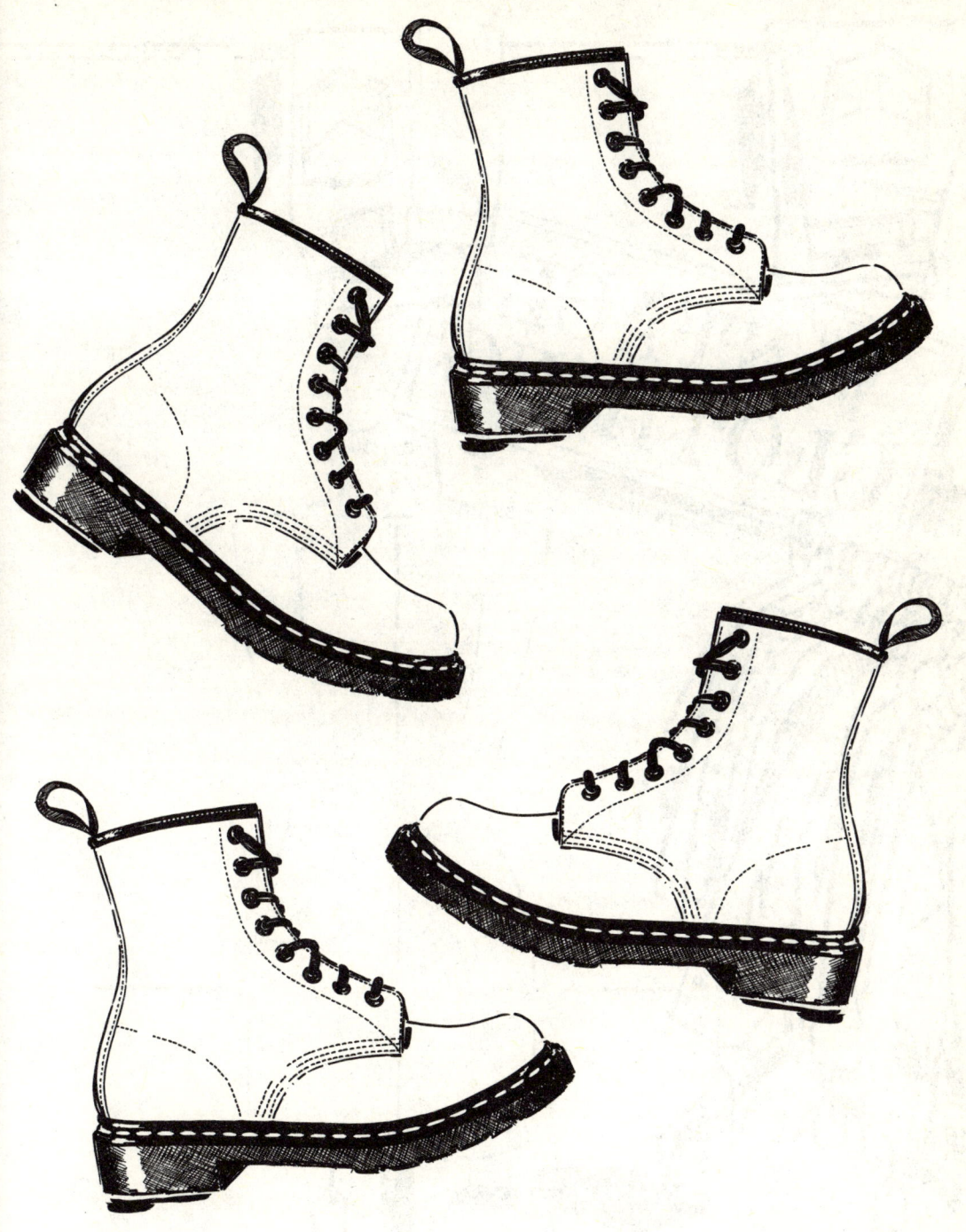

Customize and embellish them.

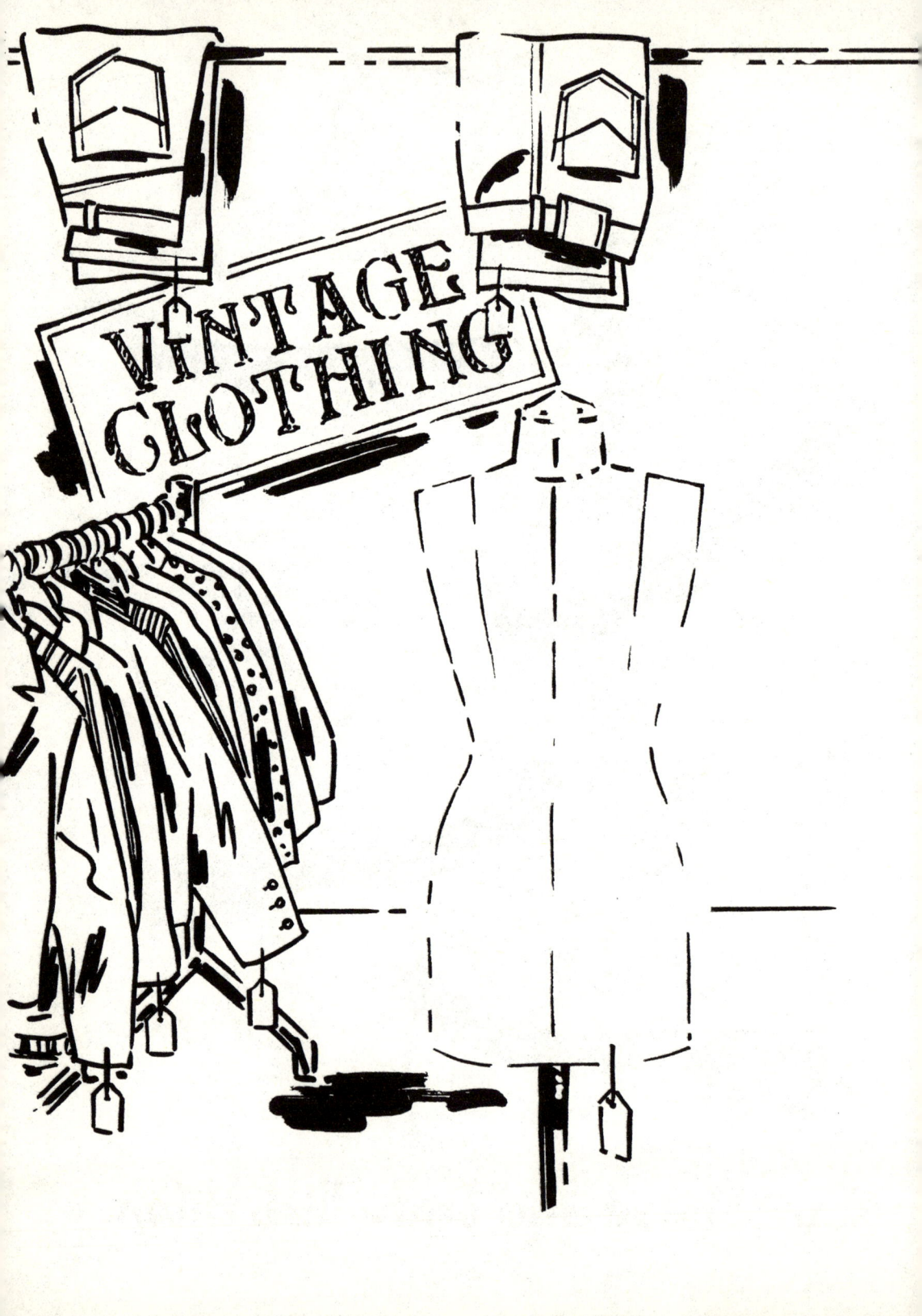

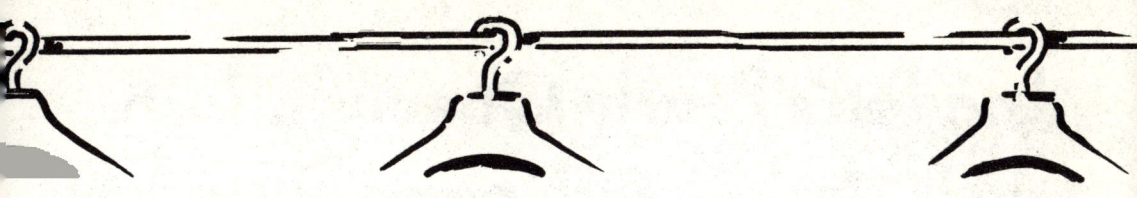

What's for sale at Brick Lane Market?

London's Pearly Queens adorn their clothes with pearl buttons. Decorate this outfit.

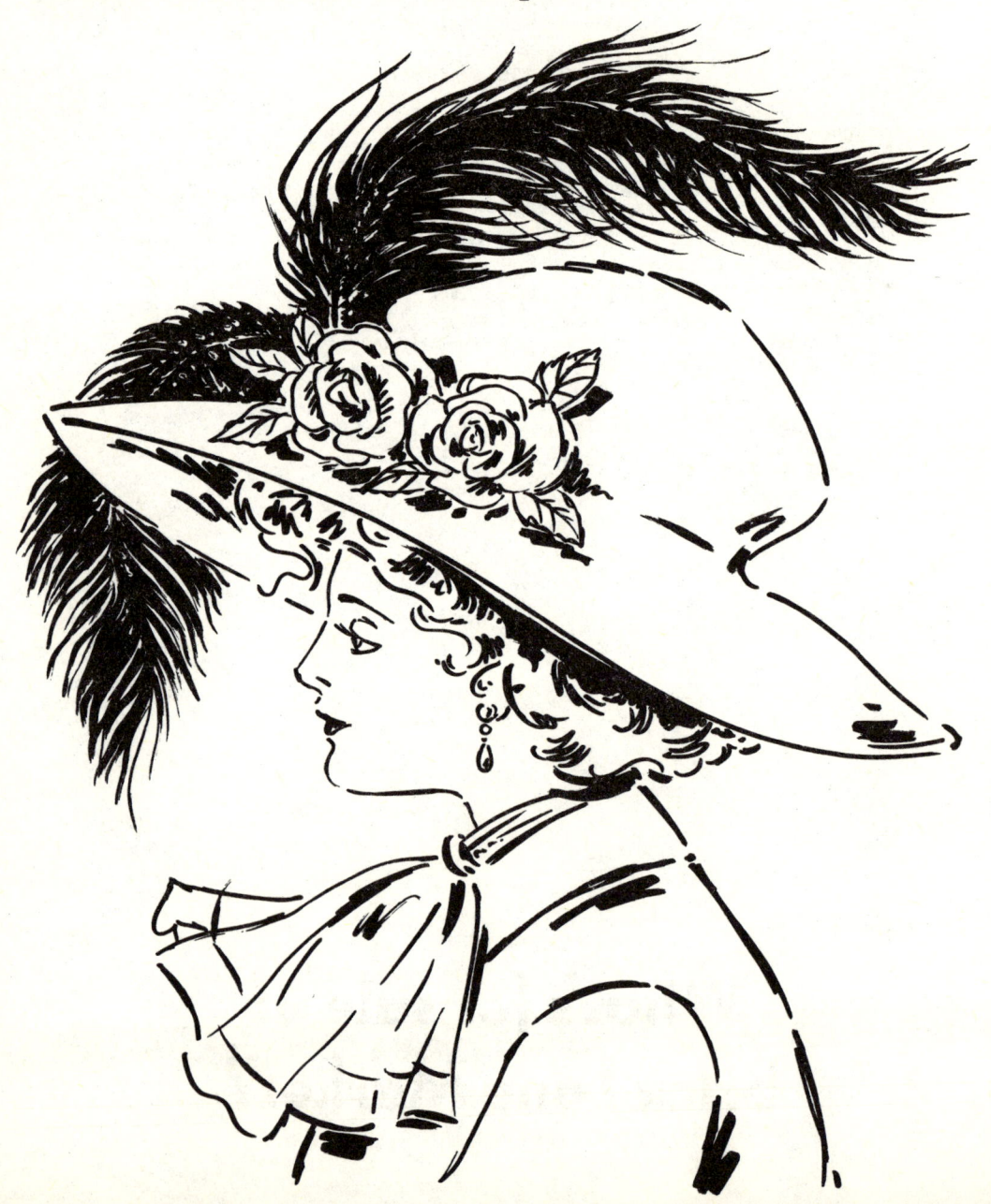

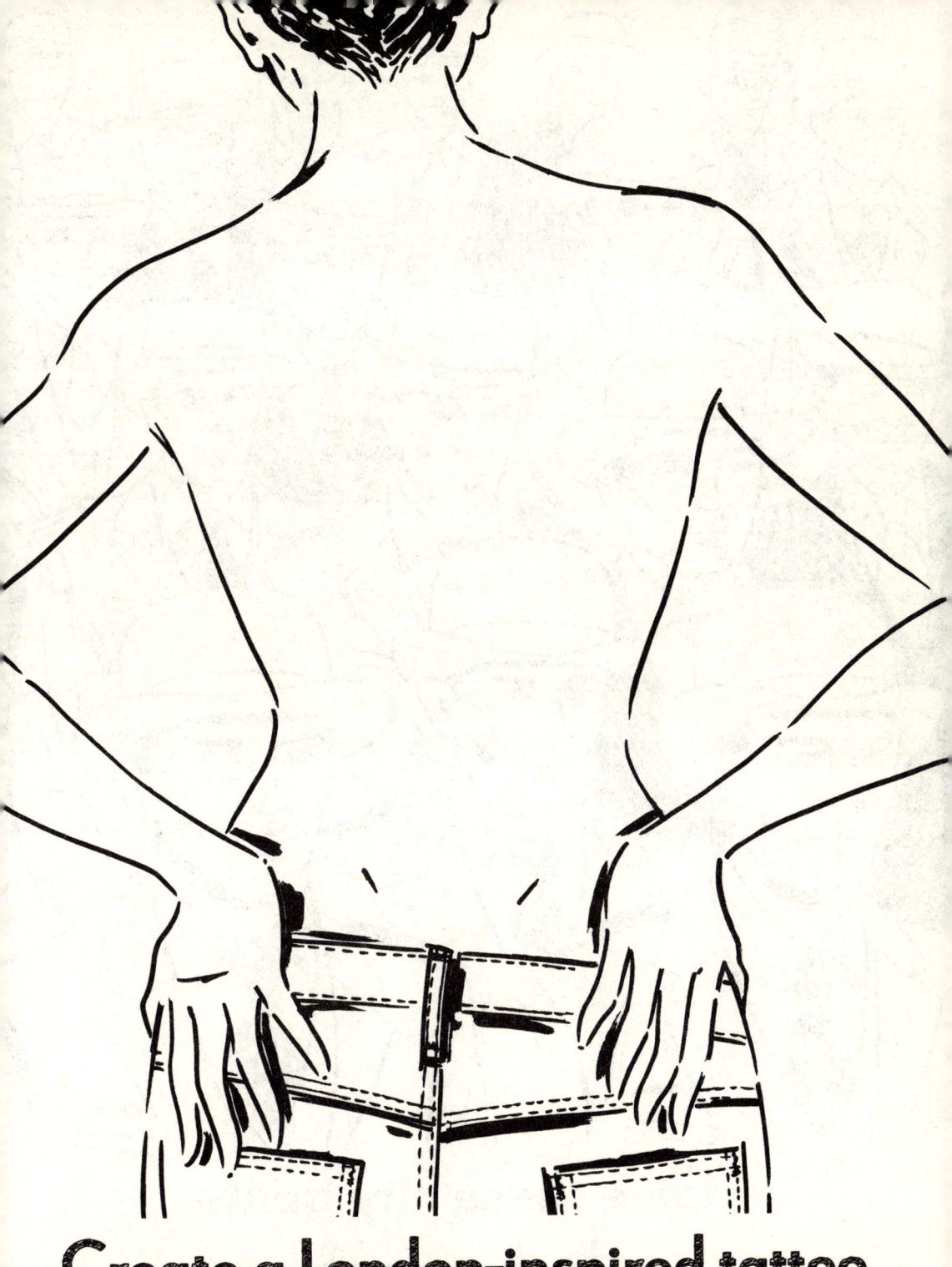
Create a London-inspired tattoo.

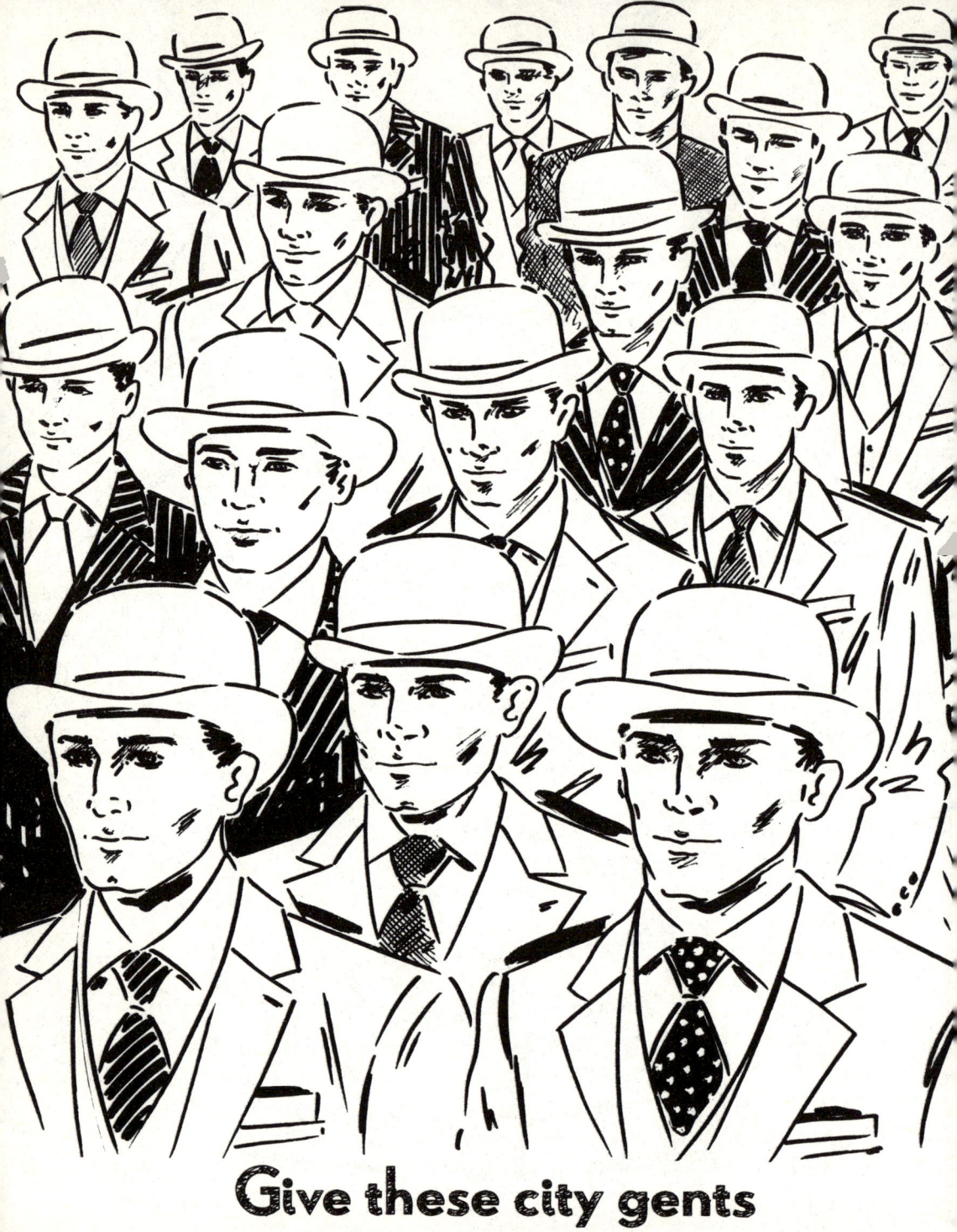

What does this shop sell? Dress the windows.

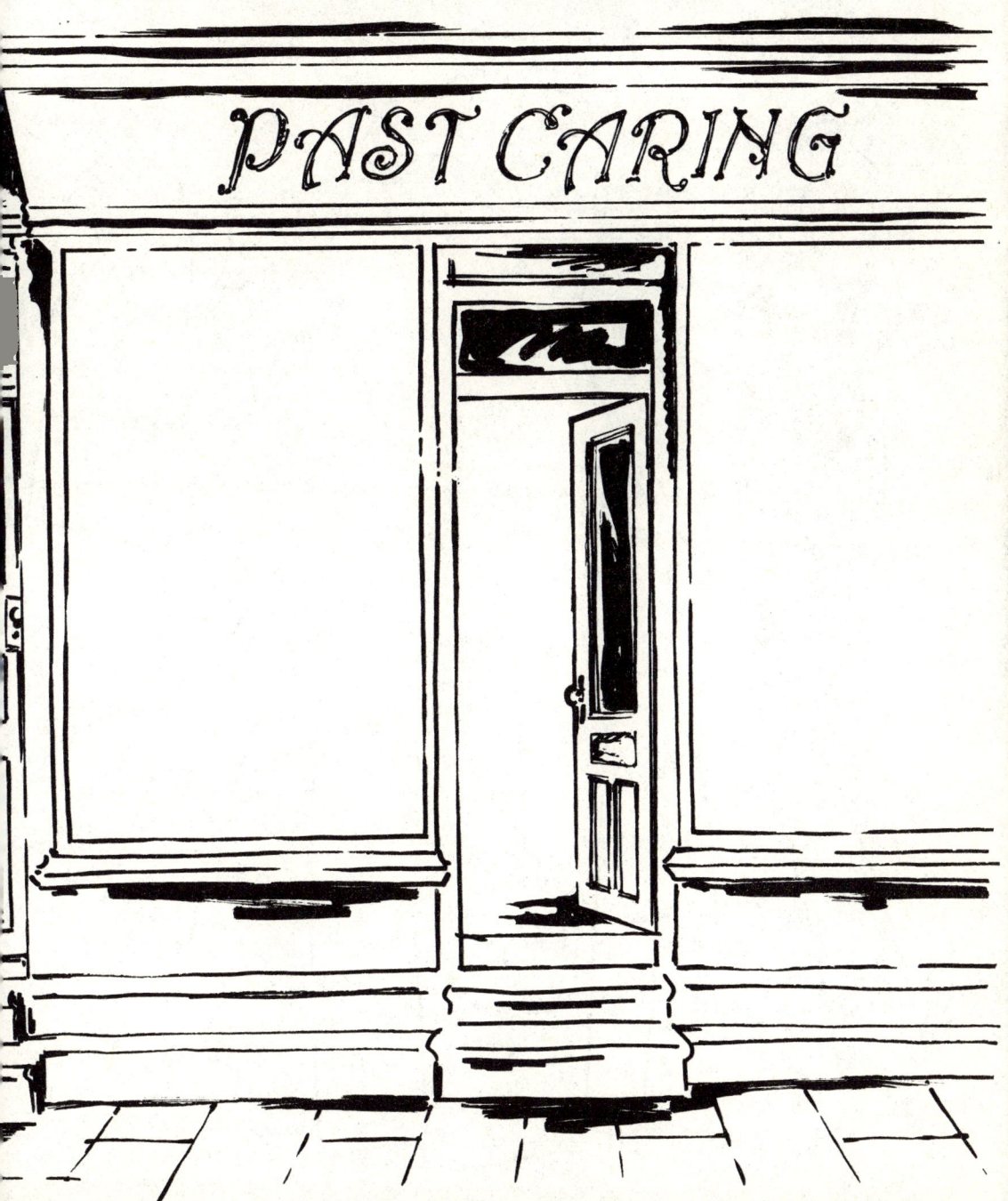

Design a gown to display at the V&A Museum.

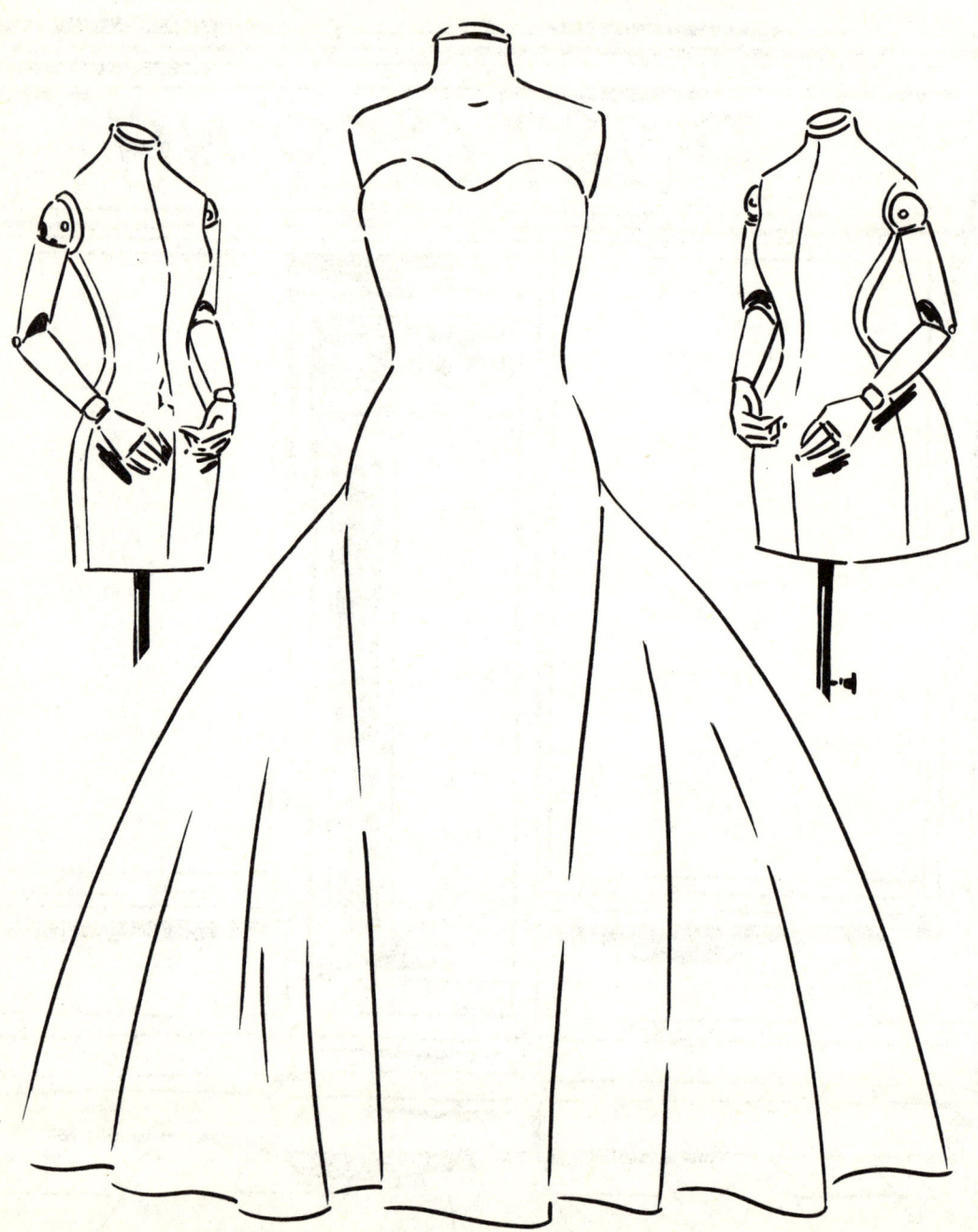

What's in this shop window?

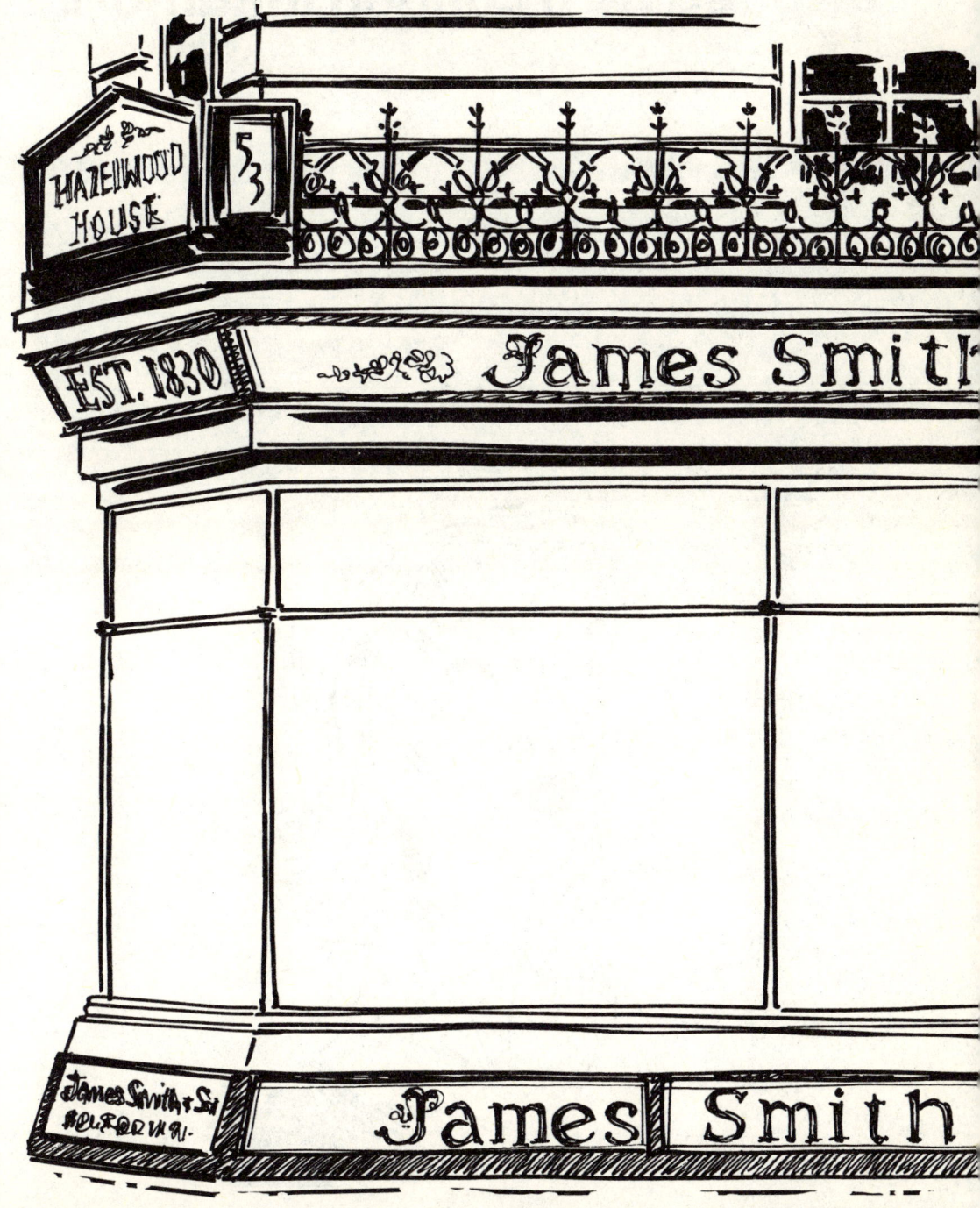

Create an outrageous hat inspired by a London landmark.

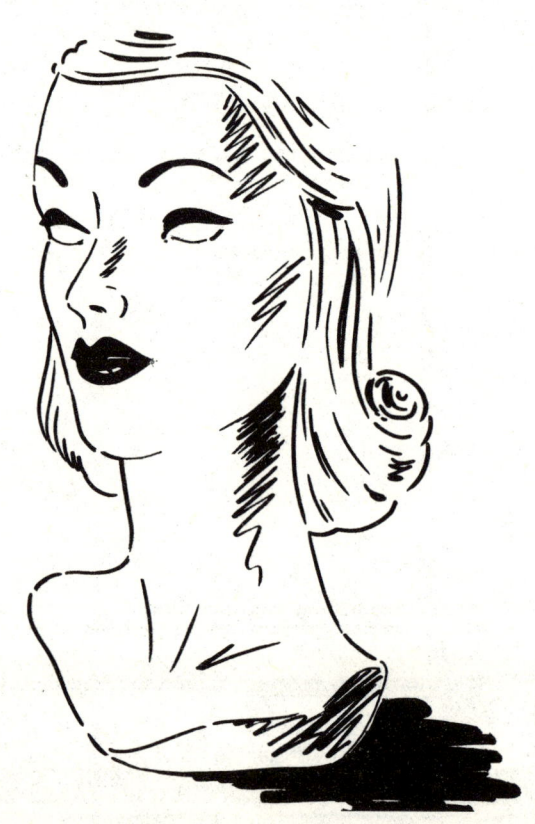

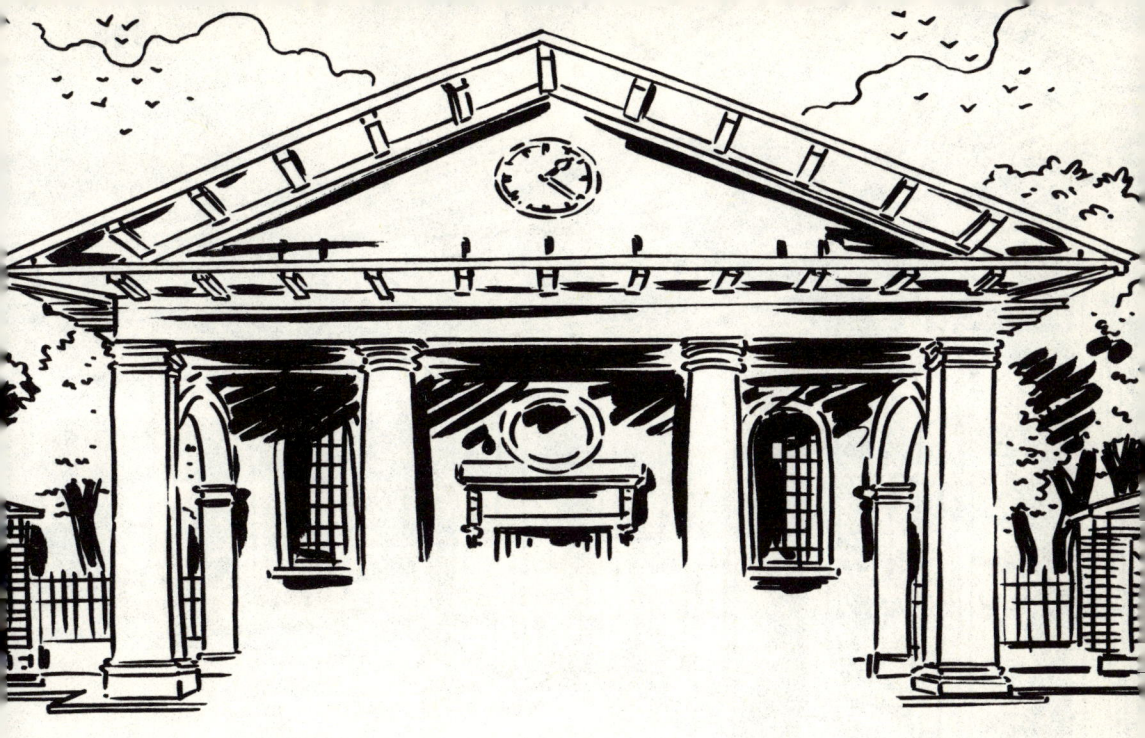

Draw a street performance in Covent Garden.

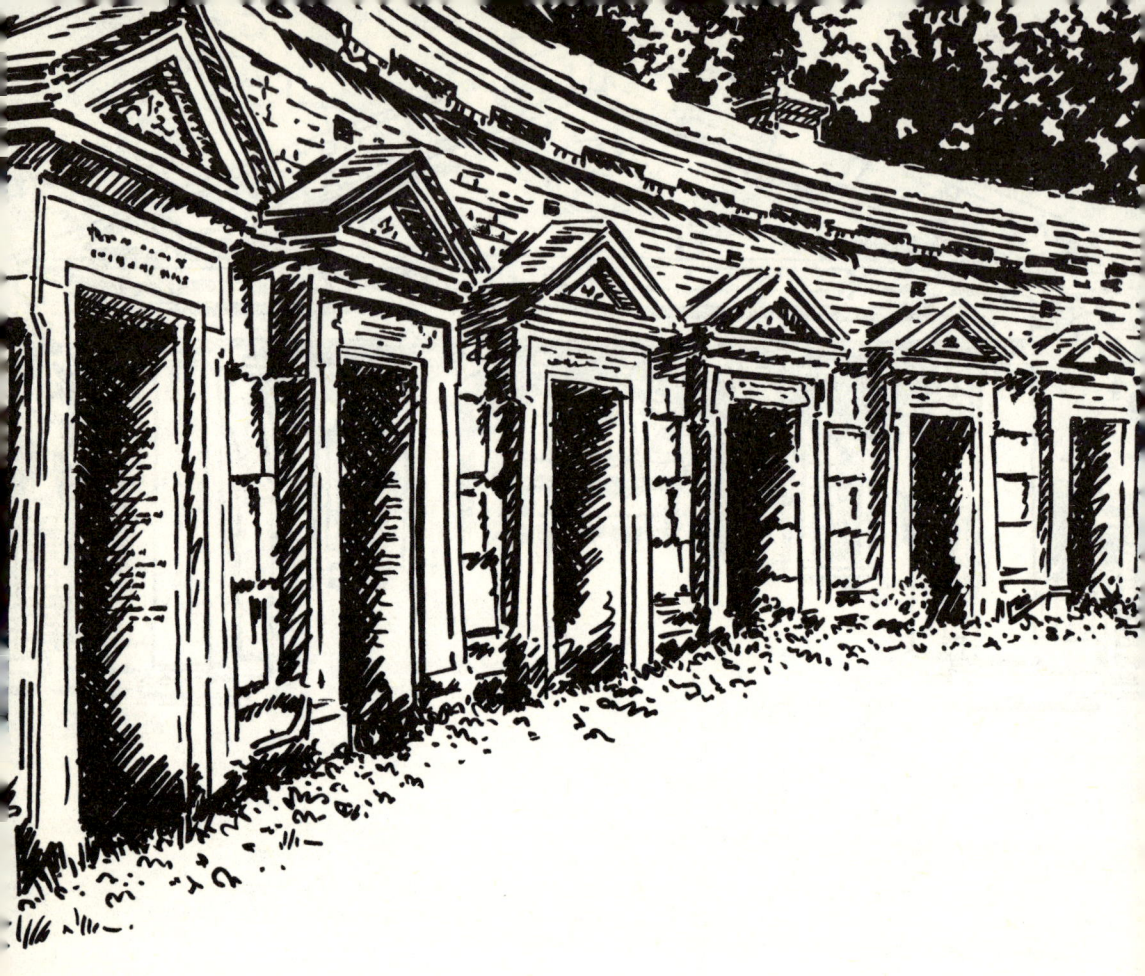

It's Halloween in Highgate Cemetery.

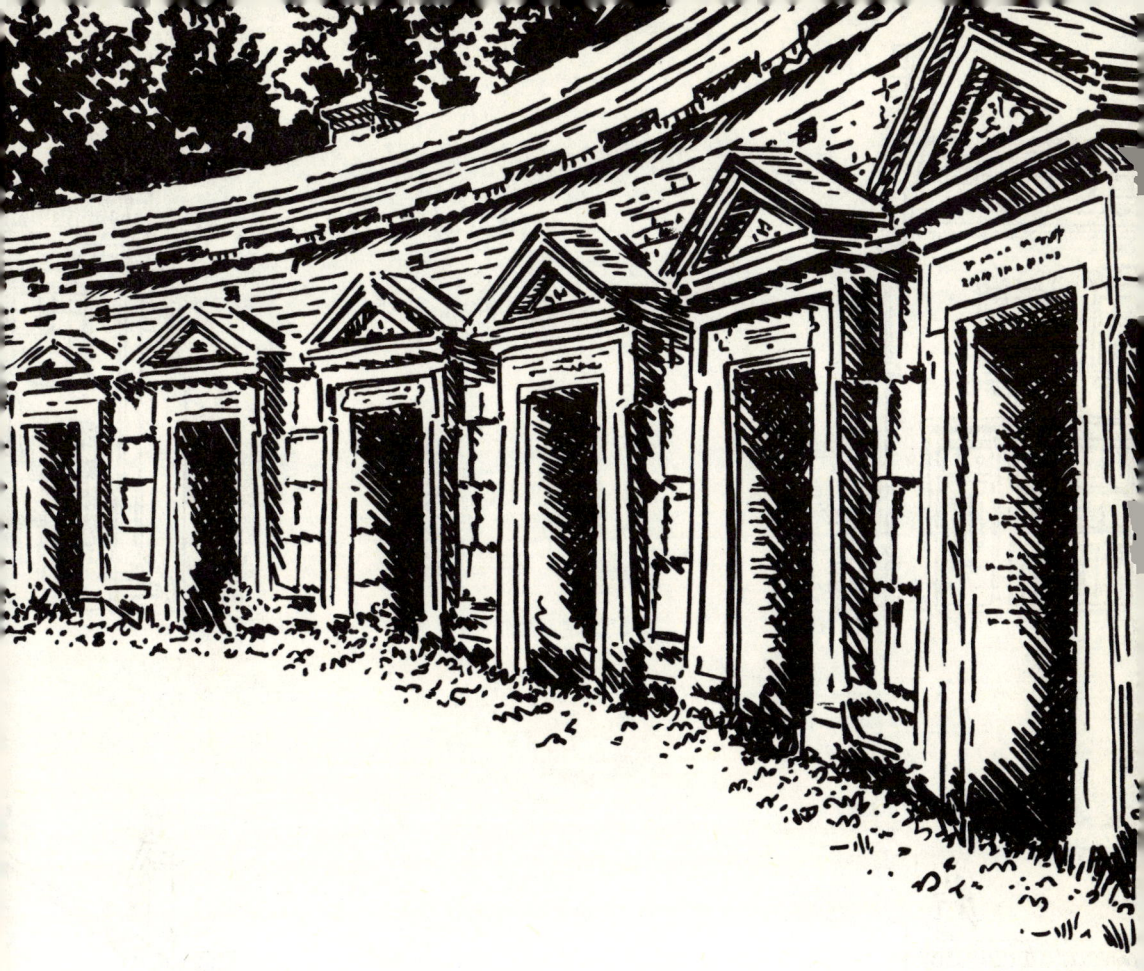

Haunt these tombs with ghosts.

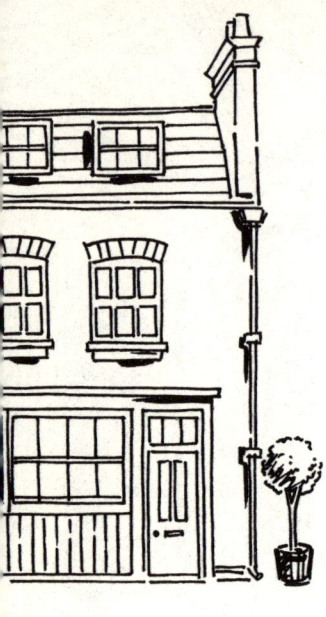
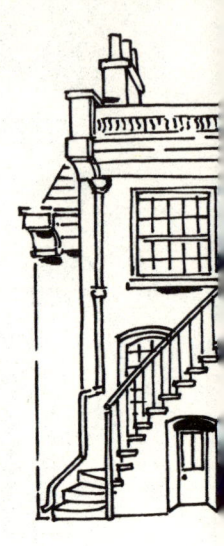
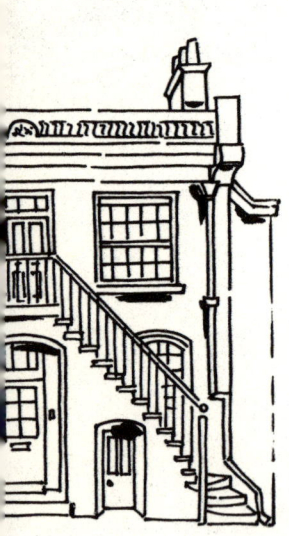
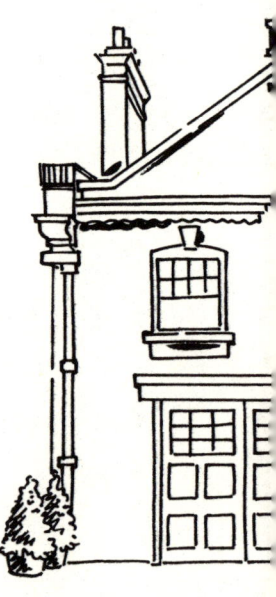

London mews were once 18th-century stables.

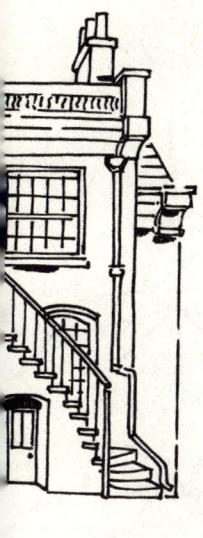
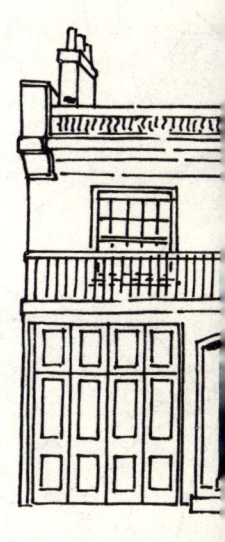
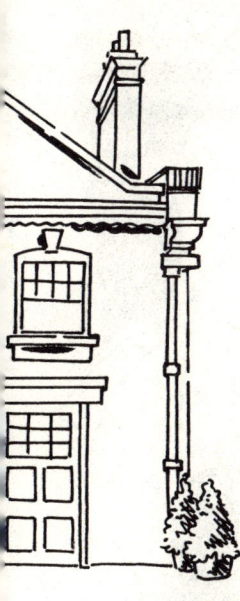
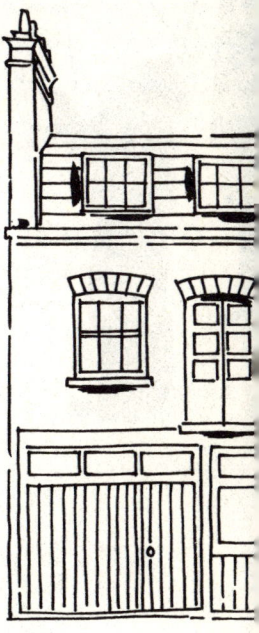

Today they are fashionable homes. Design your own row.

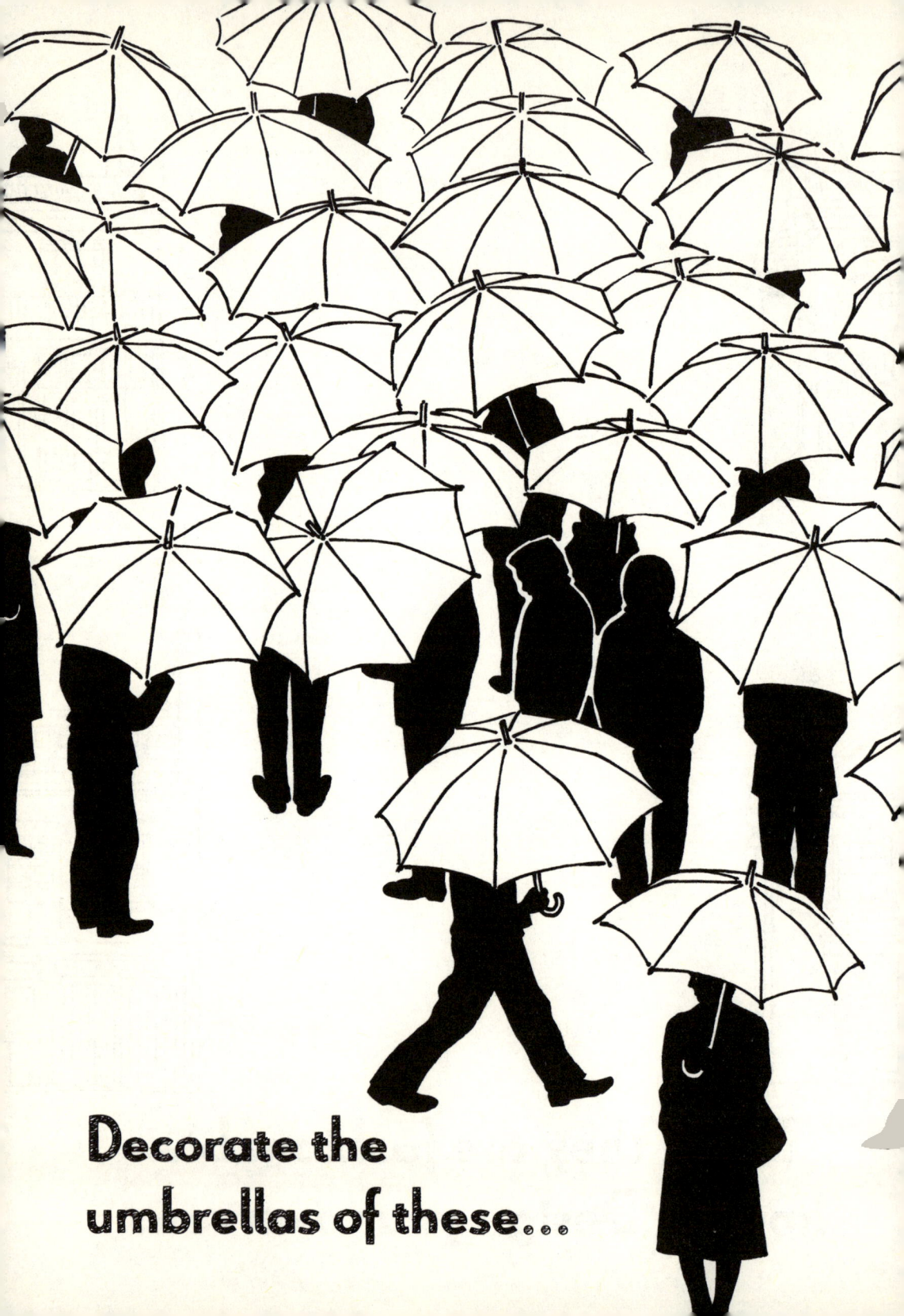

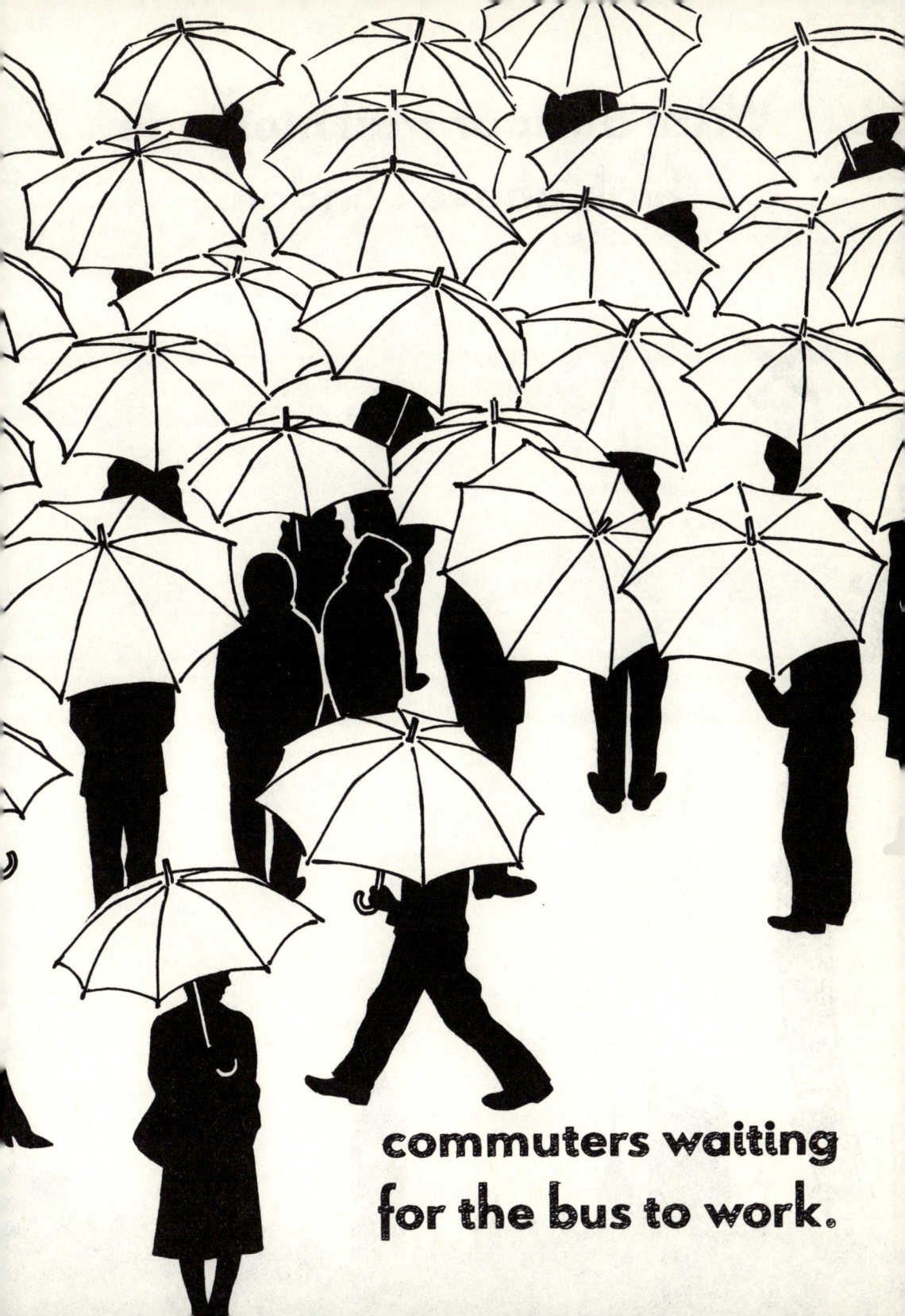

Write a vapor trail message high above London.

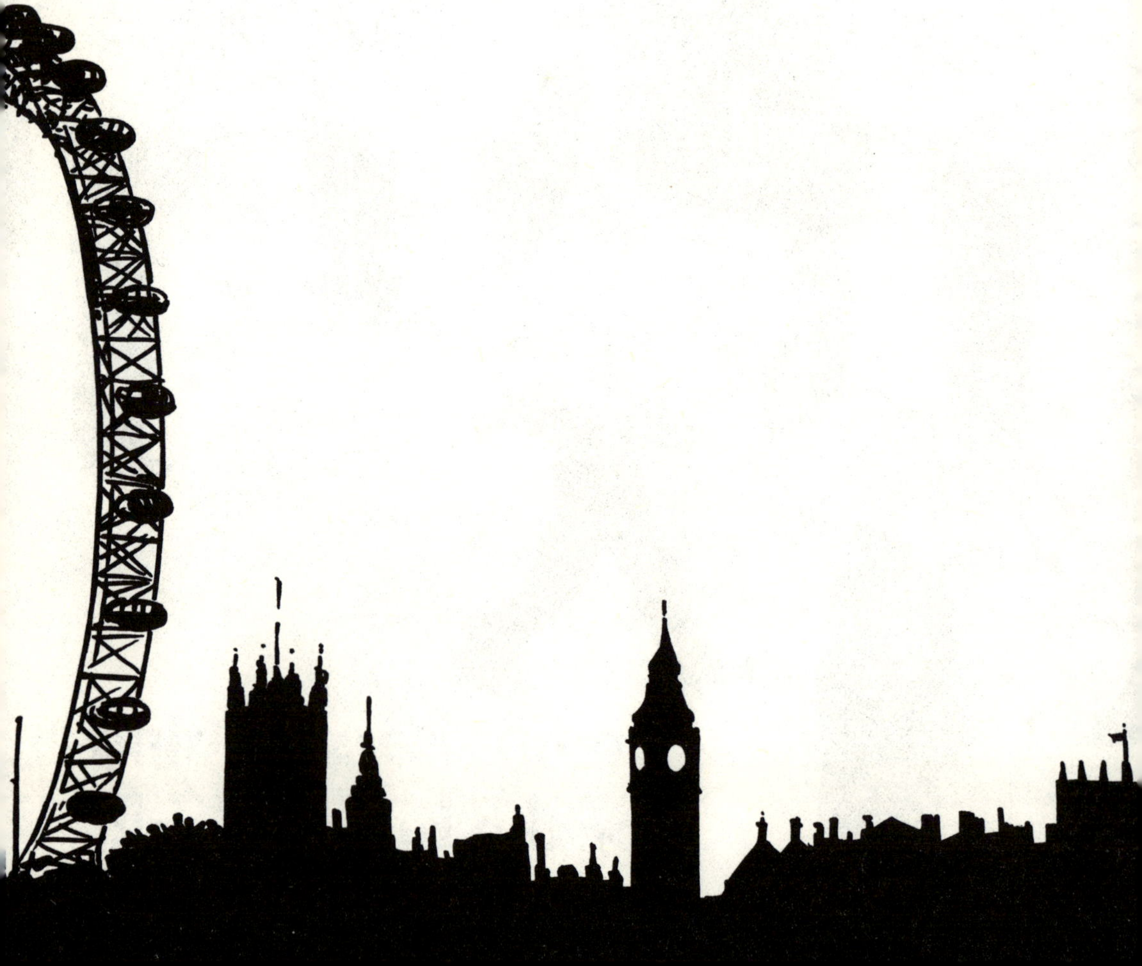

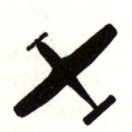
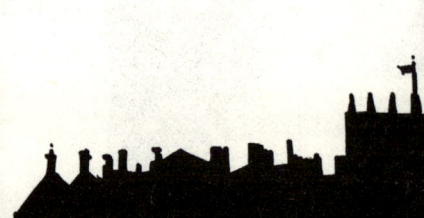

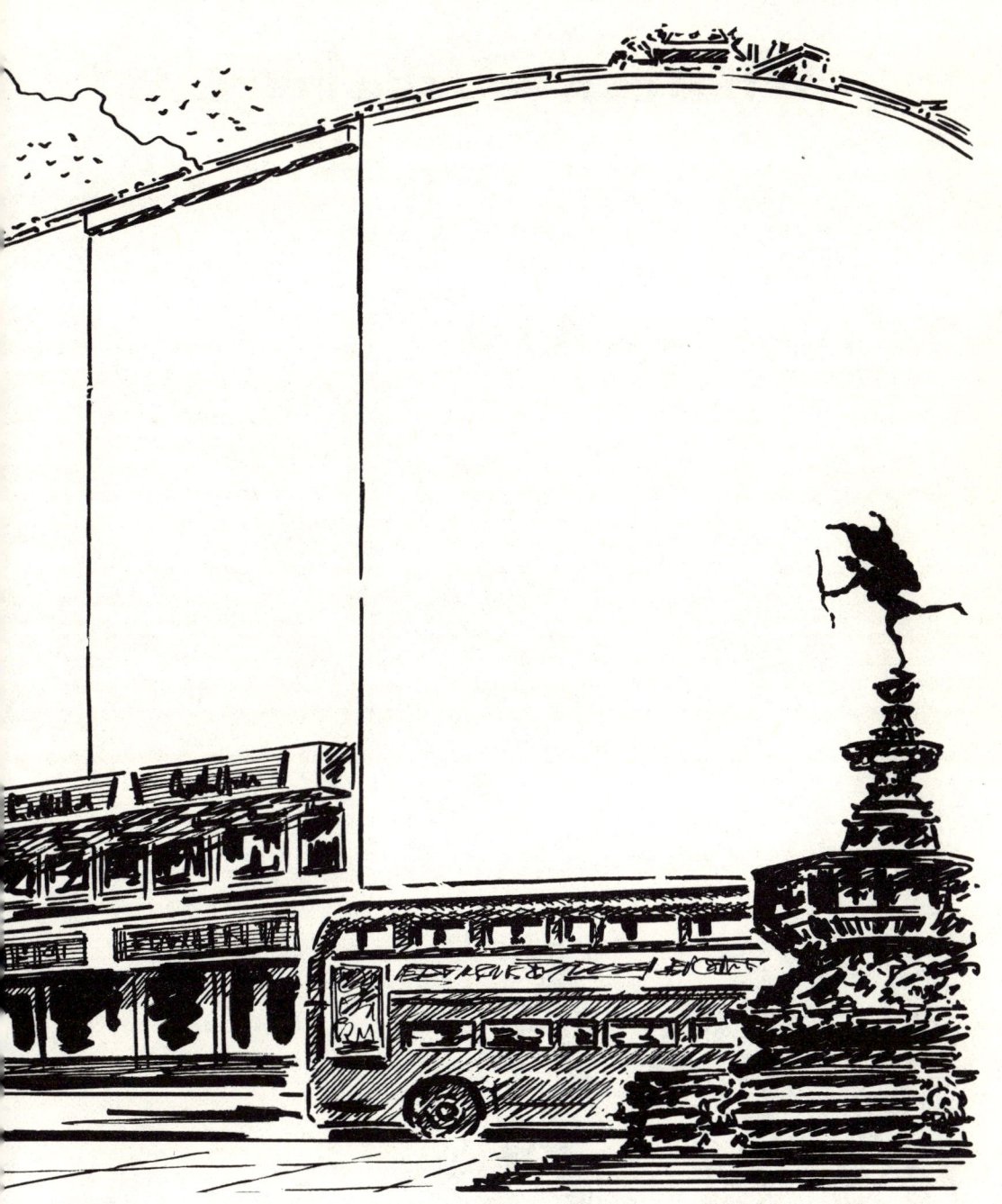

What's being advertised on the billboards at Piccadilly Circus?

What can you see lining...

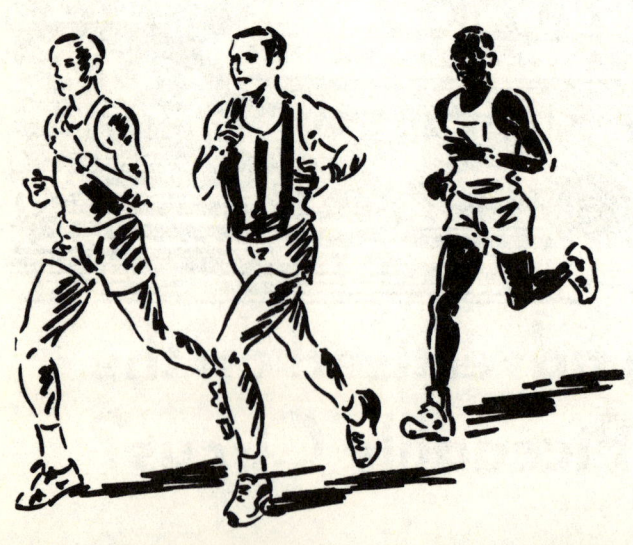

the route of the London Marathon?

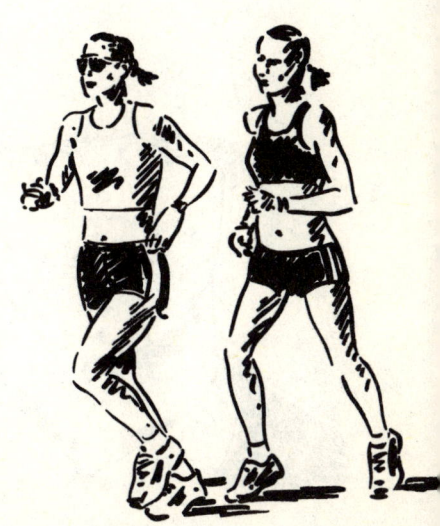

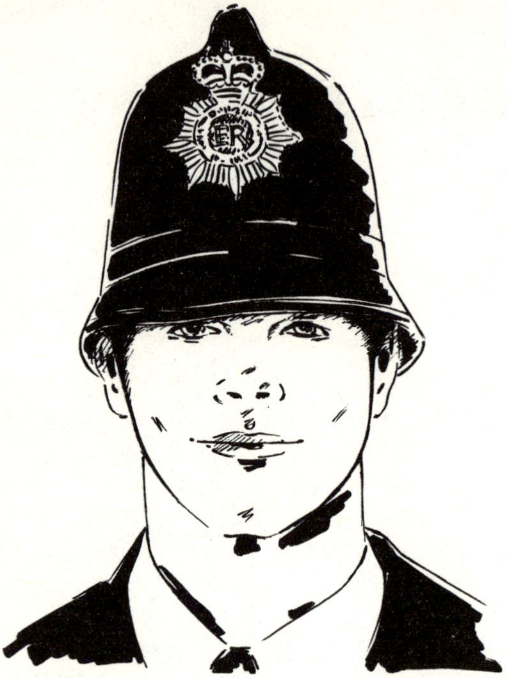

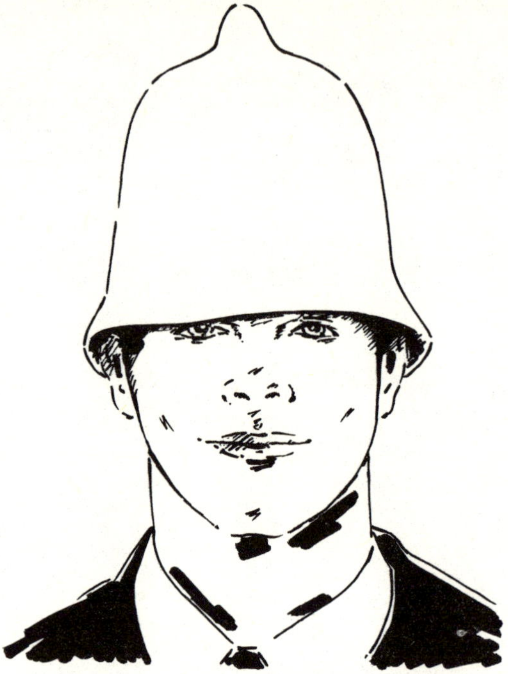

Update these policemen's helmets.

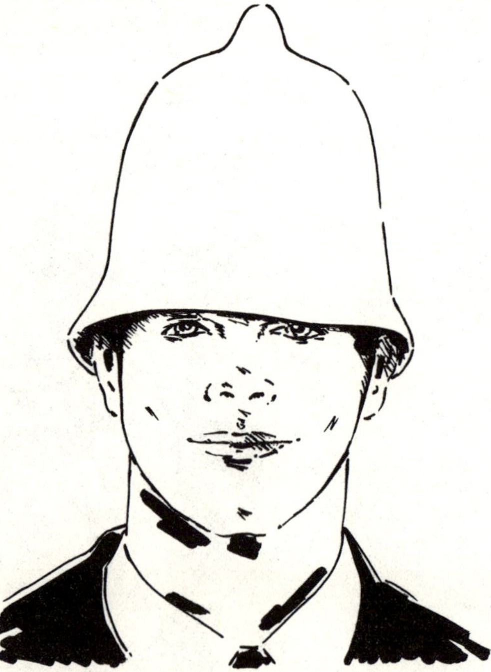

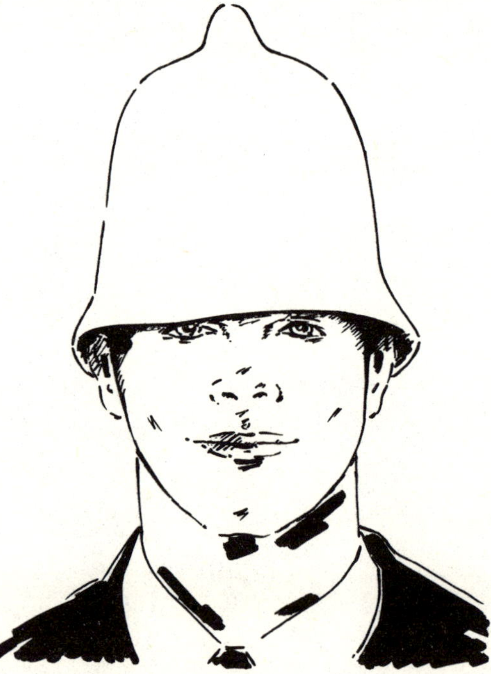

The Crown Jewels contain some of the world's biggest diamonds.

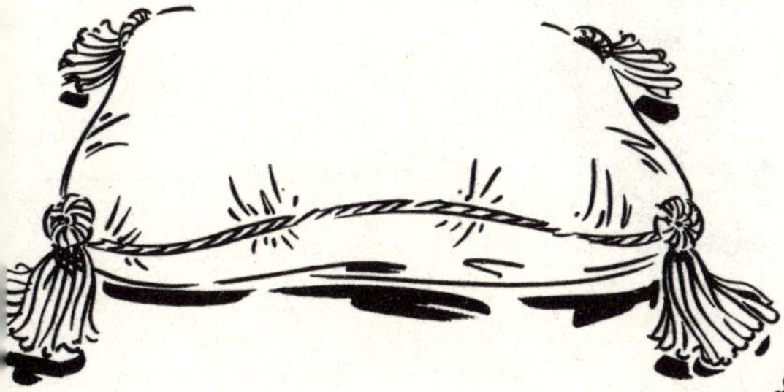

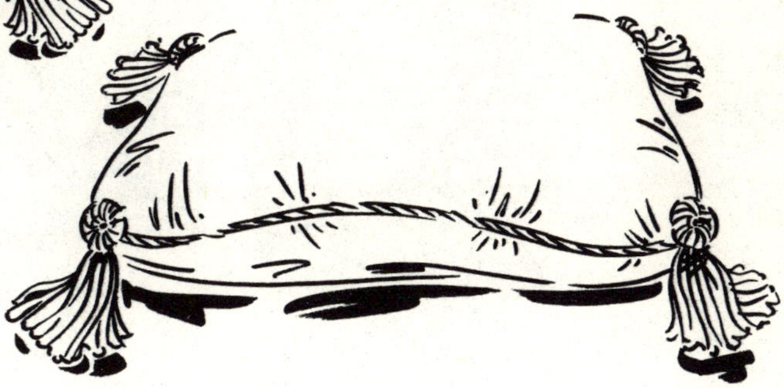

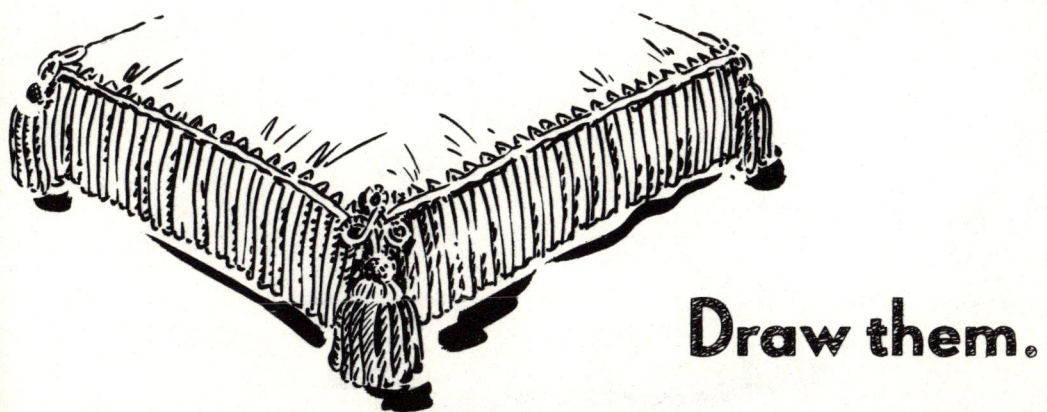

Draw them.

Dress Queen Elizabeth I in her regal finery.

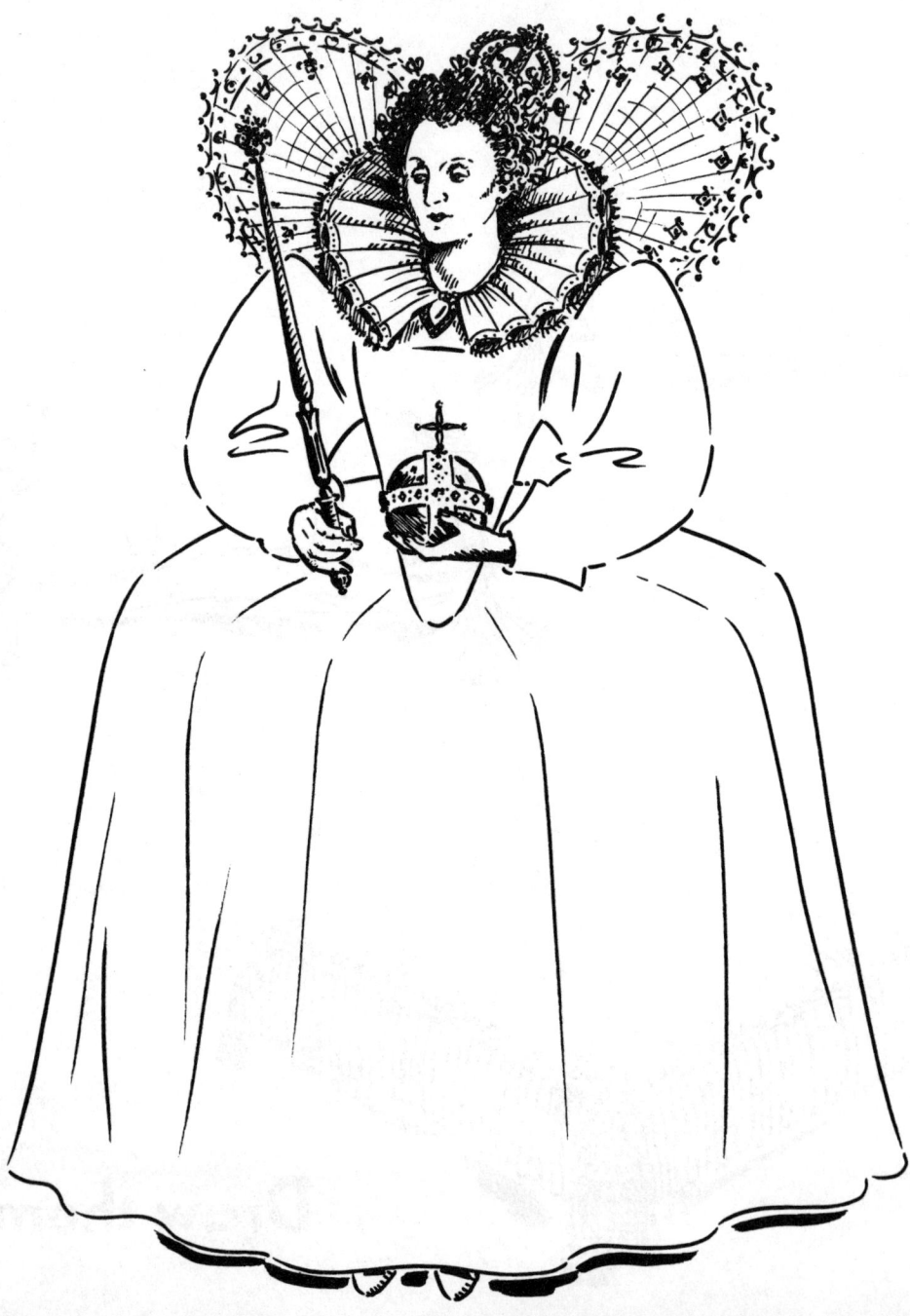

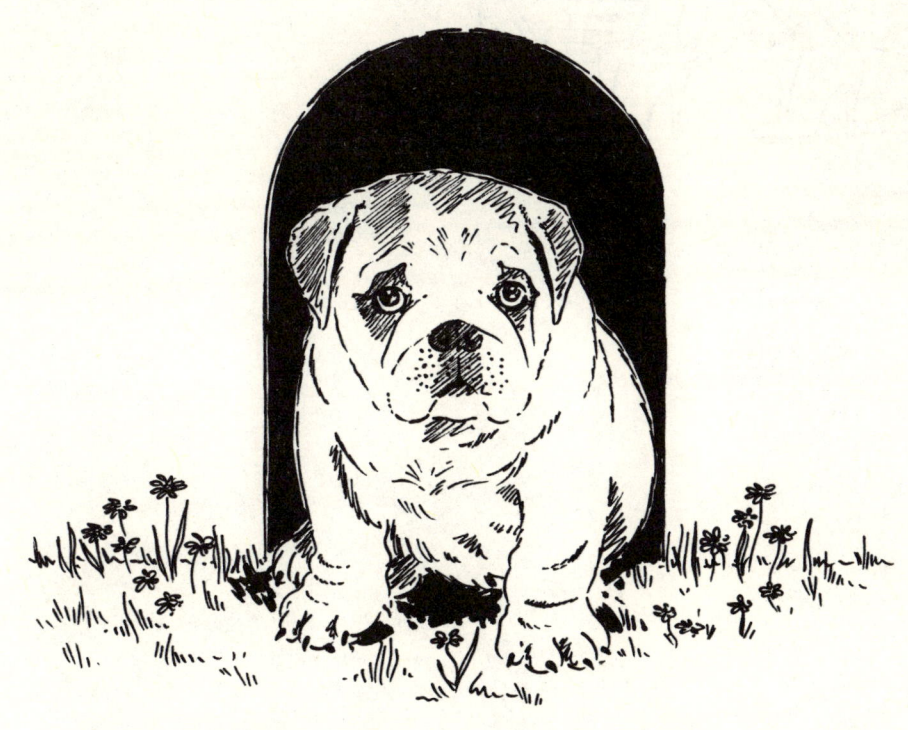

Give this British bulldog an appropriately patriotic doghouse.

Go shoe shopping on Bond Street. Which ones MUST you have?

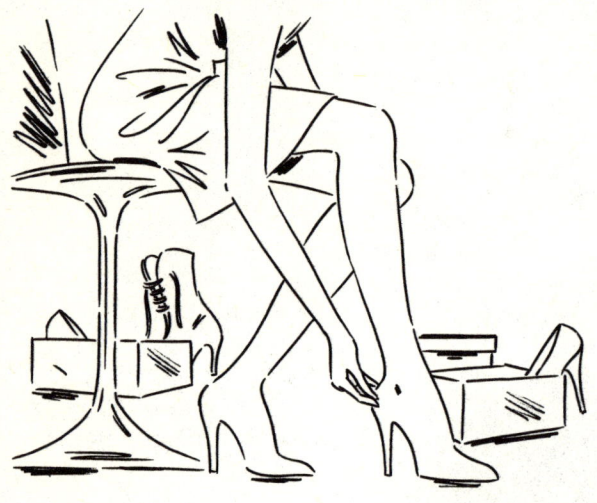

Design a pair of spectacular shoes to wear to the opera.

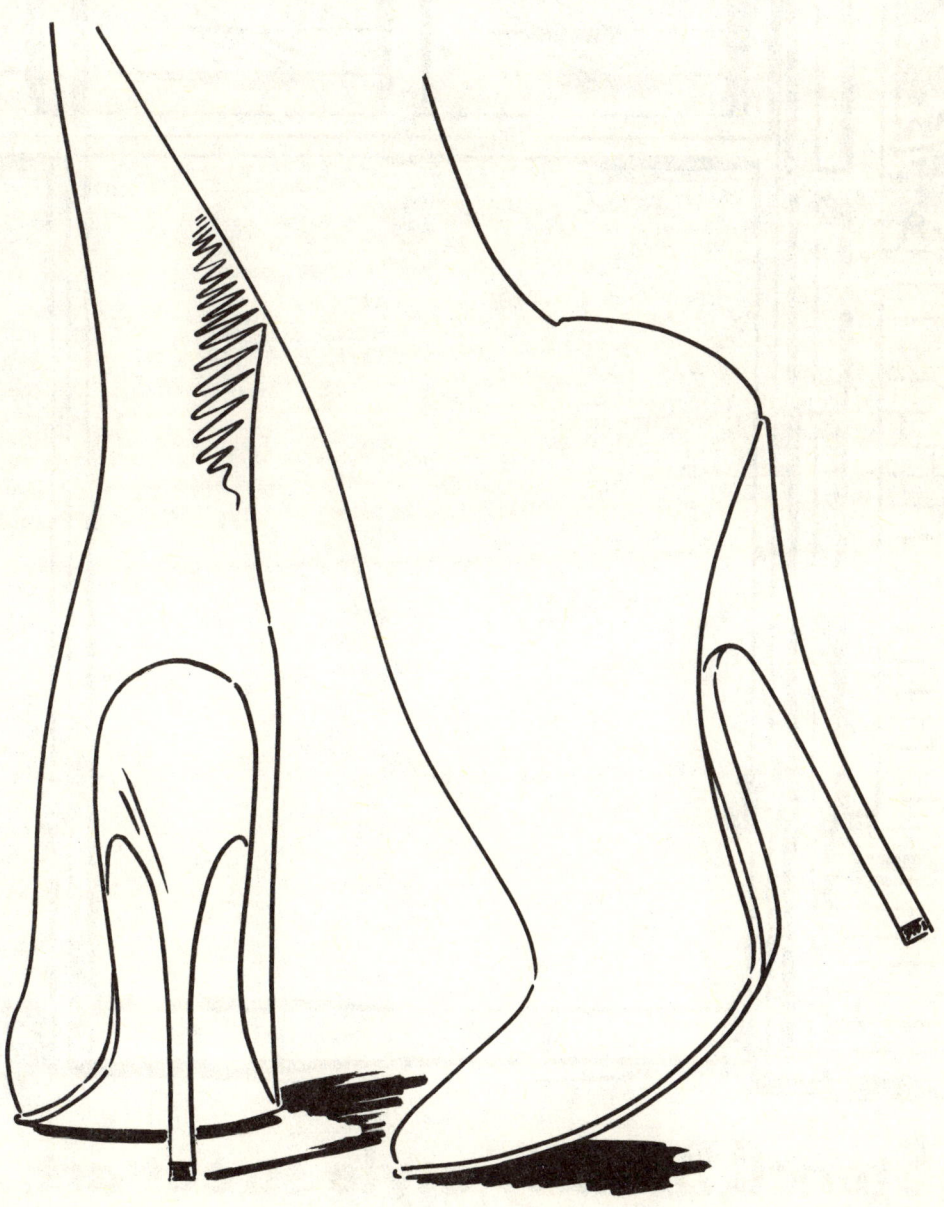

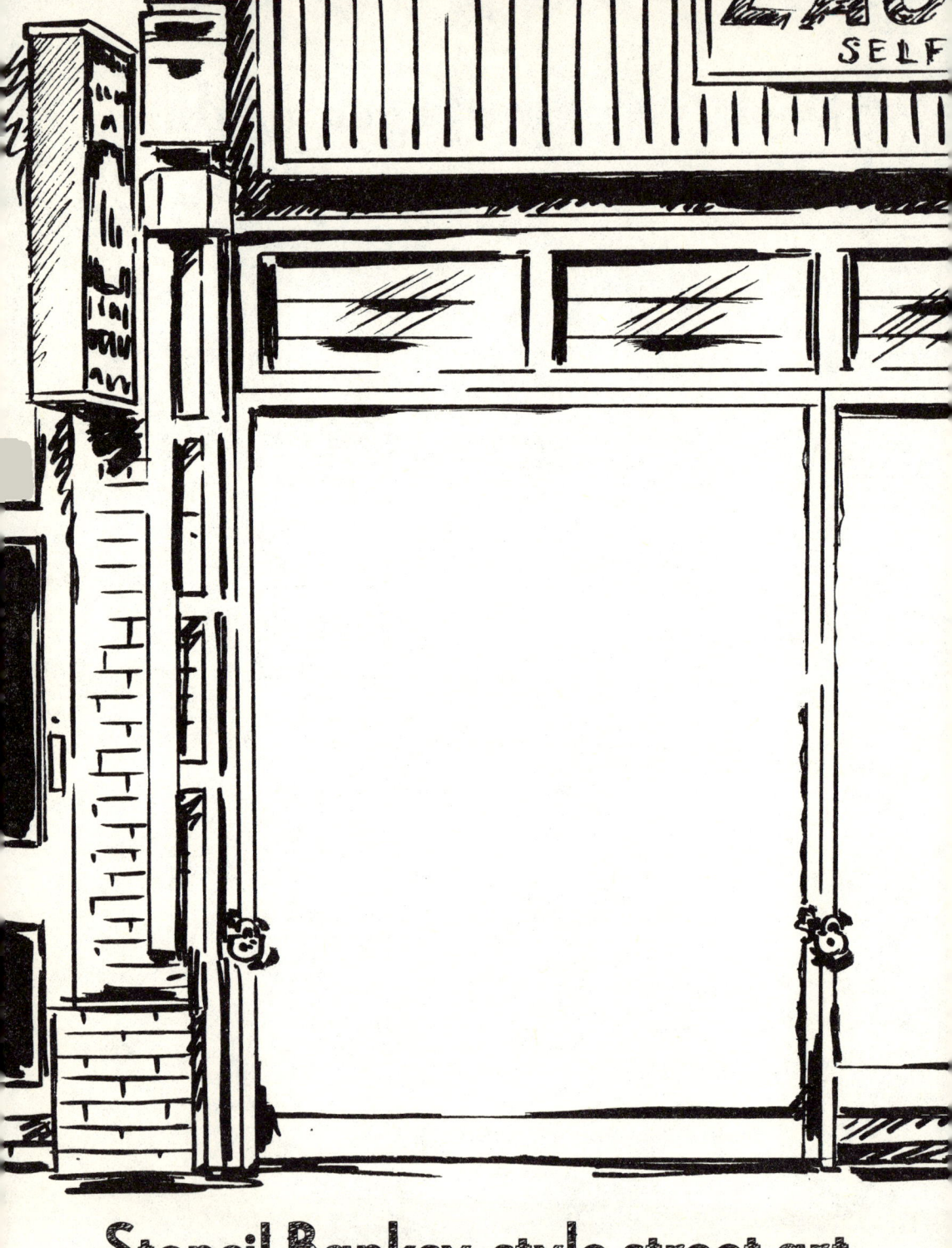

Stencil Banksy-style street art...

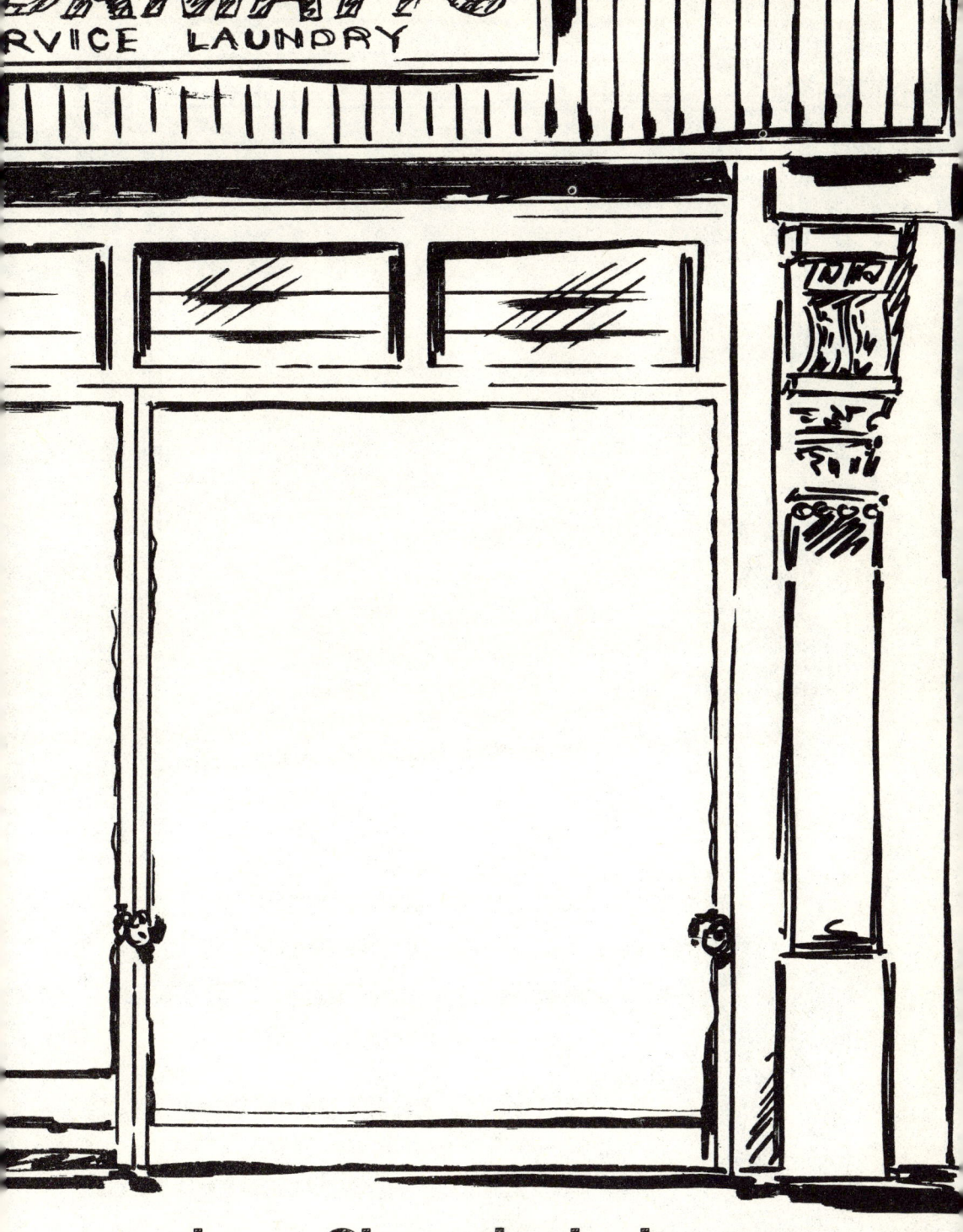
on these Shoreditch shutters.

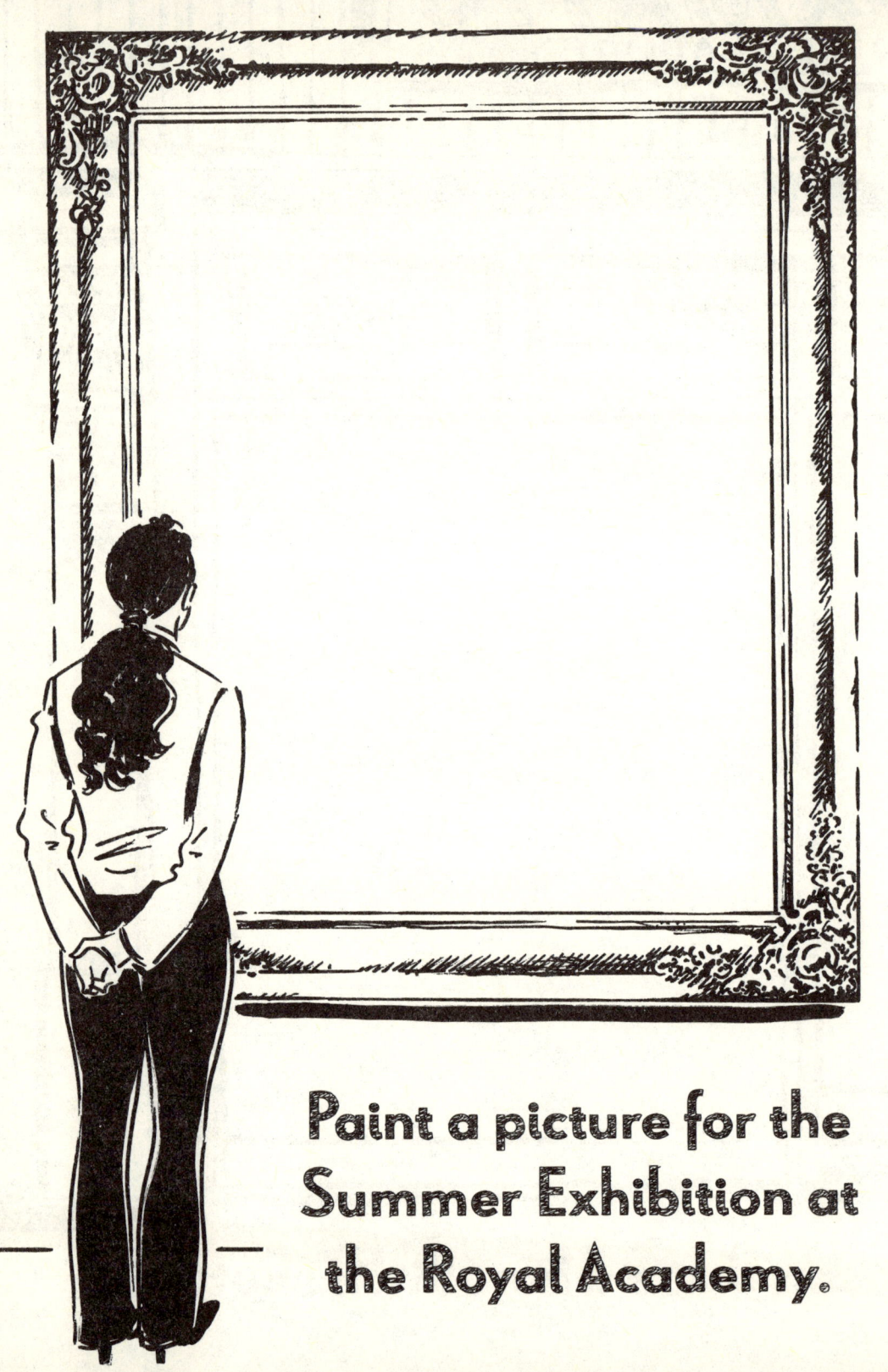

How many bangers are in this plate of mash?

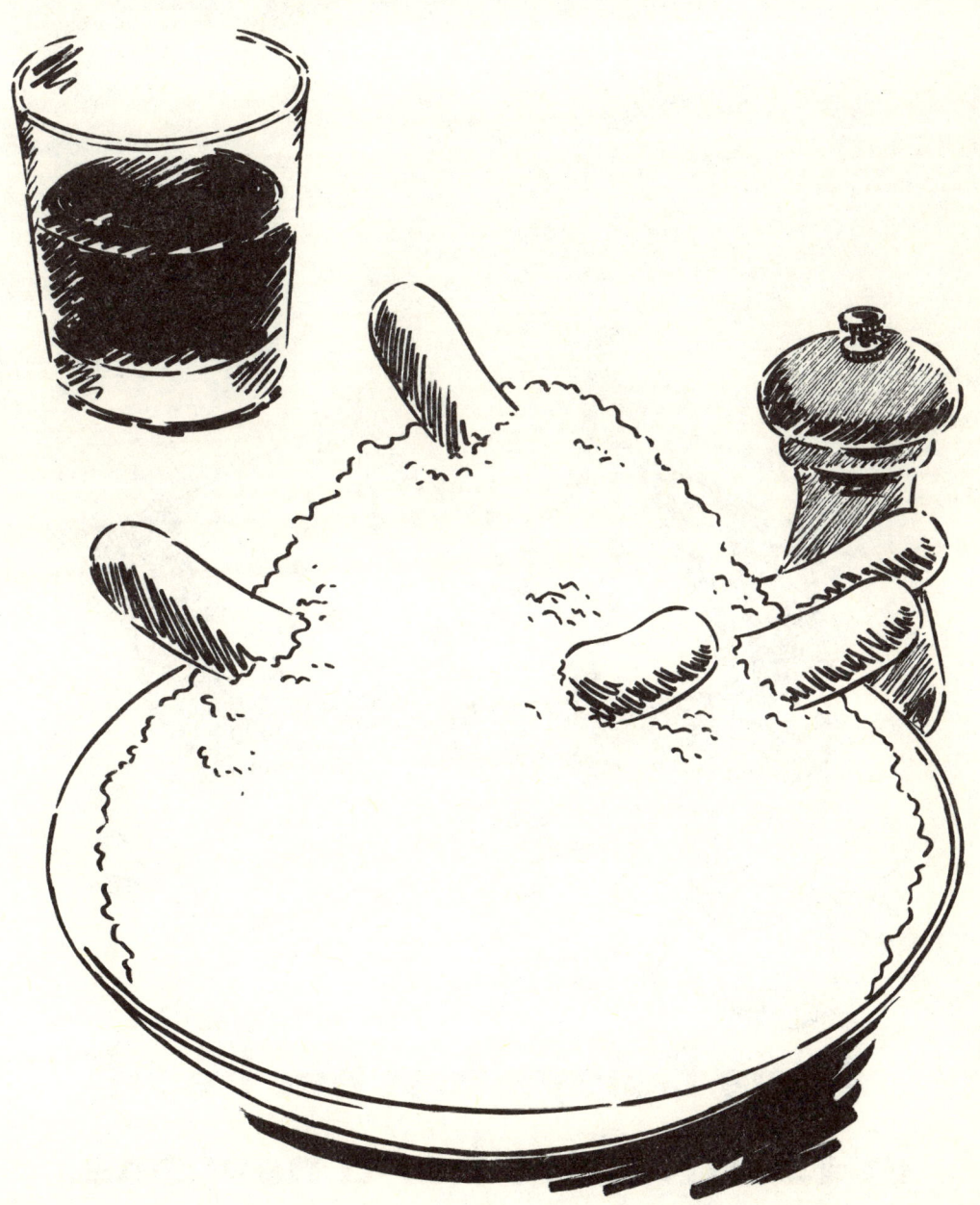

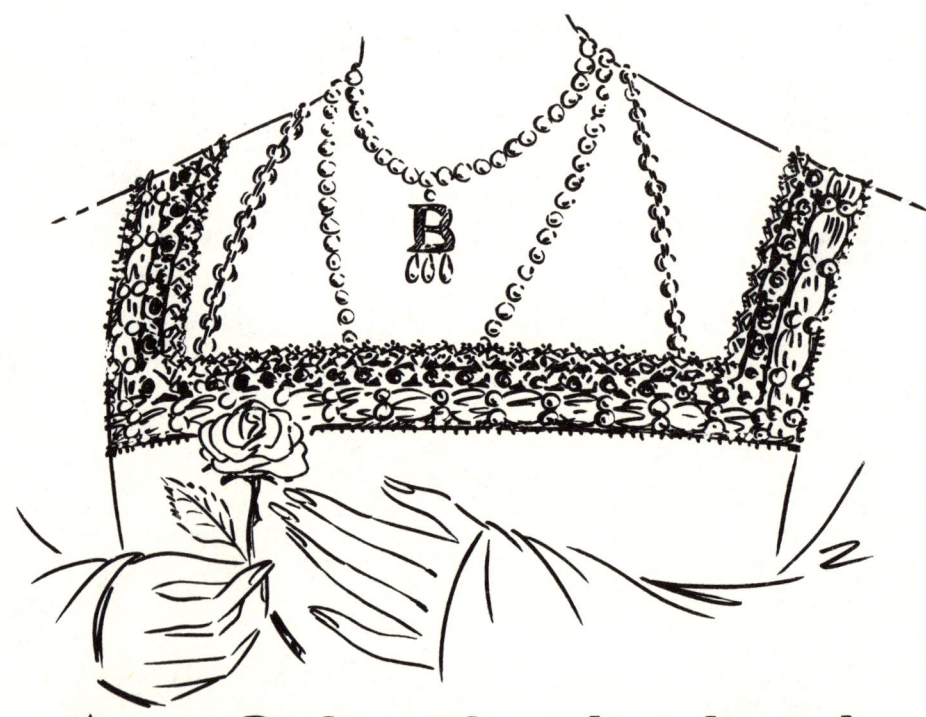

Anne Boleyn lost her head in 1536. Give her a new one.

Give Winston and Henry cold-weather cover-ups.

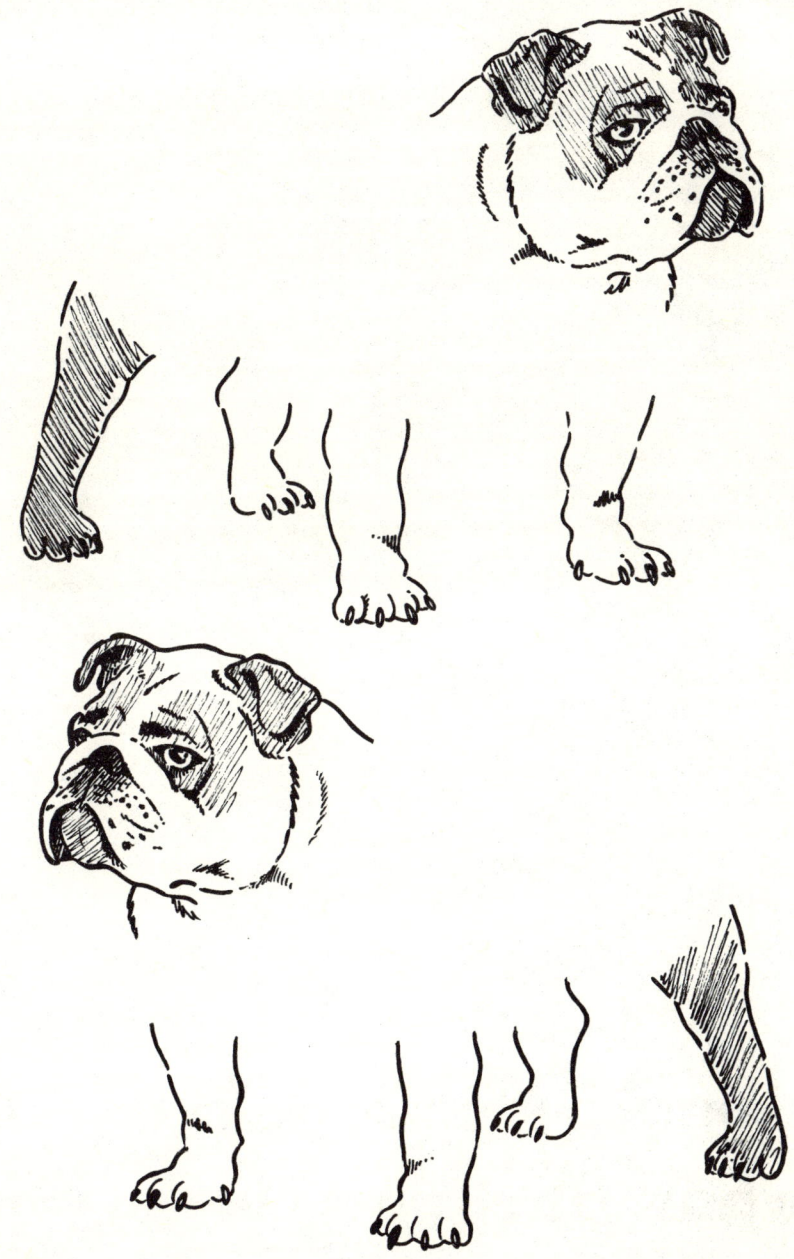

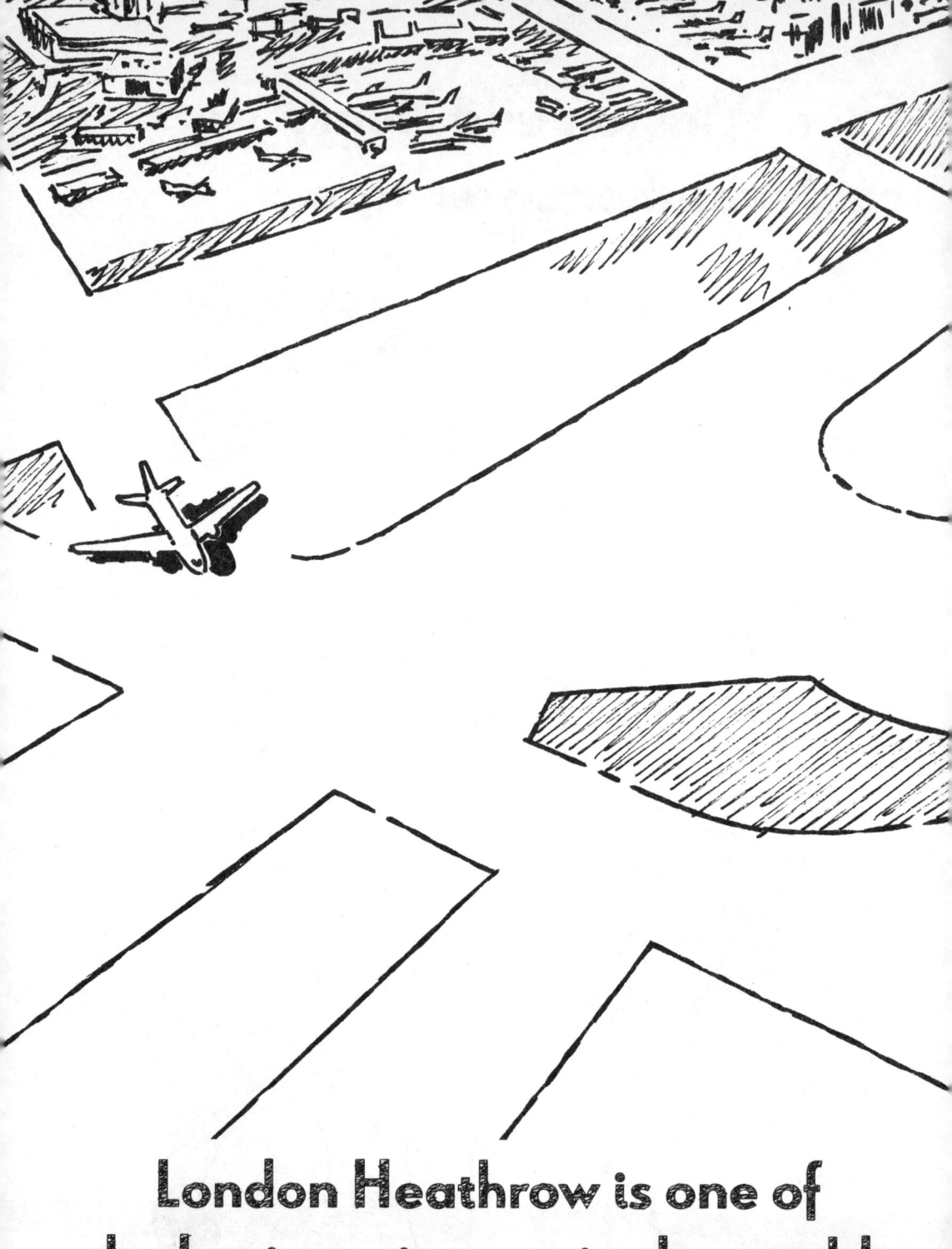

London Heathrow is one of the busiest airports in the world.

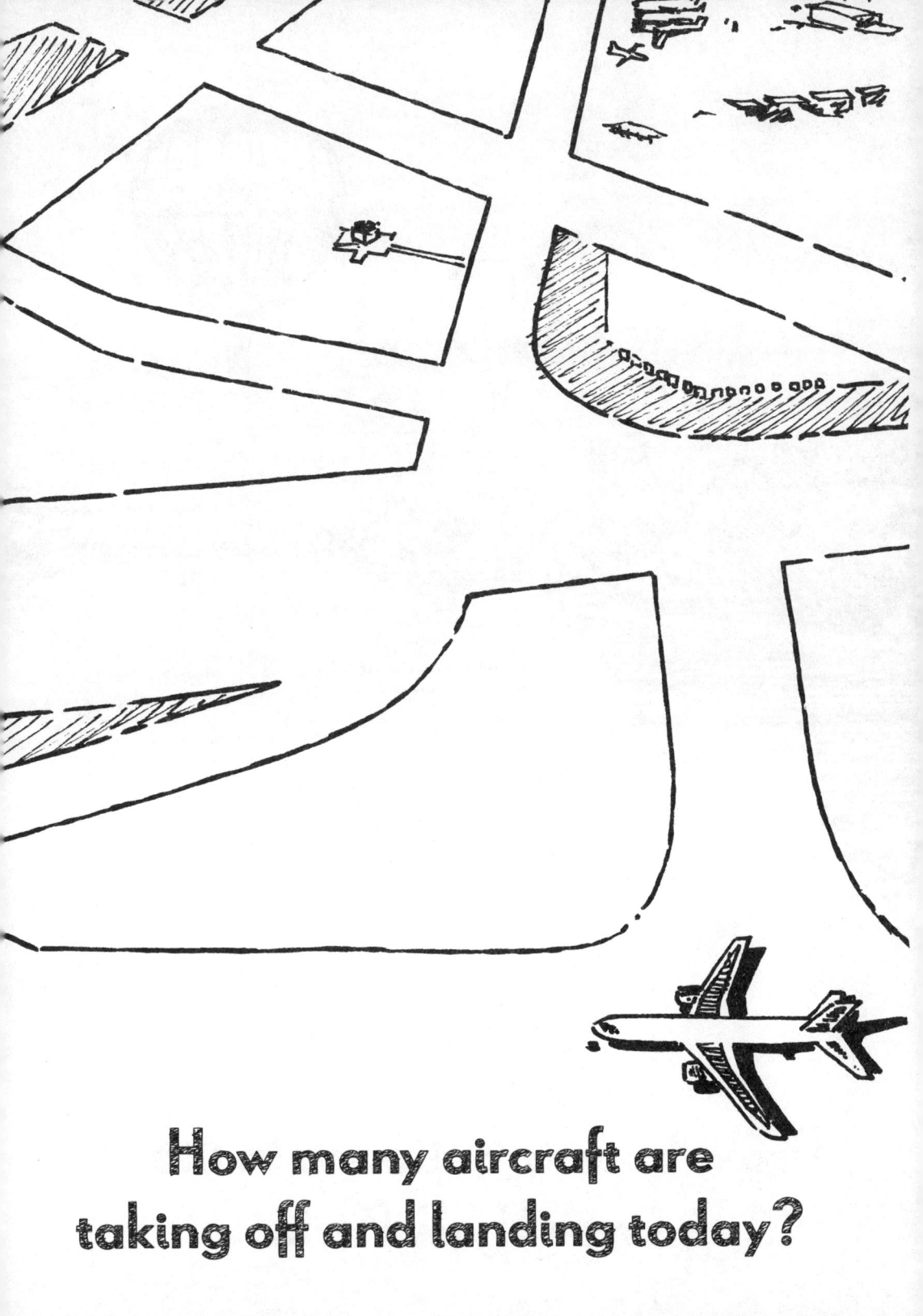

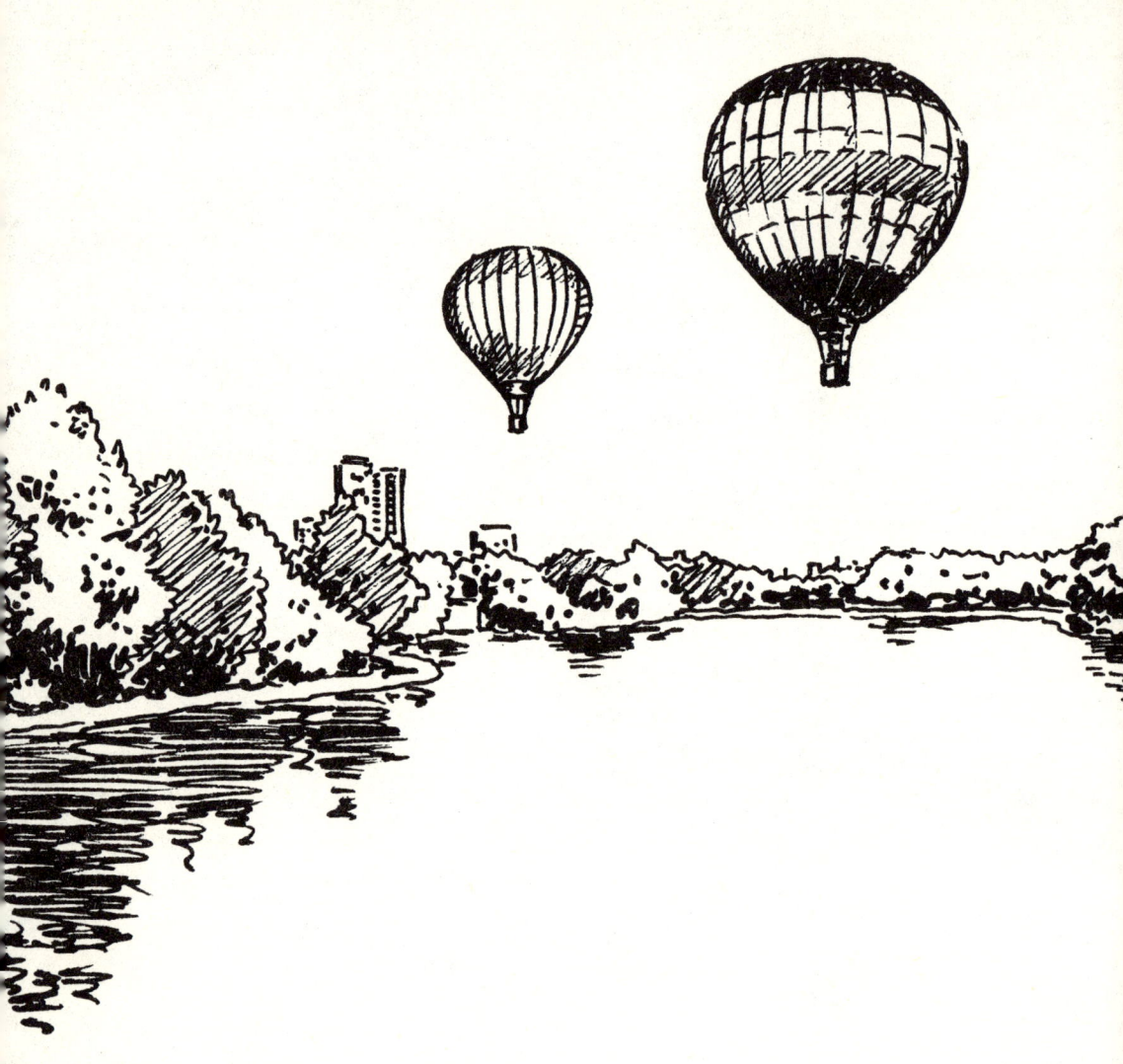

Draw hot-air balloons in the sky over Hyde Park...

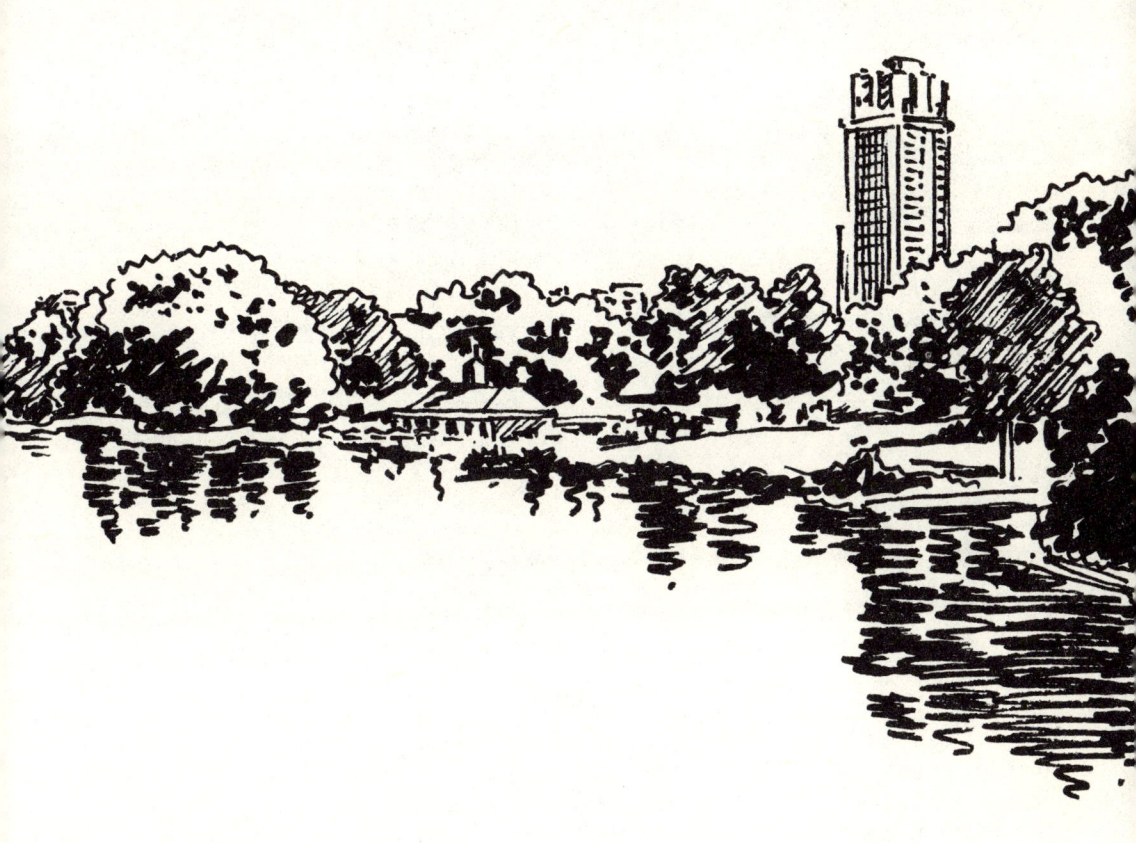

and rowing boats floating on the Serpentine Lake.

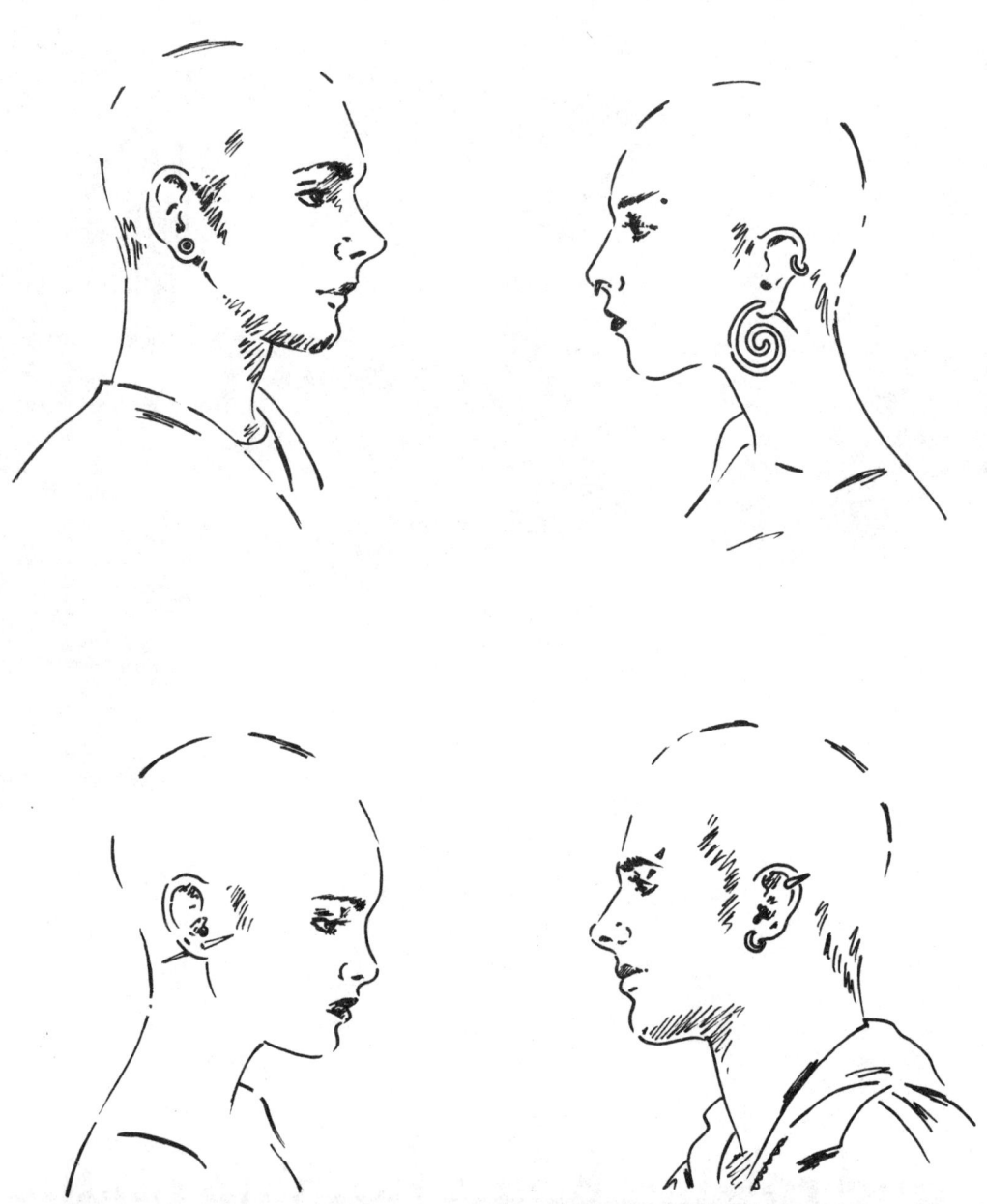

Design a new kit for your favorite London team.

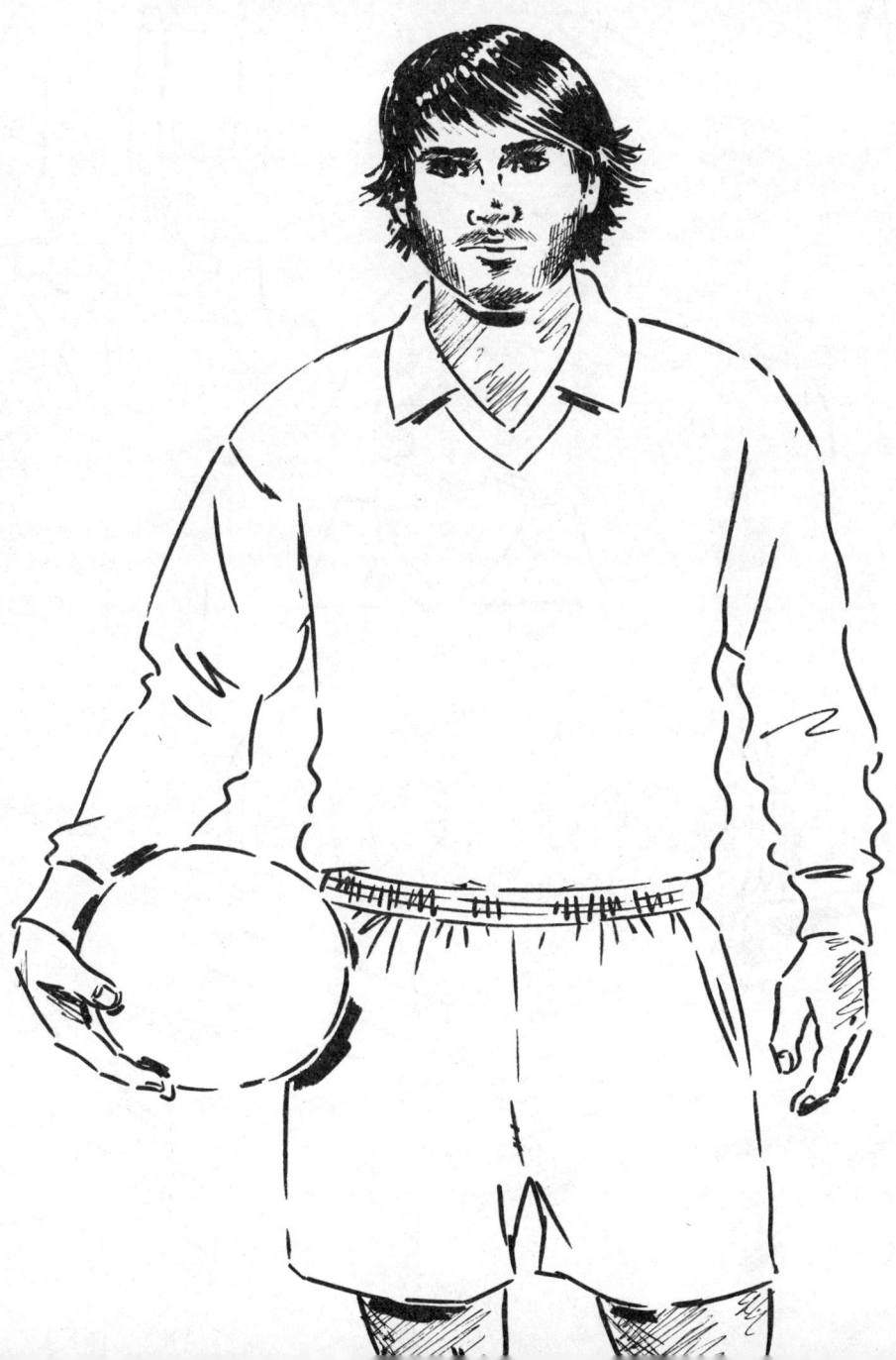

What antique trinkets can you see at Portobello Road Market?

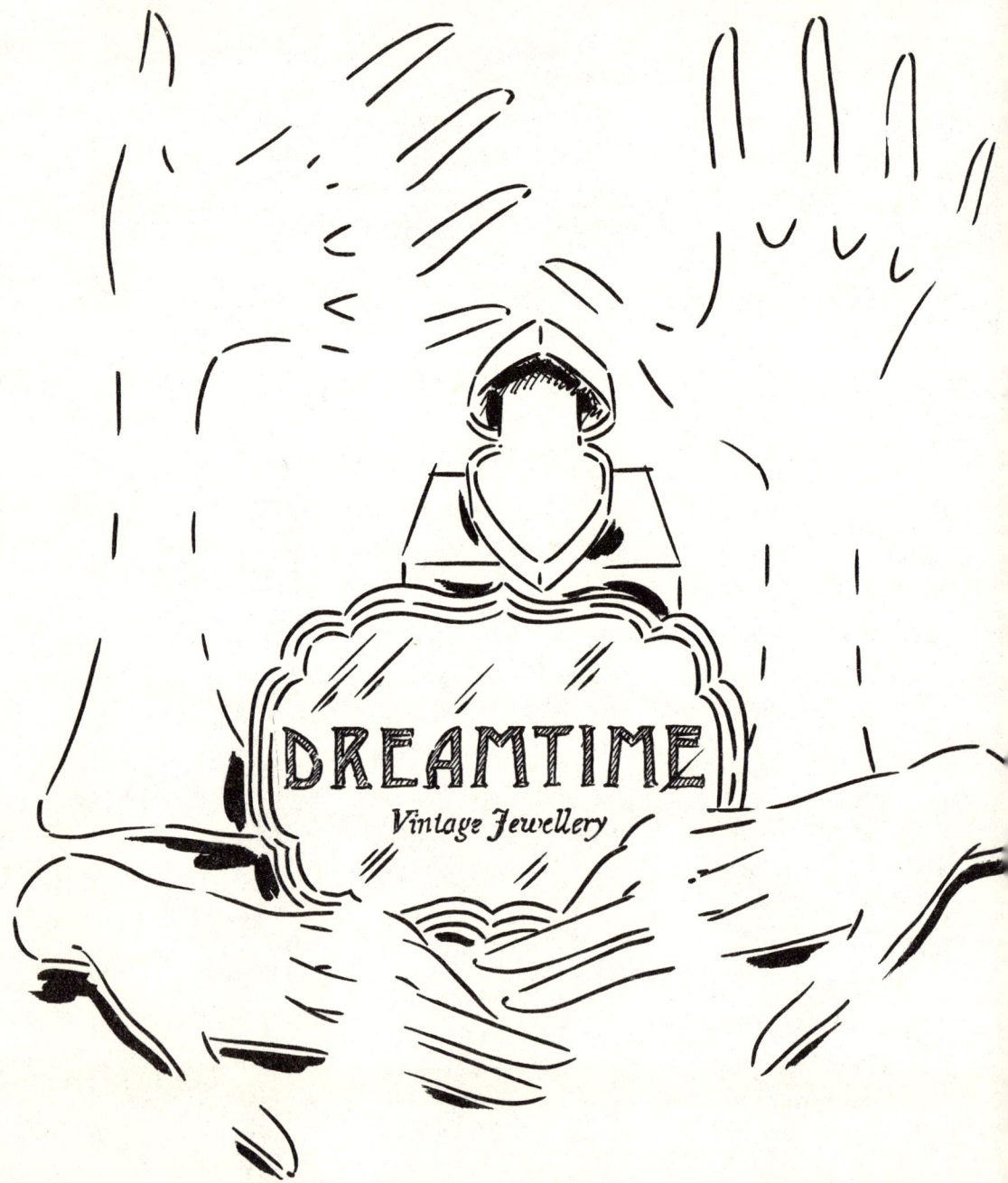

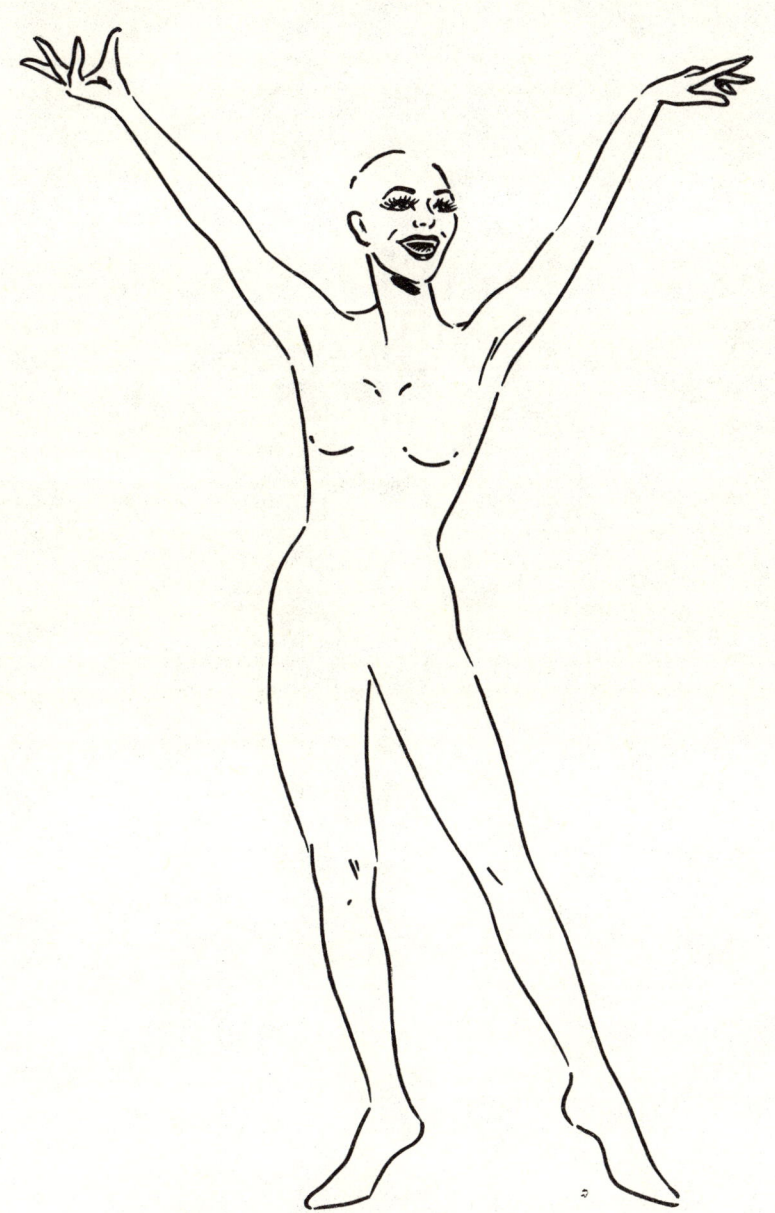

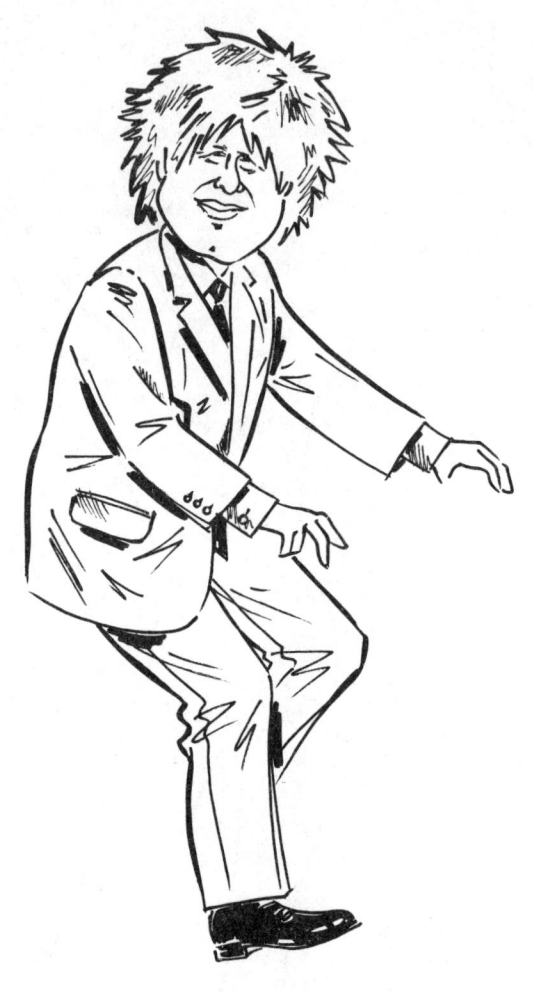

Give Mayor of London Boris Johnson a new bike to ride.

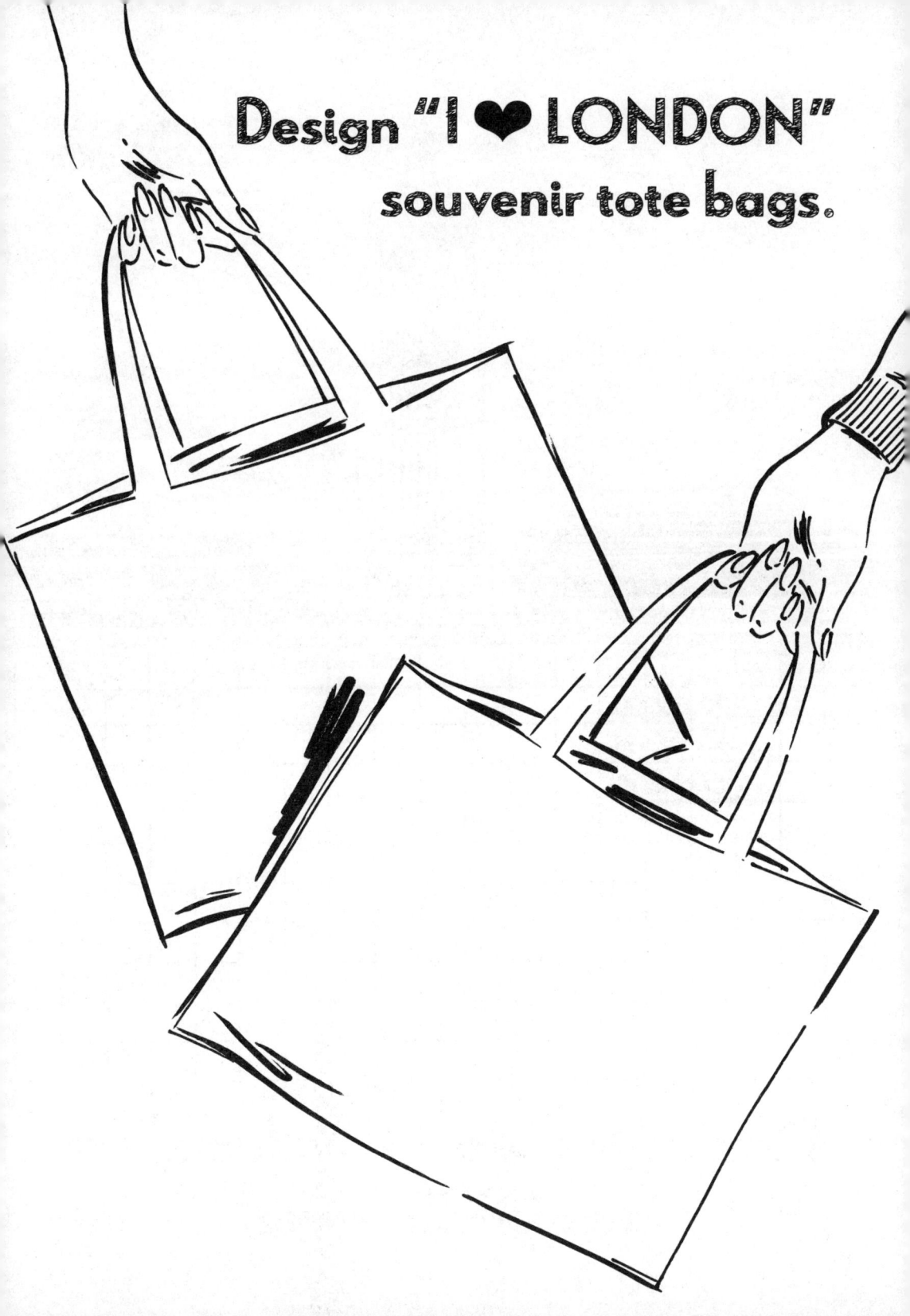

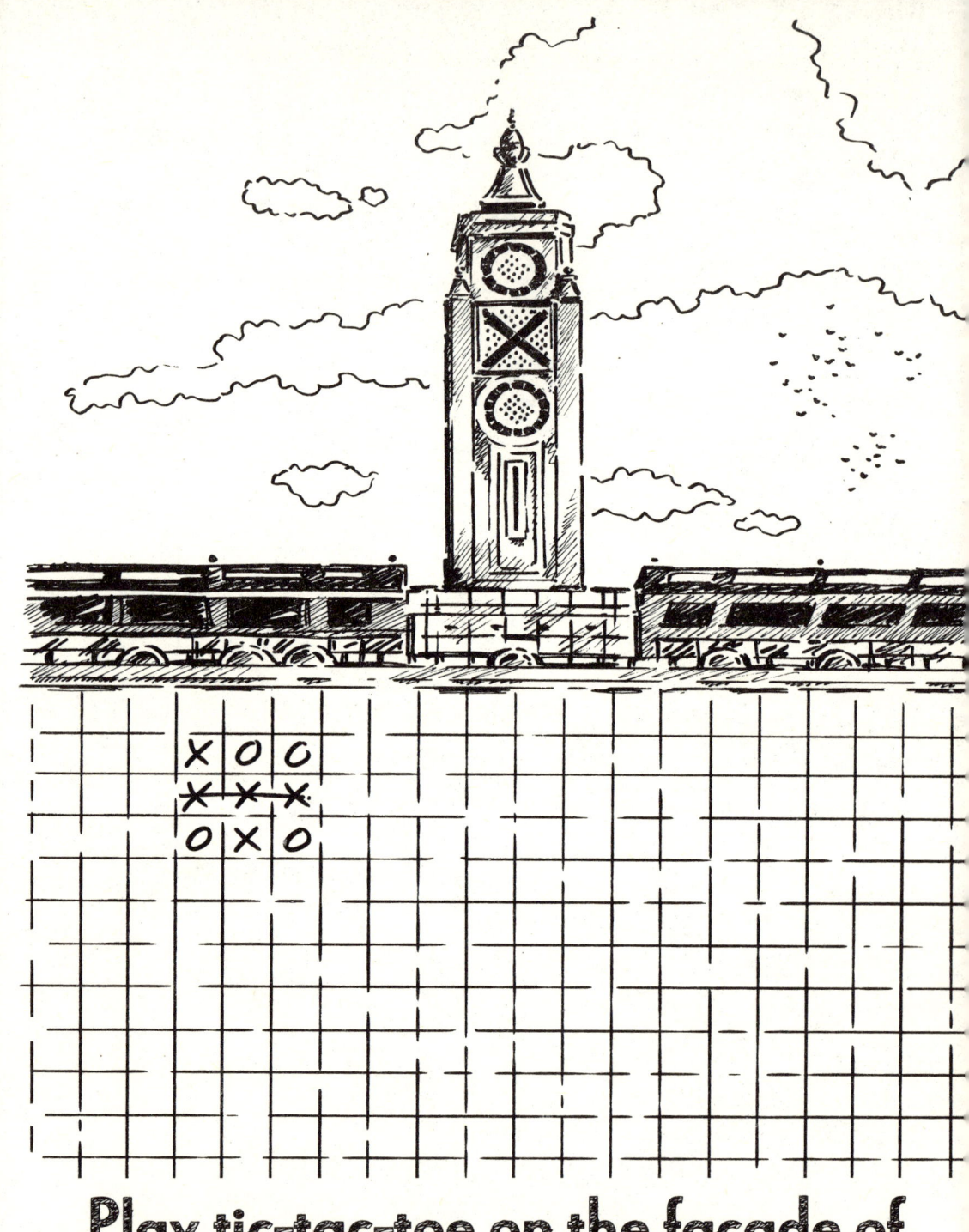

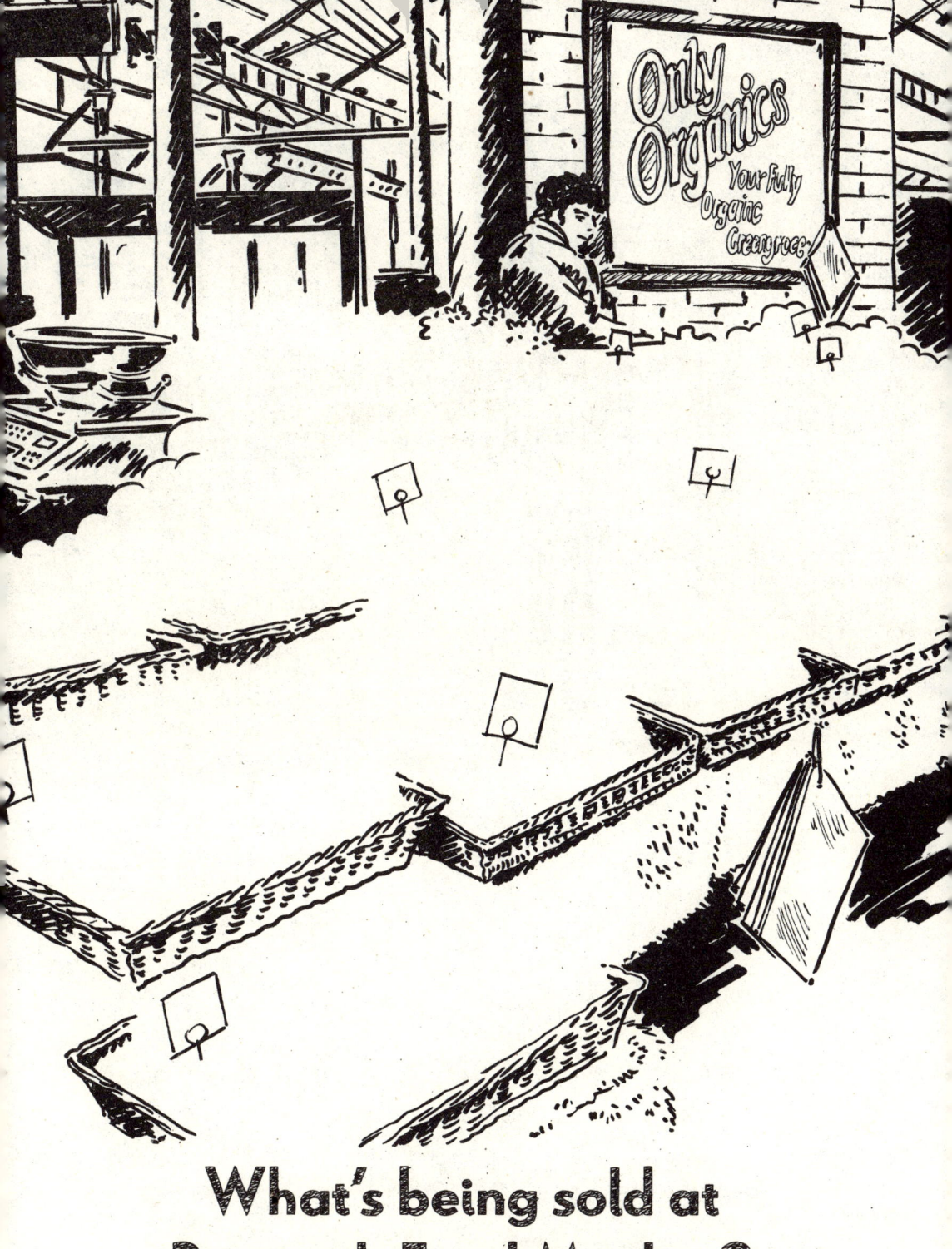

What's being sold at Borough Food Market?

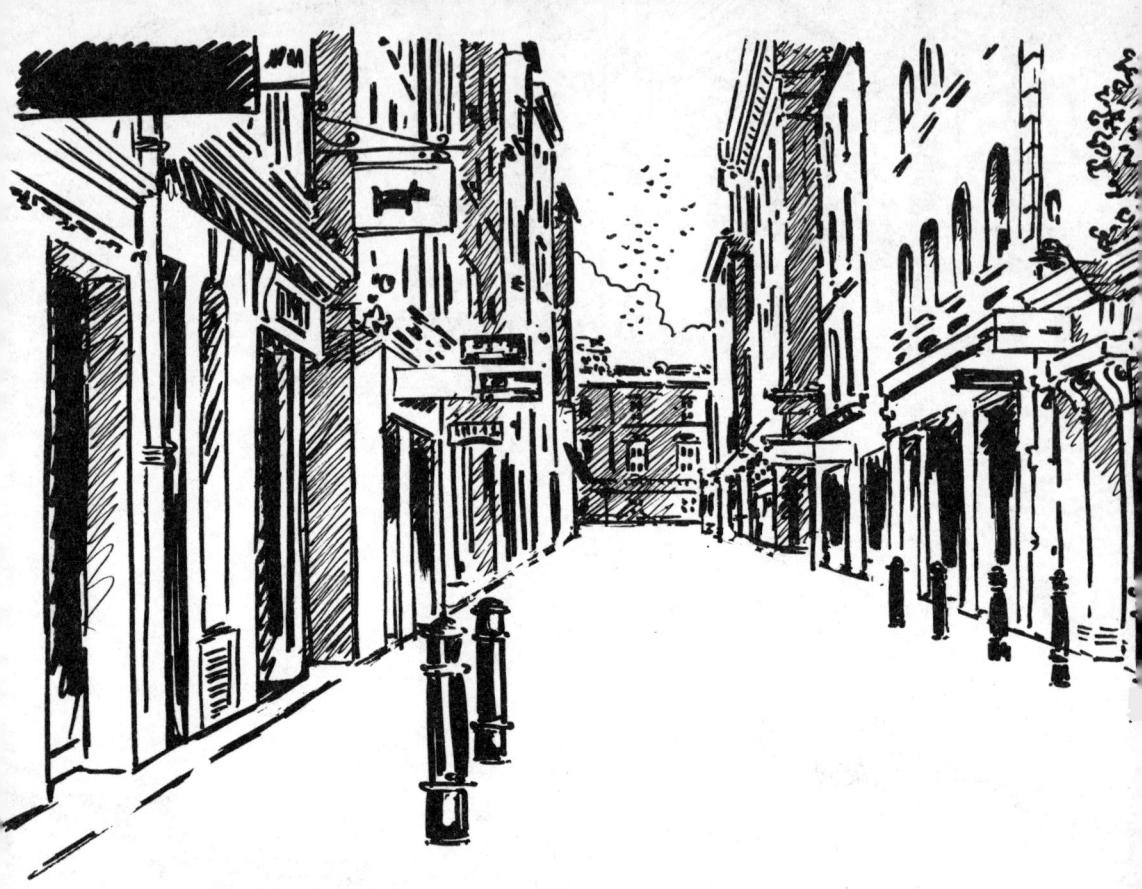

Add some cobbles to this Covent Garden street.

Create patterns for these swinging '60s-style minidresses.

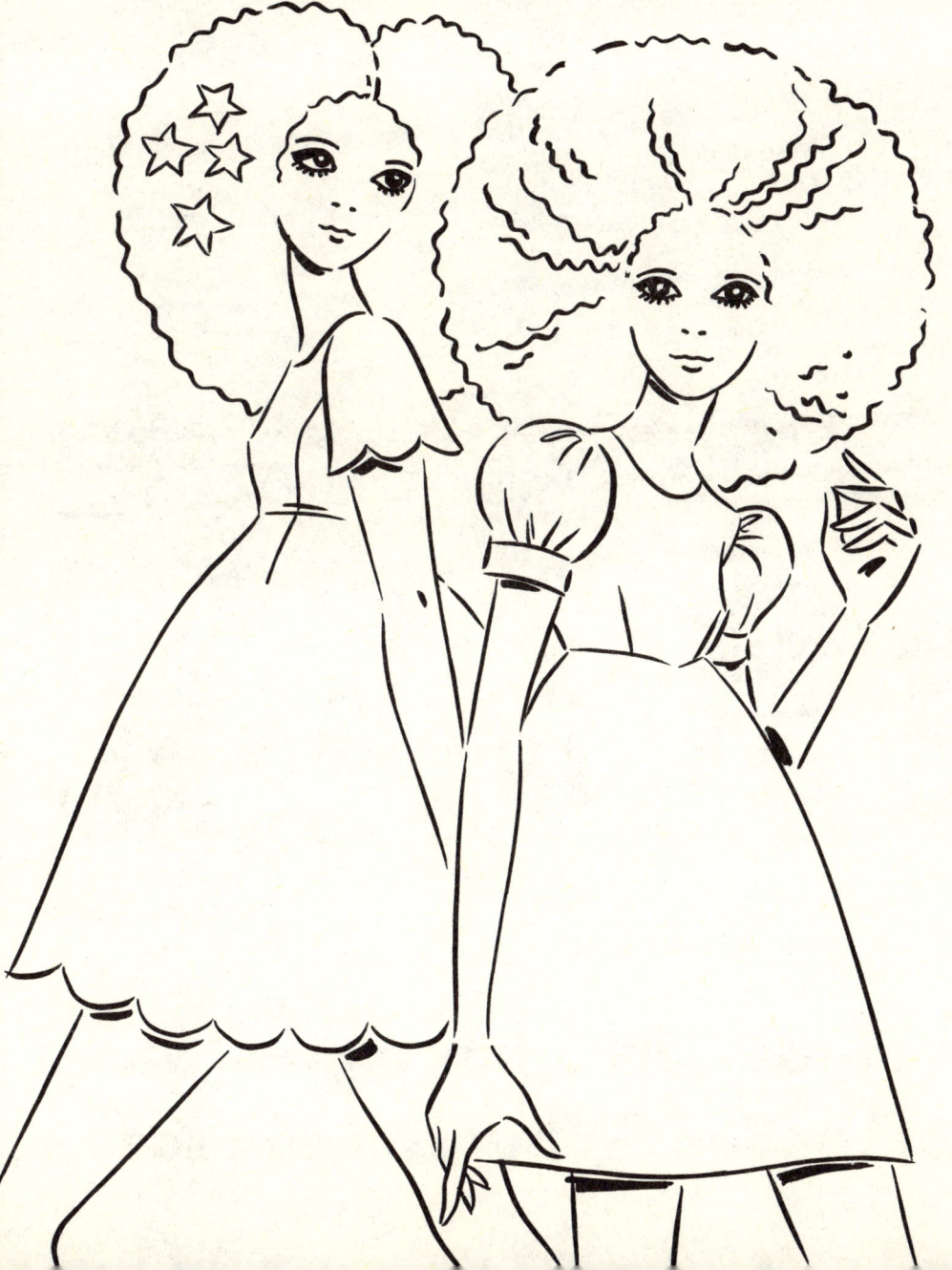

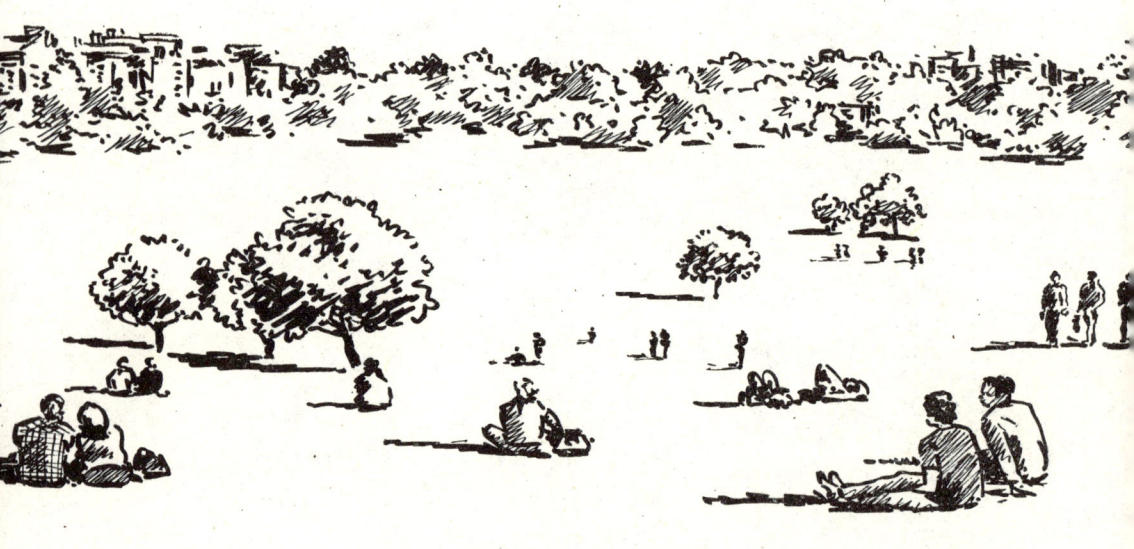

Primrose Hill offers a great view of London. What can you see?

What's going on underground at this tube station?

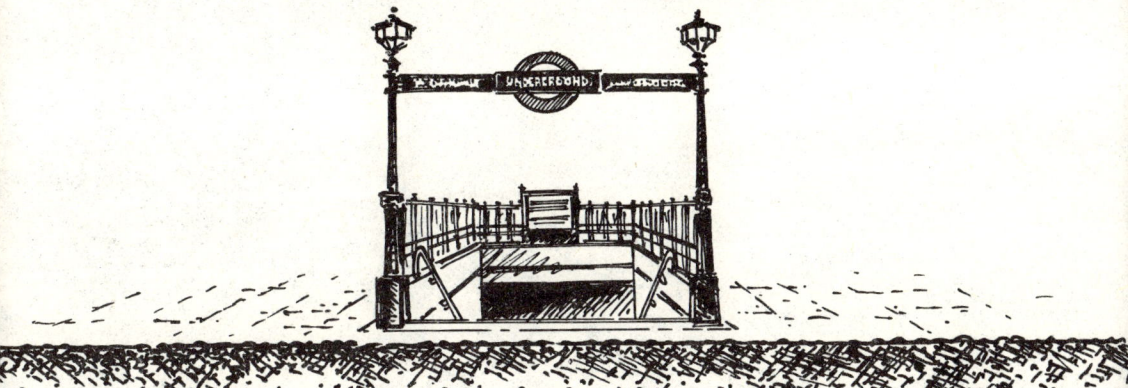

What does this leafy square in...

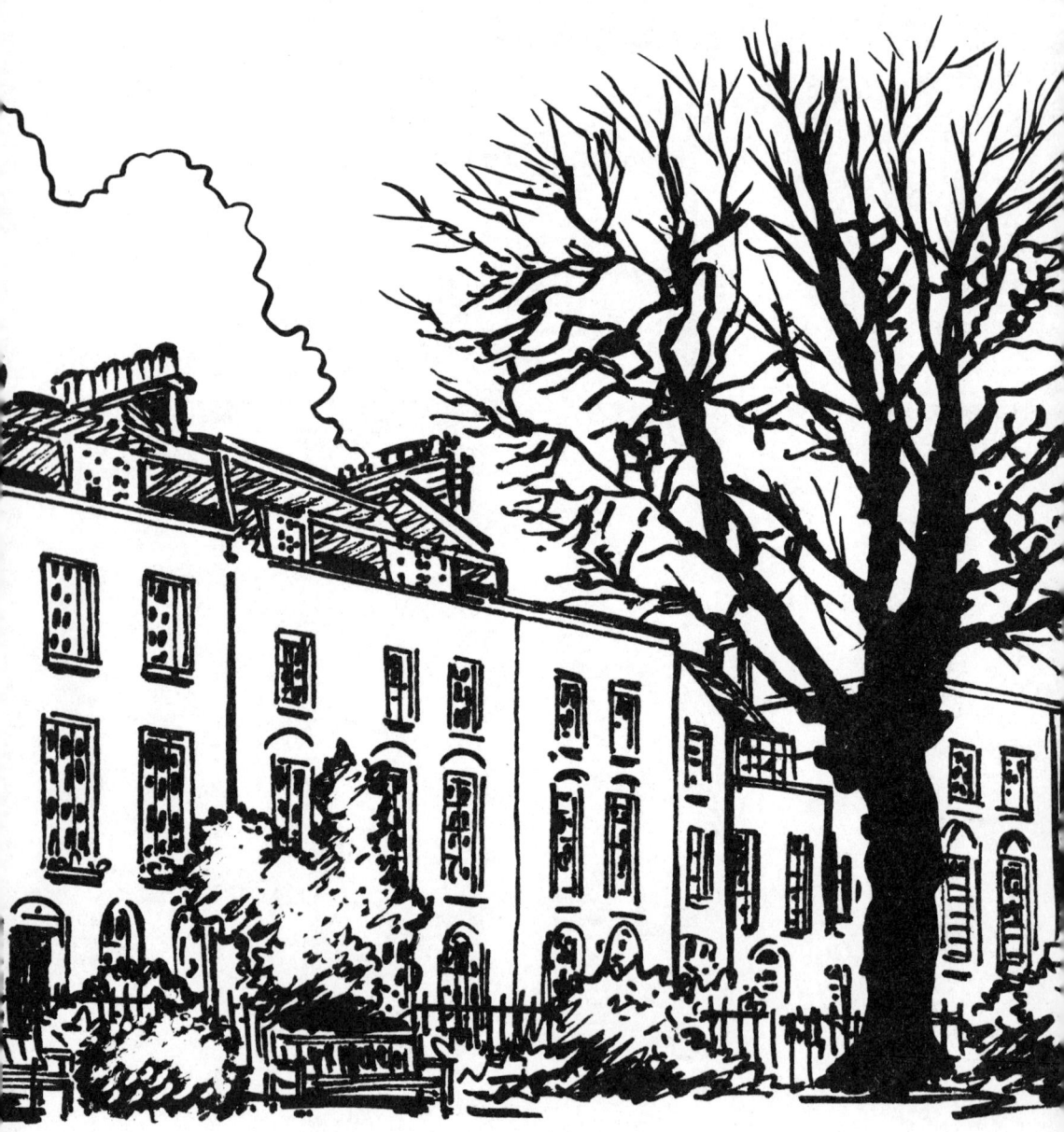

Mayfair look like in the spring?

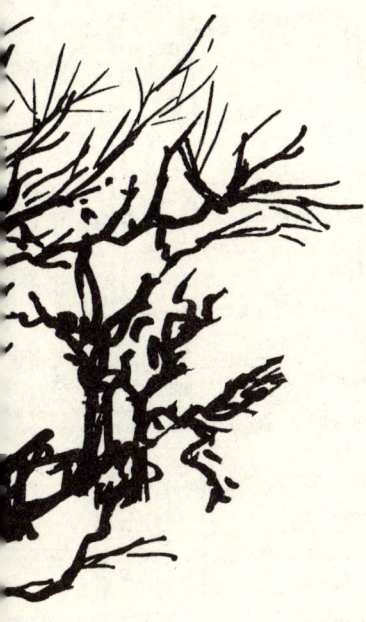

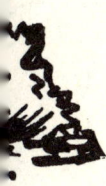

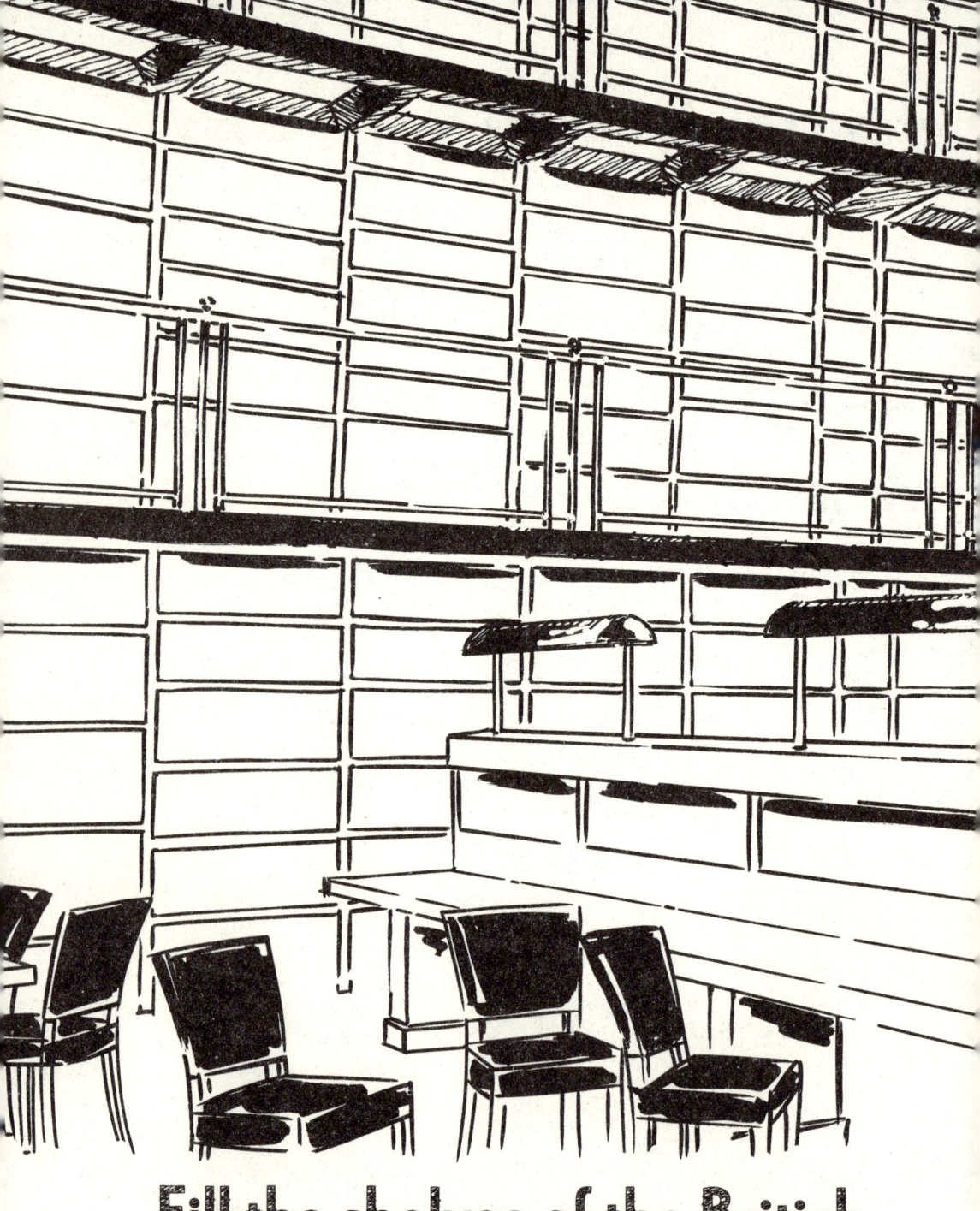

Fill the shelves of the British Library with hundreds of books.

What would you put inside this snow globe to remind you of your visit to London?

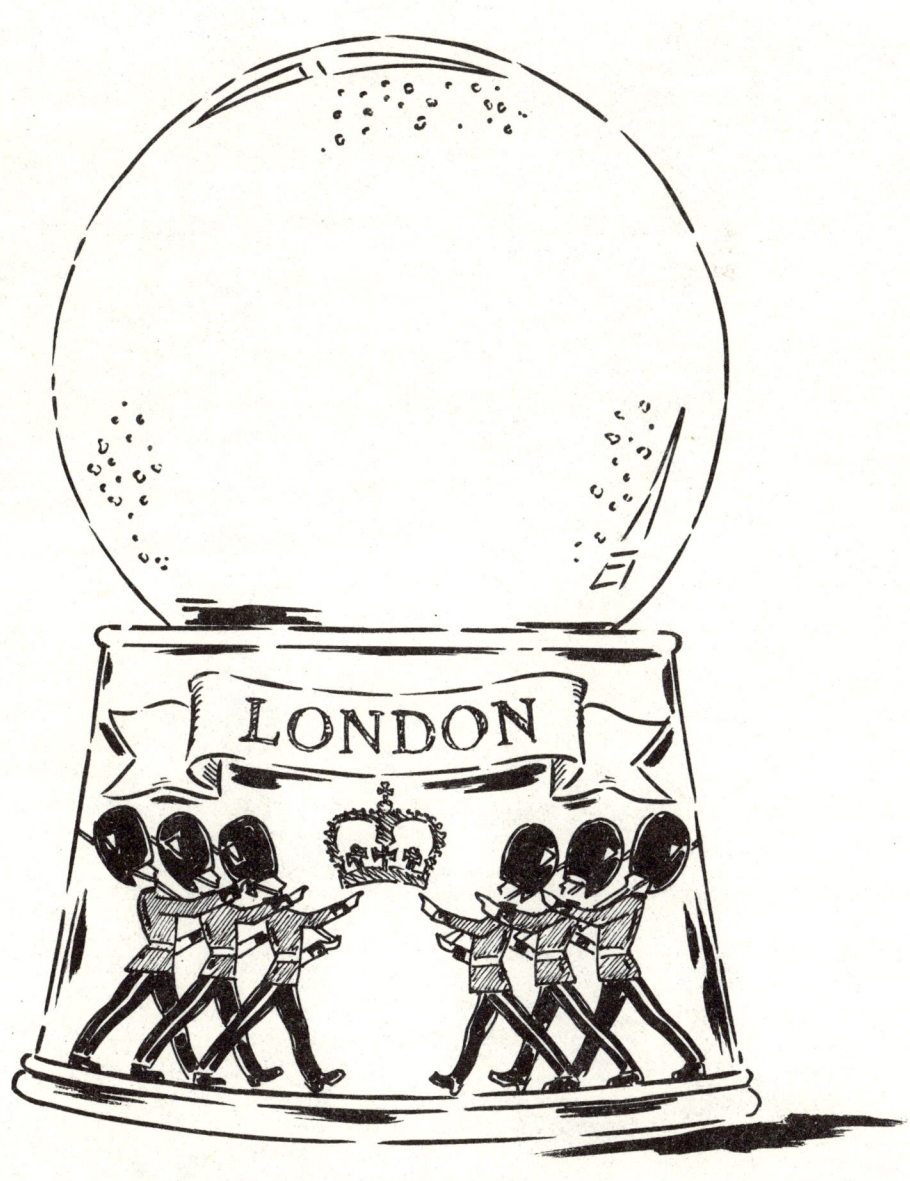

Did you know the Queen has beehives in her garden at Buckingham Palace?

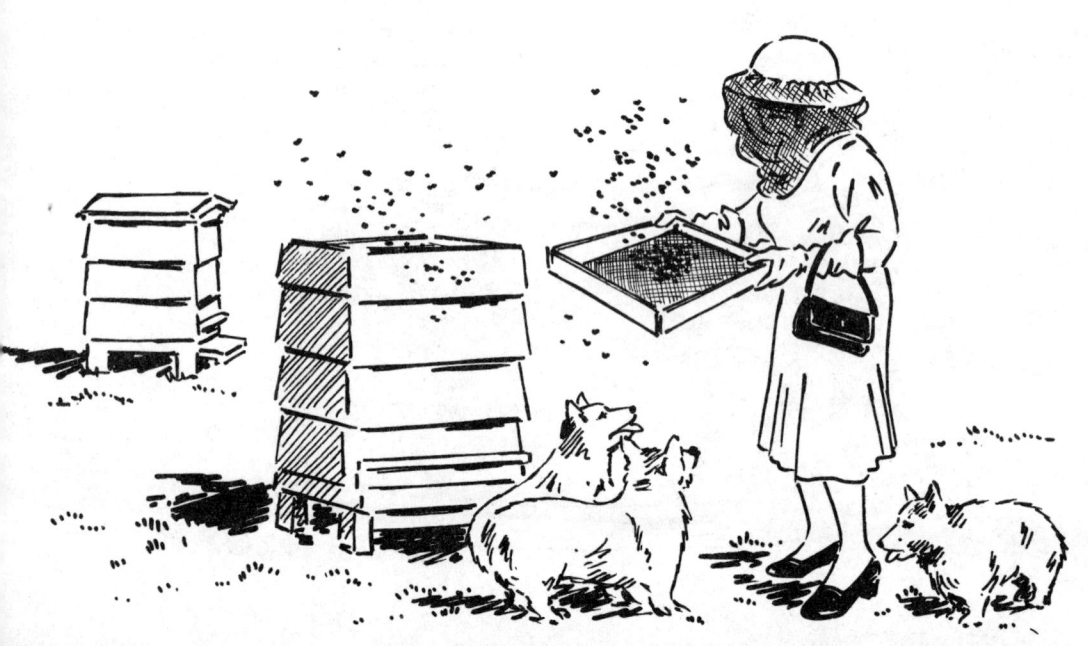

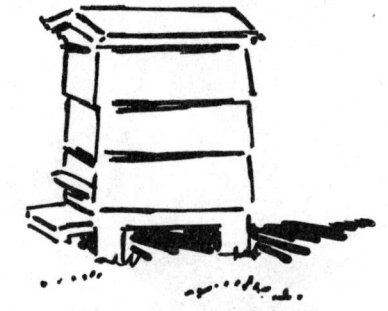

Draw a right Royal swarm.

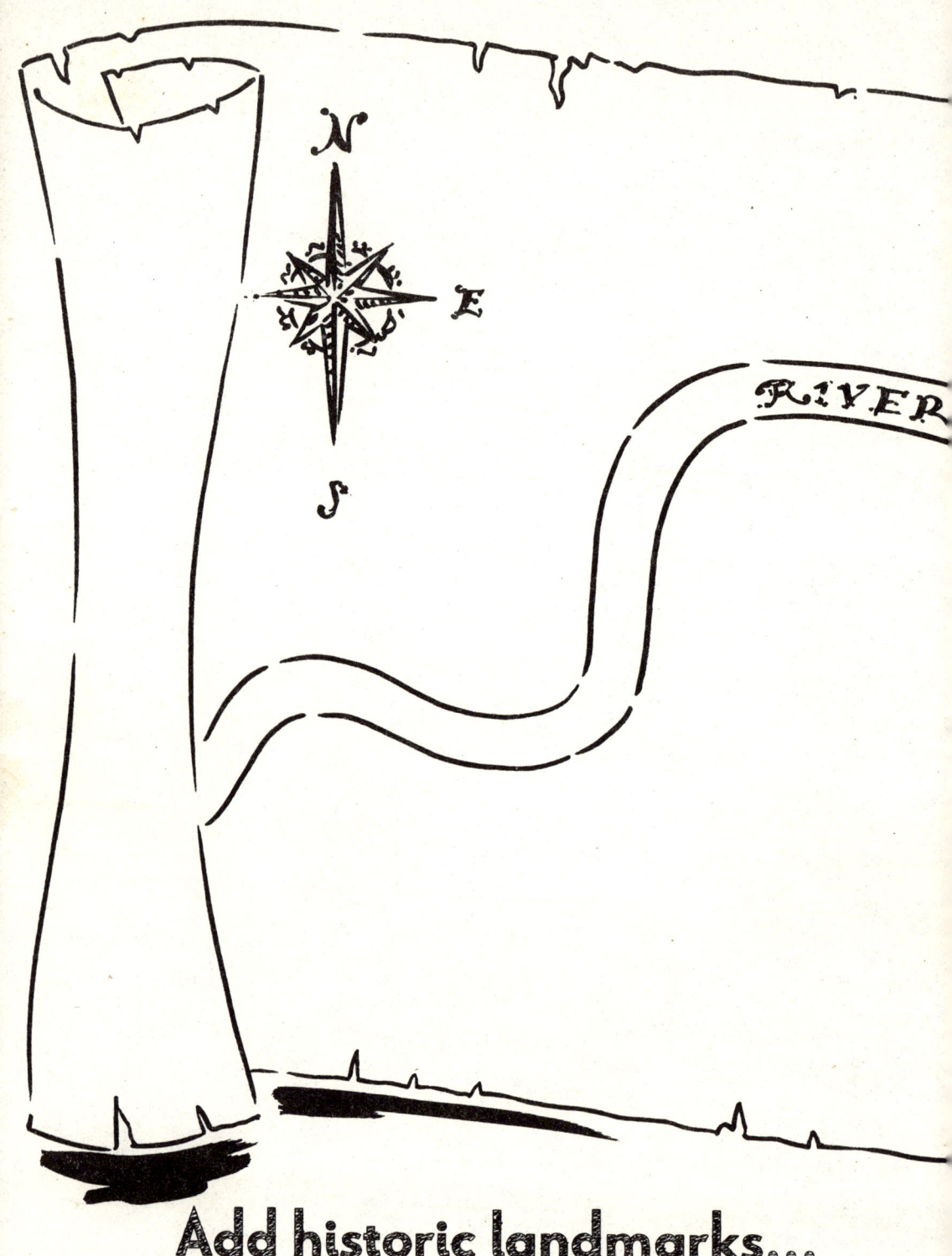

Add historic landmarks...

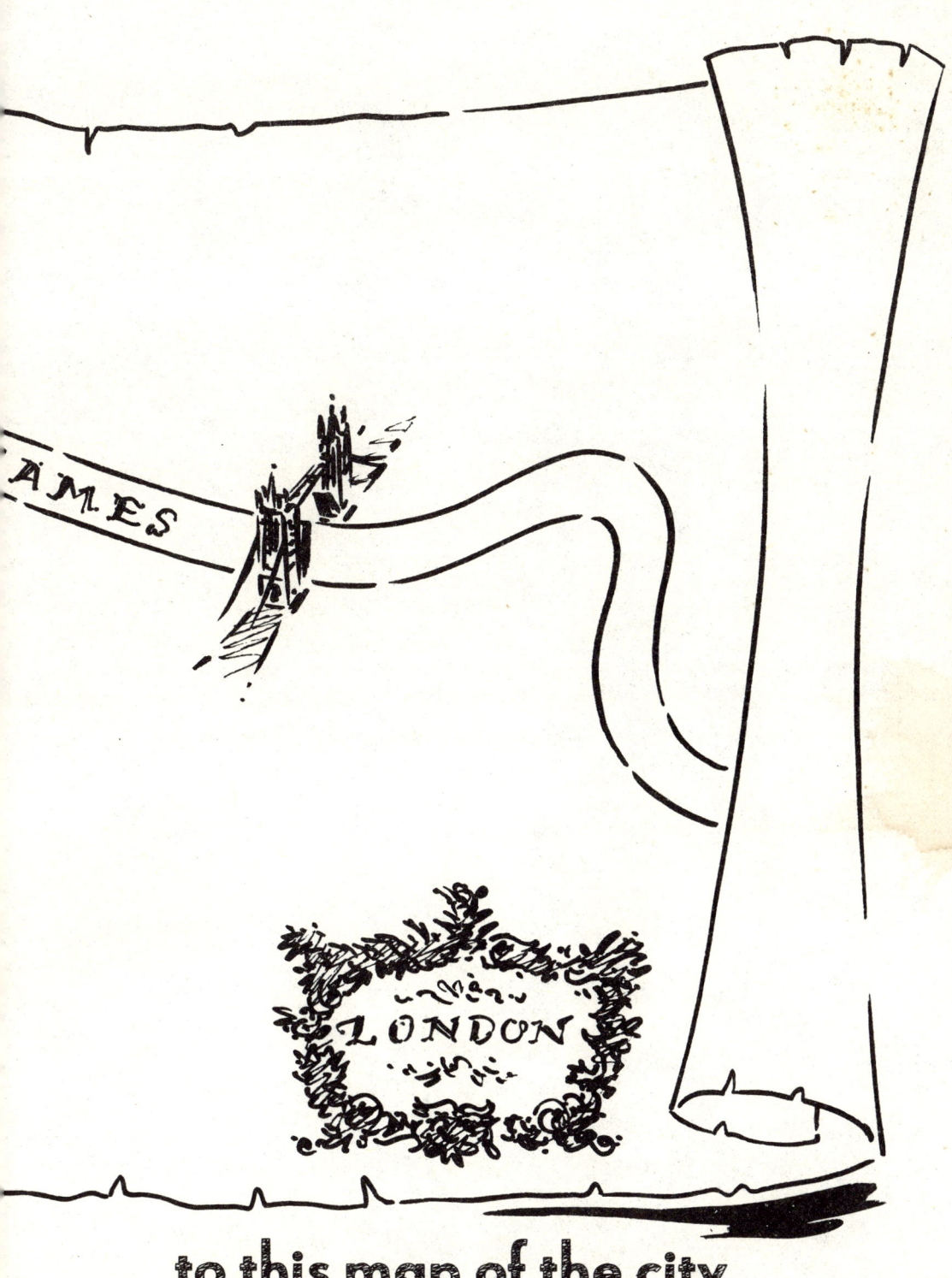

to this map of the city.

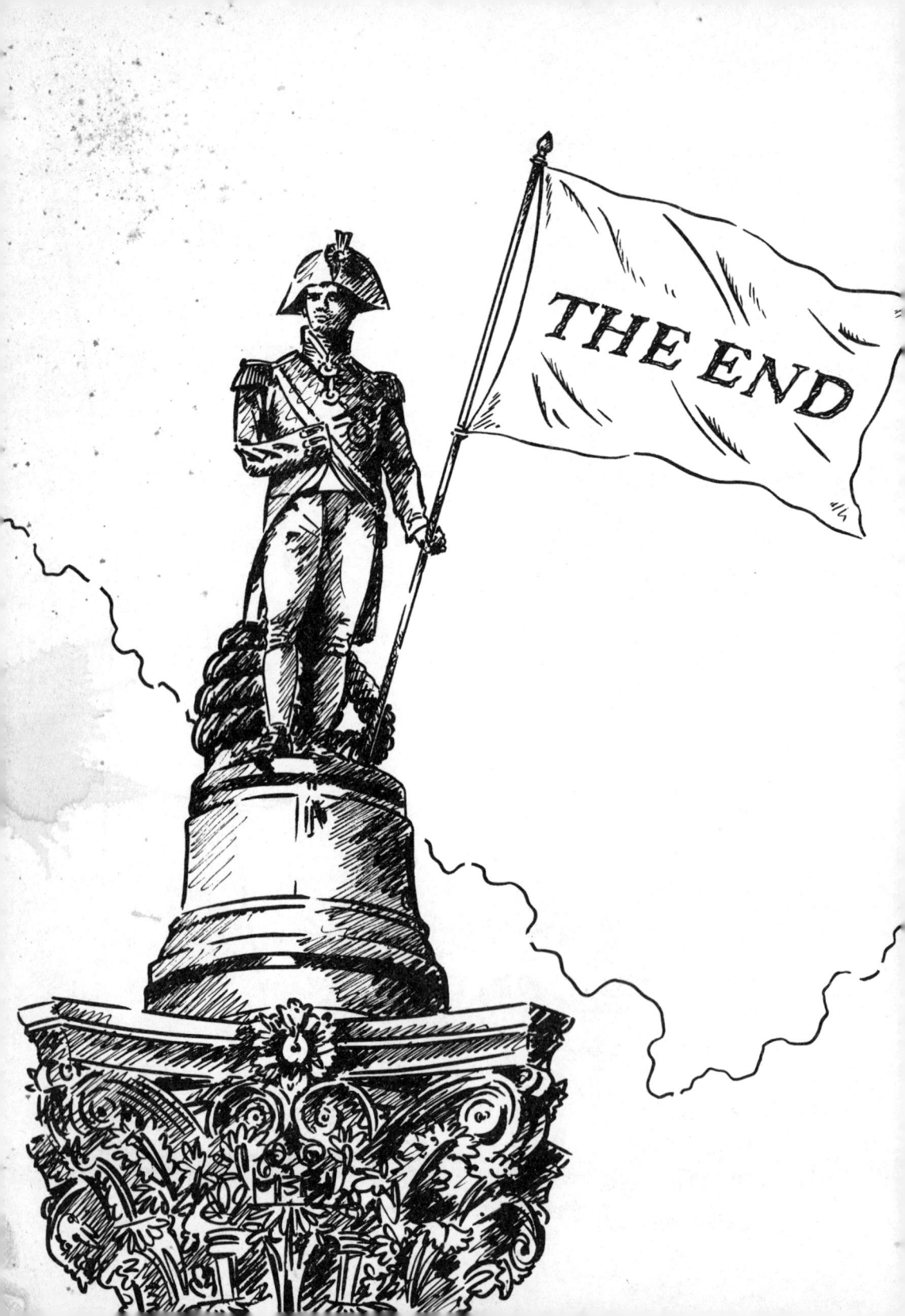